MYPHOTOWALK

A DAY
IN THE
LIFE OF GOD

Catherine Martin

myPhotoWalk
A Day in the Life of God

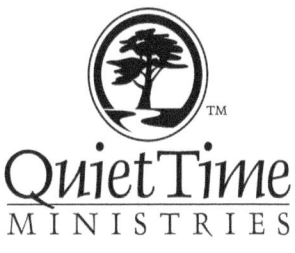

Quiet Time
MINISTRIES

PALM DESERT, CALIFORNIA

Unless otherwise indicated, all Scripture quotations in this publication are taken from the *New American Standard Bible*® (NASB), © The Lockman Foundation 1960, 1962, 1963, 1968, 1971, 1972, 1973, 1975, 1977, 1995. Used by permission. (www.Lockman.org).

Verses marked NIV are taken from the HOLY BIBLE, NEW INTERNATIONAL VERSION® (NIV®) Copyright © 1973, 1978, 1984 by the International Bible Society. Used by permission of Zondervan. All rights reserved.

Verses marked MSG are taken from The Message. Copyright © by Eugene H. Peterson 1993, 1994, 1995, 1996, 2000, 2001, 2002. Used by permission of NavPress Publishing Group.

Verses marked WMS are taken from the *Williams New Testament in the Language of the People*. Copyright © 1995, Charlotte Williams Sprawls. All rights reserved.

Verses marked TLB are taken from *The Living Bible*. Copyright © 1971, used by permission of Tyndale House Publishers, Inc., Wheaton, IL 60189, all rights reserved.

Verses marked AMP are taken from The Amplified Bible, Copyright © 1954, 1958, 1962, 1964, 1965, 1987 by The Lockman Foundation. All rights reserved. Used by permission. (www.Lockman.org)

Verses marked NLT are taken from the *Holy Bible*, New Living Translation, copyright © 1996. Used by permission of Tyndale House Publishers, Inc., Wheaton, IL 60189 USA. All rights reserved.

Verses marked GNB are taken from *The Bible In Today's English Version* published by American Bible Society © 1966, 1971, 1976. All rights reserved.

Verses marked CEV are taken from the *Contemporary English Version* published by American Bible Society © 1995. All rights reserved.

Verses marked NCV are taken from the *New Century Version*. Copyright © 2005 by Thomas Nelson, Inc. Used by permission. All rights reserved.

Verses marked PHILLIPS are taken from *The Phillips Translation* by J.B. Phillips © 1959, 1960 printed in Great Britain by Cox & Wyman Ltd., Reading for the publishers Geoffrey Bles Ltd.

Verses marked KJV are taken from the King James Version of the Bible.

Quiet Time Ministries has made every effort to trace the ownership of all poems and quotes. In the event of a question arising from the use of a poem or quote, we regret any error made and will be pleased to make the necessary correction in future editions of this book. Dramatizations of actual events are presented in the spirit of artistic license. Public photography of persons or places contained in this publication is presented in the spirit of artistic llcense as works of art, creative works, and editorial use, and does not represent advertising, infringement, endorsement, promotion, breach of privacy, or commercial association.

Cover by Quiet Time Ministries.
Cover photo by Catherine Martin—myPhotoWalk.com

Interior photos by Catherine Martin available at myPhotoWalk.com—catherinemartin.smugmug.com

myPhotoWalk—A Day In The Life Of God
Copyright © 2023 by Catherine Martin
Published by Quiet Time Ministries
Palm Desert, California 92255
www.quiettime.org

ISBN-13: 978-1-7375747-9-8

All rights reserved. No part of this publication may be reproduced, stored in a retrieval system, or transmitted in any form or by any means—electronic, mechanical, digital, photocopy, recording, or any other—except for brief quotations in printed reviews, without the prior permission of the publisher.

Printed in the United States of America

23 24 25 26 27 28 29 30 31 / LSI / 10 9 8 7 6 5 4 3 2 1

To God who created the heavens and the earth
and who made me, fashioning my days before I was even born.
"Marvelous are Your works, and that my soul knows very well."

Genesis 1:1, Psalm 139:14,16 NKJV

To my beloved husband, David G. Martin, M.D.
who has been my joy and delight for more than 40 years.
Thank you for your tireless and loving work in Quiet Time Ministries.

To those who partner with me in Quiet Time Ministries
teaching devotion to God and His Word
to men and women throughout the world.

To those who study God's Word together with me throughout the world
in our online Bible studies and in groups that use our quiet time studies.

May we all fall on our faces in awe and wonder
with hearts filled with love and trust as
we take a journey into the days of creation
and discover *a day in the life of God.*

Books by Catherine Martin

Six Secrets to a Powerful Quiet Time — A 30-Day Journey ©2005, 2014
Knowing and Loving the Bible — A 30-Day Journey ©2007
Walking with the God Who Cares — A 30-Day Journey ©2007, 2016
Set My Heart on Fire — A 30-Day Journey ©2008
Trusting in the Names of God — A 30-Day Journey ©2008
Passionate Prayer — A 30-Day Journey ©2009
Pilgrimage of the Heart — Quiet Times for the Heart ©2003, 2016
Revive my Heart — Quiet Times for the Heart ©2003, 2011
A Heart that Dances — Quiet Times for the Heart ©2003, 2022
A Heart on Fire — Quiet Times for the Heart ©2002, 2012
A Heart to See Forever — Quiet Times for the Heart ©2003, 2011
Passionate Prayer — A Quiet Time Experience ©2009
Trusting in the Names of God — A Quiet Time Experience ©2008, 2015
A Heart that Hopes in God — A Quiet Time Experience ©2007, 2011
Run Before the Wind — A Quiet Time Experience ©2008, 2012
Walk on Water Faith — A Quiet Time Experience ©2014
One Holy Passion — A Quiet Time Experience ©2017
A Woman's Heart that Dances — A Devotional Journey ©2009
A Woman's Walk in Grace — A Devotional Journey ©2010
The Calling — A Devotional Journey ©2019
The Quiet Time Notebook — A Quiet Time Notebook ©1994, 2013
The Quiet Time Journal — A Quiet Time Notebook ©1994, 2012
The Devotional Bible Study Notebook — A Quiet Time Notebook ©2010, 2013
The Passionate Prayer Notebook — A Quiet Time Notebook ©2013
myPhotoWalk—Quiet Time Moments — Devotional Photography ©2016
myPhotoWalk—Savoring God's Promises of Hope — Devotional Photography ©2017
myPhotoWalk—The Story of Your Life — Devotional Photography ©2020

Contents

PROLOGUE
When You Need To Trust God 9

A Brief Interlude Called Time
Chapter 1: Before Time Began 15
Chapter 2: Elohim The Creator 19
Chapter 3: Elohim's Creation 23

First Day: Light
Chapter 4: The Power Of God's Word 31
Chapter 5: Painting The Empty Canvas 35
Chapter 6: From Darkness To Light 39

Second Day: The Heavens
Chapter 7: Looking Up 47
Chapter 8: God's Chariot Of Clouds 51

Third Day: Earth, Ocean, Vegetation
Chapter 9: The Beauty Of The Earth 59
Chapter 10: When God Made The Ocean 63
Chapter 11: A New Kind Of Beauty 67
Chapter 12: God Saw That It Was Good 71

Fourth Day: Sun, Moon, Stars
Chapter 13: A Standing Ovation 79
Chapter 14: The Blood Red Moon 83
Chapter 15: Painting The Sky 87

Contents

Fifth Day: Fish, Birds

Chapter 16: Life In The Water 95

Chapter 17: When Birds Dance 99

Chapter 18: A Bird In A Tree 103

Sixth Day: Animals, Man

Chapter 19: God's Creatures 111

Chapter 20: When God Surprises You 115

Chapter 21: God's Masterpiece 119

Chapter 22: Every Life Tells A Story 123

Seventh Day: Rest

Chapter 23: The Day God Rested 131

Chapter 24: A Time Of Refreshing 135

Chapter 25: Trusting God 139

Epilogue

The End Of The Beginning 145

Appendix

myPhotoWalk SmugMug 150

Photography 151

About The Author 155

About myPhotoWalk 156

Acknowledgments 157

You Might Also Like 158

When You Need To Trust God

The starry night was just so incredibly beautiful there on Oahu, Hawaii. Why was I so uneasy? I was standing on the slopes of Diamond Head, a majestic volcanic cone, and I was trying to absorb the magnificent views of the restless Pacific Ocean and the sparkling lights of Honolulu. Age twenty-one, I was entirely alone in a grassy field at La Pietra Hawaii School for Girls, my place of residence to attend a summer project with Campus Crusade for Christ. It suddenly hit me. *What was I thinking? Was this leap of faith more leap than faith?* First of all, I didn't know anyone. Then, it was my first time away from home. And finally, I was scared. What to do? Coming from the bustling city of Phoenix, Arizona, I was accustomed to traffic all around me at all times of the day and night. So, I had ventured outside to be alone with a God I barely knew. I really needed to talk with Him in quiet and solitude about this new adventure. The questions swirling in my mind and the silence all around me was unnerving. Indeed, in that moment, there was nothing familiar or peaceful about this tropical wonderland of Hawaii.

But in that lonely moment in Hawaii, I looked up at the sky, searching for God, searching for answers. Suddenly, I gasped in awe and wonder. I marveled at the blanket of stars sparkling like diamonds covering the entire expanse of the heavens. I just stood completely still at attention in that field for a long time. I *knew* I was in the presence of God. I sensed Him there with me as I looked at countless stars that no one on earth could possibly create. In just this one glance at something mirroring infinity, there was no question in my mind as to the existence of Eternal God, Creator of Heaven and Earth. A heart of worship and a trust in God grew stronger and deeper that pivotal night, and, as it turned out, in many subsequent times alone with Him throughout that illuminating summer in Hawaii.

When you look all around at the wonder and beauty of nature in God's creation — the stars in the sky, the petals of a flower, the veins of a leaf, the wings of a bird — you can't help but be overwhelmed by the design and intricacy in all you see. When you see this beauty, what goes through your mind? A thought one can't help but consider is that a design must imply a designer. This kind of thinking speaks directly to the heart and can fuel one's faith.

The Bible explains the voice behind creation — God's voice — and invites us to listen: "The heavens are telling of the glory of God; And their expanse is declaring the work of His hands. Day to day pours forth speech, And night to night reveals knowledge. There is no speech, nor are there words; Their voice is not heard. Their line has gone out through all the earth, And their utterances to the end of the world" (Psalm 19:1-4).

So when you see the awesome wonder of creation all around you, what does it do for your belief and trust in God? How can it help you in practical everyday living? In a turbulent time many years ago, the Lord led me to walk with Him out in the California desert near where I live and capture images with my Nikon camera. The result is that He taught me to slow down and take a long look at everything I saw. The veins in the leaves on a tree, ripple designs of sand on the desert floor, colorful birds singing as they clung to branches of sagebrush, and beautiful shapes of branches in the chaparral spread out in what might appear to be a desolate place. Here are questions I asked myself as I took time to

Prologue

see God's creation through the lens of my camera. If God can create the heavens and the earth, then what can He do in my life? If He can paint beauty and color into the sky in a magnificent sunrise, and design colorful petals on a rose, then what kind of loveliness can He bring into the landscape of my own personal world? If He can sculpt Sedona Red Rocks like those on this book cover, then imagine His plan for our lives. Realizing God's power in creation pushes us beyond our present spiritual capacity and moves us to a deeper life of faith and trust in God.

Jeremiah, the great prophet of God, demonstrates the power of a deep and profound contemplation of God's creation for his own life. He wrote, "Ah Lord God! Behold, You have made the heavens and the earth by Your great power and by Your outstretched arm! Nothing is too difficult for You" (Jeremiah 32:17). God confirmed that discovery when He told Jeremiah, "Behold, I am the Lord, the God of all flesh; is anything too difficult for Me?" (Jeremiah 32:27).

What will help you when you need to trust God? When you realize that nothing is too difficult for God, then you discover a deeper trust in Him for all the impossible situations in your own life. Years ago, when I was writing my first book on the names of God, *Trusting in the Names of God*, I began with a contemplation of the name, Elohim, found in Genesis 1:1. As a result of my own personal study, I wrote a message "A Day in the Life of God," where I examined all that God did in each day of creation. Now, many years later, I have often thought about all God can do in a day when I need to trust Him in difficult circumstances where I have no answers. Then I respond, "If God can do that in a day, then my situation is not too hard for Him." I basically arrive at Jeremiah's conclusion: "Nothing is too difficult for You." And I trust God more — total reliance under stress and trial. I gain an eternal perspective with faith in His promises, and set my sights on eternity where I will live forever with Him. And then I watch Him answer my cries in unique and creative ways that never even entered my mind. And that's when I come to the oft-expressed conclusion that life is indeed the great adventure of knowing God.

The Lord says that "in the last days difficult times will come" (2 Timothy 3:1). These times call for a deep trust in God. I want you to know God and trust Him more. The book you hold in your hands, *A Day in the Life of God*, will help you have a greater belief and trust in God. We are going to explore each day of creation in Genesis 1 and 2, and take a photographic adventure together as I share my journey looking at God's creation through the lens of my camera. So dear friend, I invite you to linger long with each image and devotion in *A Day in the Life of God*. Whatever turbulent time you may be facing, as you discover what God can do in a day, and you see His magnificent beauty in His creation, you will be encouraged to draw closer to Him and trust Him more. Then, you will say along with the psalmist, "The Lord is my strength and shield. I trust Him with all my heart" (Psalm 28:7).

In His love,
Catherine Martin

"Since the creation of the world His invisible attributes,
His eternal power and divine nature, have been clearly seen,
being understood through what was made."

Romans 1:20

In seasons of severe trial, the Christian has nothing on earth that he can trust to,
and is therefore compelled to cast himself on his God alone.
When his vessel is on its beam-ends, and no human deliverance can avail,
he must simply and entirely trust himself to the providence and care of God.
Happy storm that wrecks a man on such a rock as this!
O blessed hurricane that drives the soul to God and God alone!

Charles Haddon Spurgeon

"The LORD is my strength and shield. I trust Him with all my heart.
He helps me and my heart is filled with joy.
I burst out in songs of thanksgiving."

Psalm 28:7 NLT

INTERLUDE

Time has been called a "brief interlude between eternity past and eternity future." This interlude is comprised of 24-hour days, and we have our own interlude of time on earth, living out the days God gives us. Think of all the things you do in a day. Now imagine what God can do in a day (Exodus 20:11). The first verse in God's Word helps us understand the meaning of this interlude in life called "time" — "In the beginning, God created the heavens and the earth" (Genesis 1:1). Who is this God and what does He want us to understand? Let's begin the journey of *A Day in the Life of God*.

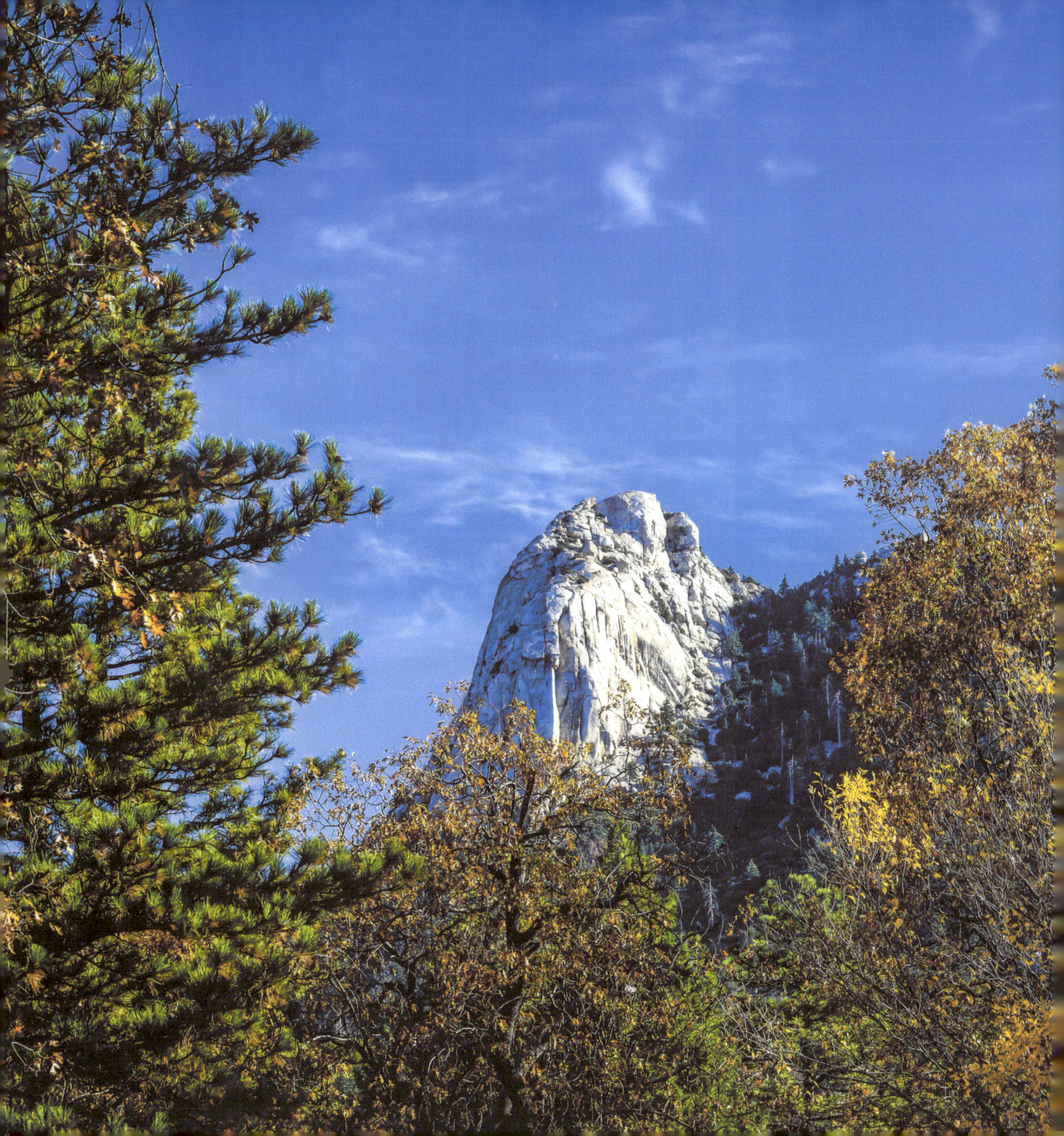

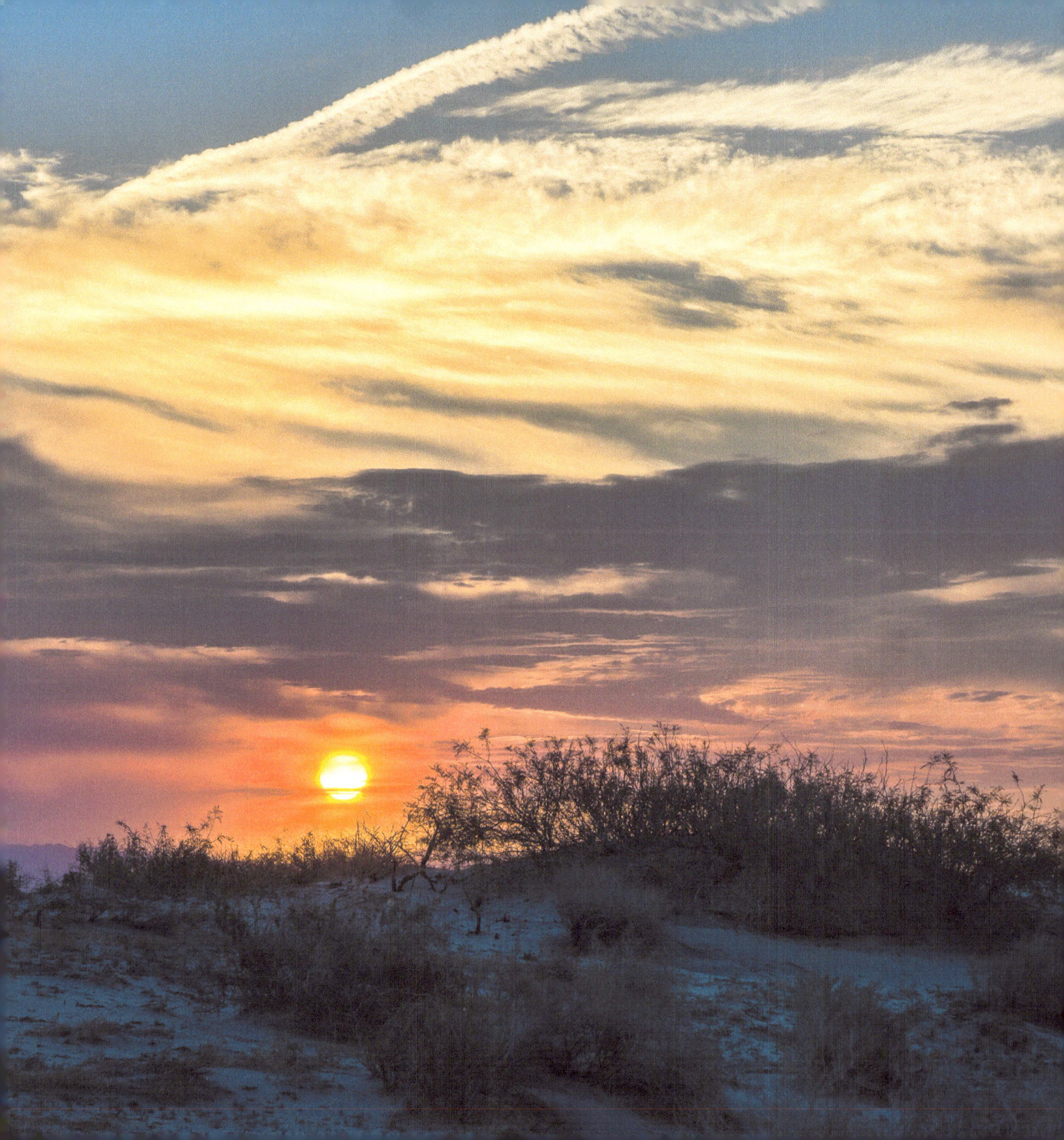

I
BEFORE TIME BEGAN

In the beginning God created the heavens and the earth.

GENESIS 1:1

Donald Grey Barnhouse wrote of a "brief interlude between eternity past and eternity future called time." Eternity means there is no beginning and no end. Tucked somewhere in eternity is the beginning and ending of time. C.S. Lewis invites us to take a sheet of paper representing eternity and imagine it to be extended infinitely in all directions. Then, draw a short line representing time. In so doing, you realize the eternal God is self-existent with no beginning and no end, and is outside the boundaries of time. He created time. He is not bound by time. The first verse in the Bible introduces us to the concept of time and eternity. "In the beginning God created the heavens and the earth" (Genesis 1:1). To say "In the beginning" implies eternity past and the existence of God before time began and creation was accomplished. God wants you to know He is outside the boundaries of time, and is greater than any circumstances or troubles you face today. The eternal nature of God, His very existence, and His revelation to you form the foundation of your trust in Him today.

Before the mountains were born or You gave birth to the earth and the world, even from everlasting to everlasting, You are God.

PSALM 90:2

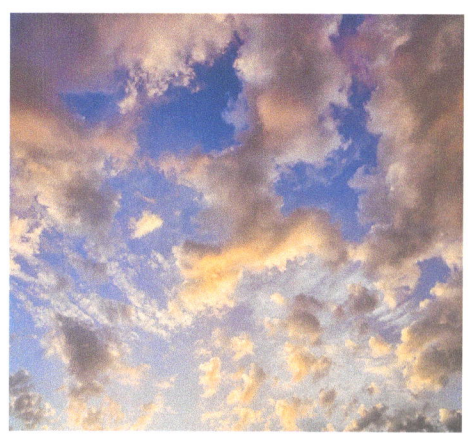

O God, our help in ages past, our hope for years to come,
Our shelter from the stormy blast, and our eternal home.
Under the shadow of Thy throne, still may we dwell secure,
Sufficient is Thine arm alone, and our defense is sure.
Before the hills in order stood, or earth received her frame,
From everlasting Thou art God, to endless years the same.
A thousand ages in Thy sight are like an evening gone
Short as the watch that ends the night, before the rising sun.
O God, our help in ages past, our hope for years to come,
Be Thou our guide while life shall last, and our eternal home.

O GOD, OUR HELP IN AGES PAST — ISAAC WATTS

The eternal God is your refuge, and His everlasting arms are under you.

DEUTERONOMY 33:27 NLT

Because God lives in an everlasting now, He has no past and no future. When time words occur in the Scriptures, they refer to our time, not His…God dwells in eternity but time dwells in God. He has already lived all our tomorrows as He has lived all our yesterdays…That God appears at time's beginning is not too difficult to comprehend, but that He appears at the beginning and end of time *simultaneously* is not so easy to grasp, yet it is true.

THE KNOWLEDGE OF THE HOLY — A.W. TOZER

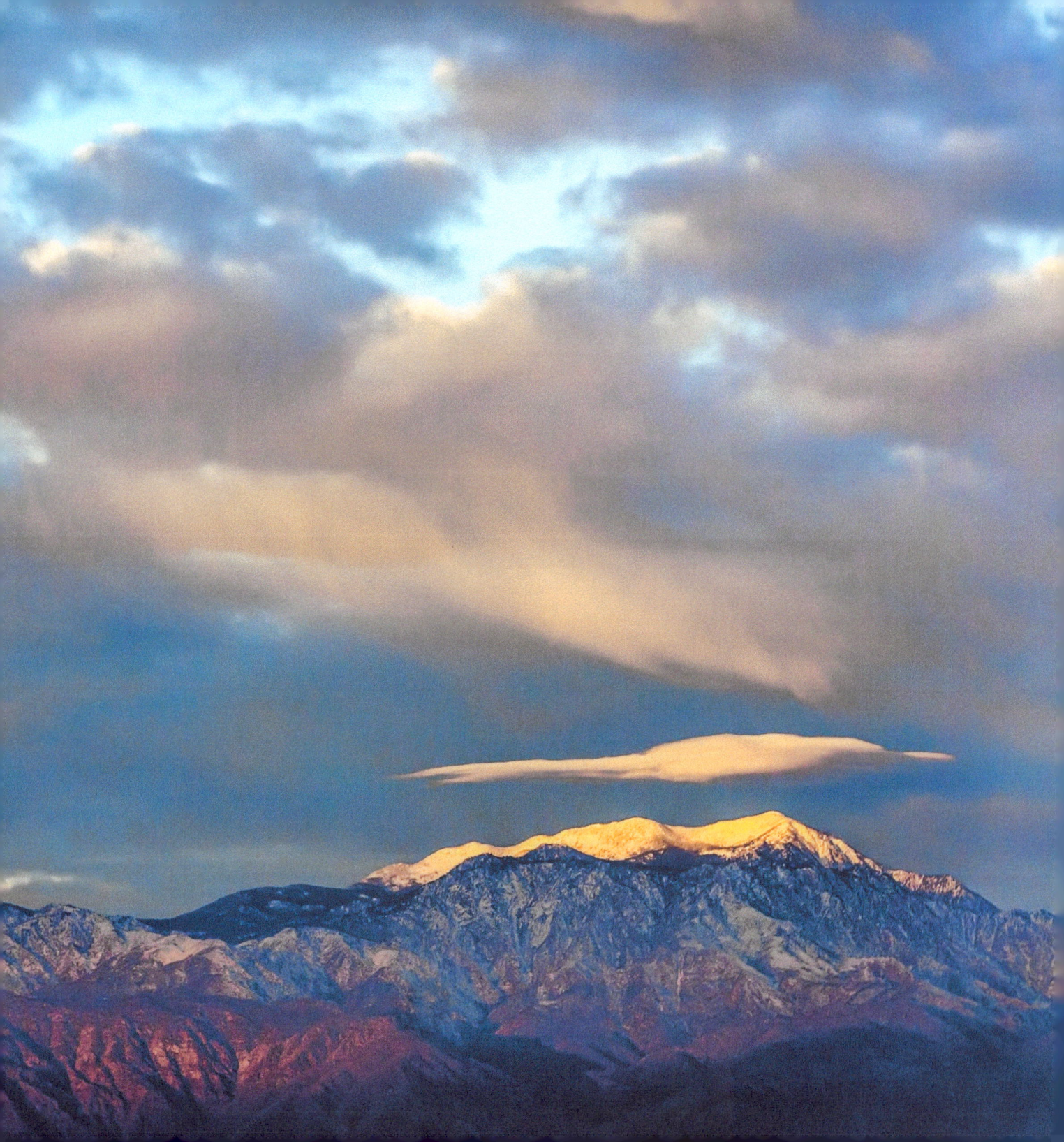

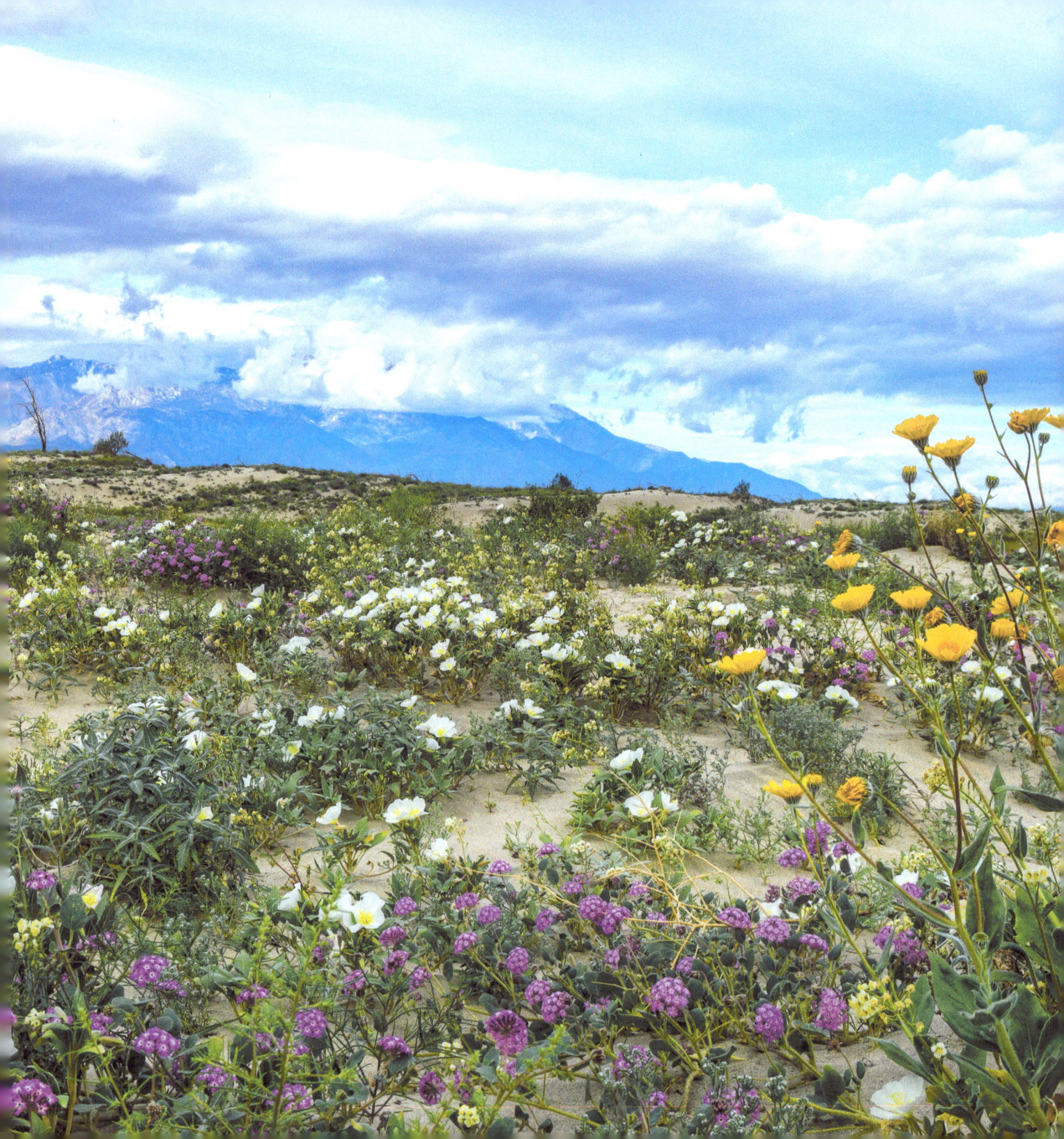

2
Elohim The Creator

In the beginning God…

Genesis 1:1

The first revelation given by God in His Word for you to discover is the fact of His existence and the introduction of His name, Elohim. Beginning the Bible with His name is like putting His own signature on the book He has written to reveal Himself to you. His name, Elohim, is used 35 times in the first two chapters of Genesis and is associated with His power in creation. The plural form of Elohim reveals the Triune God—Father, Son, and the Holy Spirit. The Triune God said, "Let Us make man in Our image" (Genesis 1:26). Many questions are answered with this beginning statement by God. Yes, there is a God. Yes, He desires to be known because He has revealed Himself to us. He is self-existent, uncreated, and outside the boundaries of time and space. He is infinite and eternal. And He is Triune. Because He tells you His name, He is building a basis for trust and faith in a relationship with Him. He desires your trust in Him. David, the psalmist, experienced this when he wrote, "Those who know Your name will put their trust in You" (Psalm 9:10).

Those who know Your name will put their trust in You, for You, O Lord, have not forsaken those who seek You.

Psalm 9:10

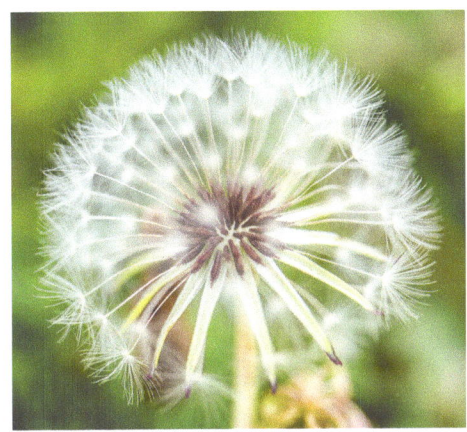

I know not, but God knows; Oh, blessed rest from fear!
All my unfolding days to Him are plain and clear.
Each anxious, puzzled "why?" from doubt or dread that grows,
Finds answer in this thought; I know not, but He knows.
I cannot, but God can; Oh, balm for all my care!
The burden that I drop His hand will lift and bear.
Though eagle pinions tire, I walk where once I ran,
This is my strength to know; I cannot, but He can.
I see not, but God sees; Oh, all sufficient light!
My dark and hidden way to Him is always bright.
My strained and peering eyes may close in restful ease,
And I in peace my sleep; I see not, but He sees.

But God — Annie Johnson Flint

Don't be afraid, for I am with you. Don't be discouraged, for I am your God.
I will strengthen you and help you.

Isaiah 41:10 NLT

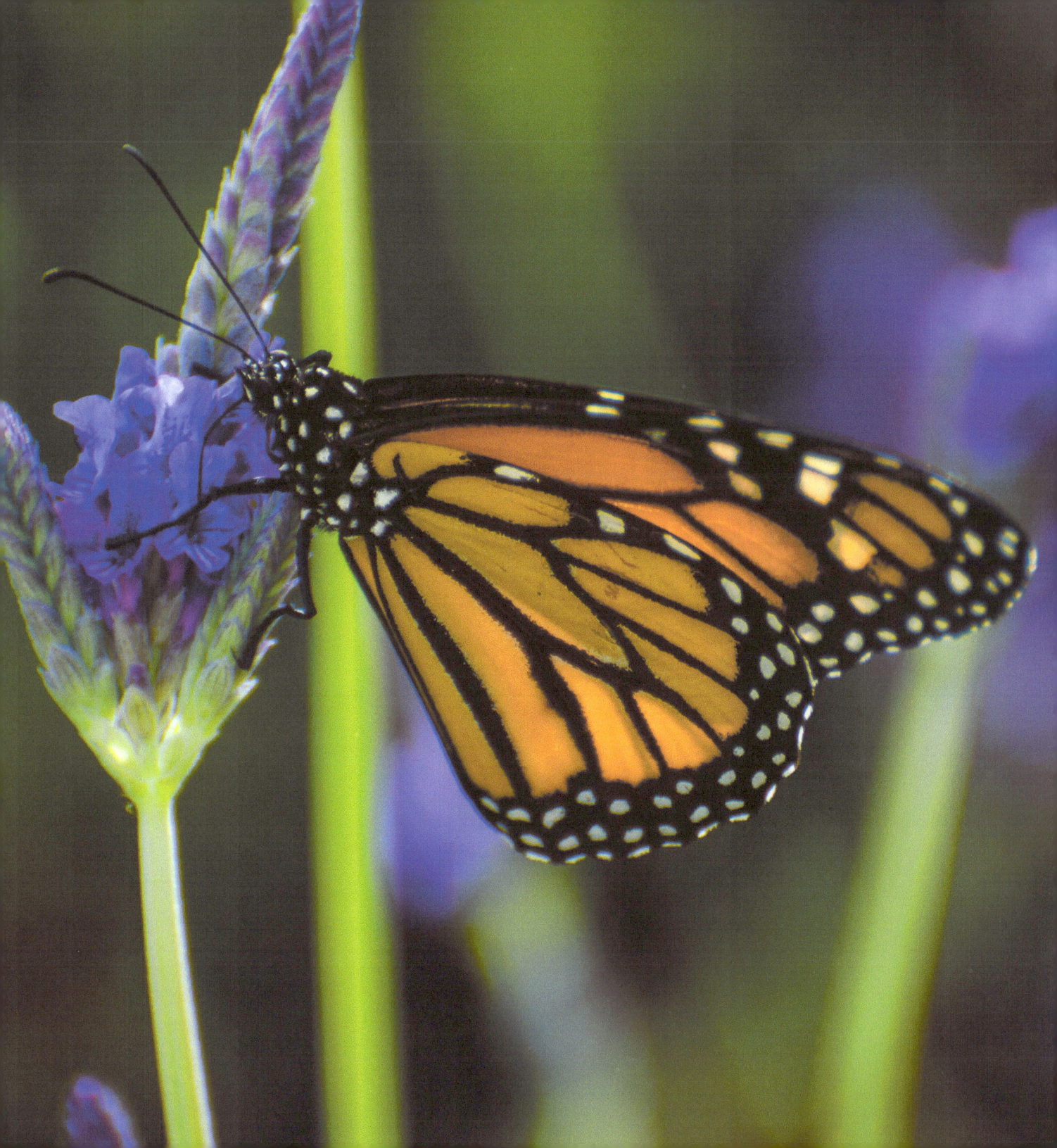

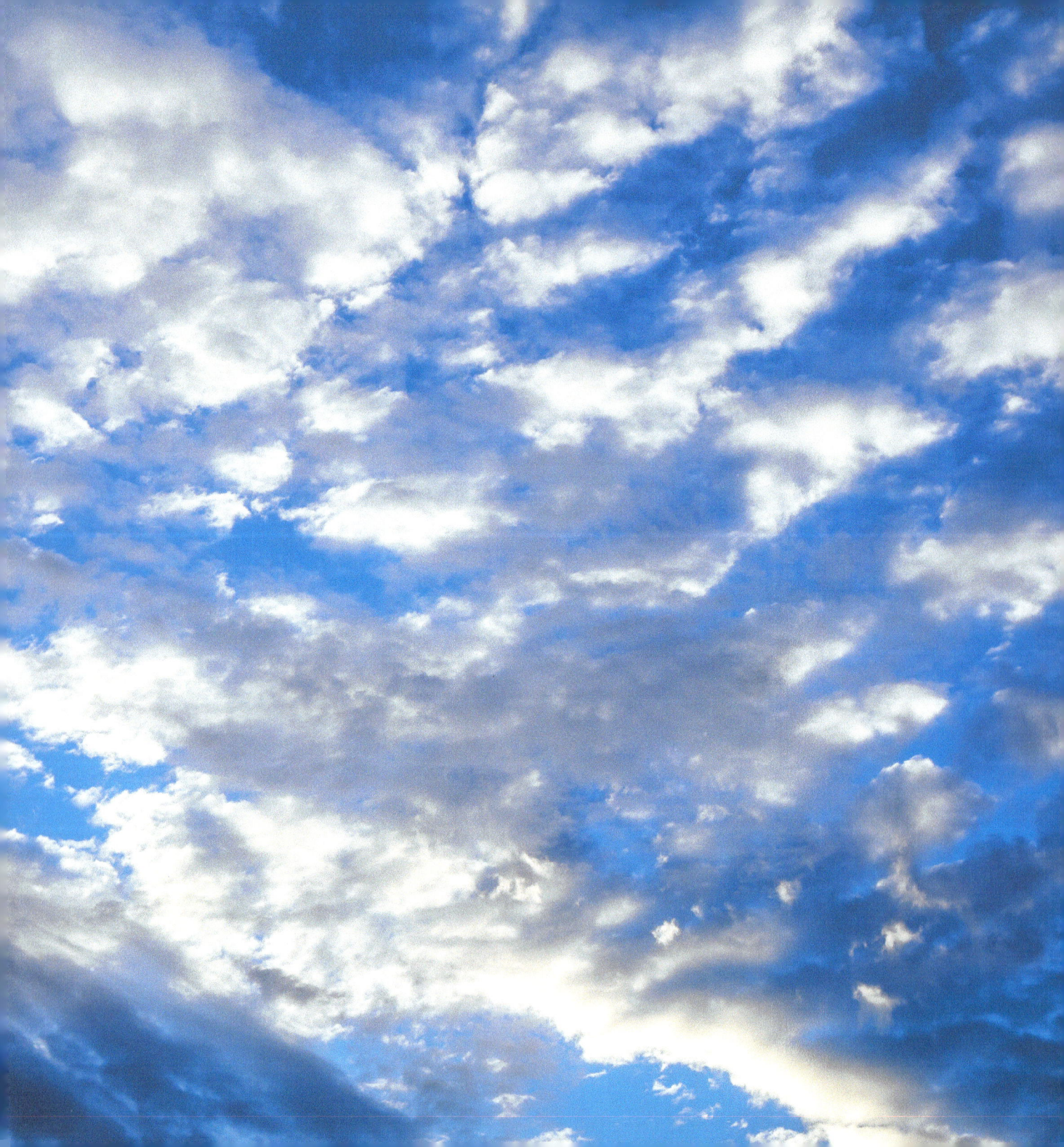

3
Elohim's Creation

...God created the heavens and the earth.

Genesis 1:1

When you find yourself in an impossible situation with no earthly answer, where will you go and what will you do? Knowing that your God created the heavens and the earth gives you the answer when there is nothing on earth to help you. Just look around at God's magnificent creation. Elohim is the One who can create something out of nothing and "makes the clouds His chariot" (Psalm 104:3). God's creation proves He can paint beauty and meaning into the "nothing" any person experiences in their lives. Paul wrote in Ephesians 3:20 that "God is able to do immeasurably more than all we ask or imagine, according to His power that is at work within us." In the Bible you discover the Triune God at work in creation. Genesis 1:2 says that the Spirit of God was hovering over the surface of the waters. And John 1:3 explains Jesus was present and working in creation as the Word—"All things came into being through Him, and apart from Him nothing came into being that has come into being." Elohim is more than enough for all your impossibles. You can trust Him today.

The earth was formless and void, and darkness was over the surface of the deep, and the Spirit of God was moving over the surface of the waters.

Genesis 1:2

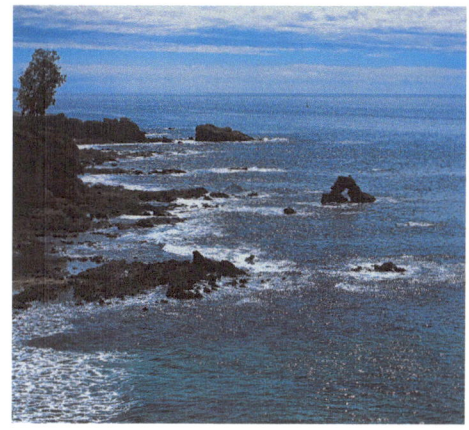

The story is told that one day a group of scientists got together and decided that man had progressed and advanced and no longer needed God. So they chose one of the scientists to go and tell God that they were finished with Him. The scientist walked up to God and told Him about all their advances and abilities and that indeed they no longer needed Him. God listened with patience and kindness. He said, "Okay, how about this? Let's have a man-making contest." The scientist replied enthusiastically, "Great!" God told him that they would do it the same as He did in the days of Adam. The scientist replied, "No problem," and reached down and grabbed a handful of dirt. God looked at him and kindly said, "You will have to get your own dirt." This made-up, imaginary story shows that only God can create something out of nothing.

AS SHARED BY CATHERINE MARTIN IN HER MESSAGE A DAY IN THE LIFE OF GOD

"Creation" is defined simply as *the work of God in bringing all things into existence*. Only God is eternal — everything else in the universe had a beginning. True creation is creation *ex nihilo* (out of nothing)…

THE BEGINNING OF THE WORLD — DR. HENRY M. MORRIS

By faith we understand that the entire universe was formed at God's command,
that what we now see did not come from anything that can be seen.

HEBREWS 11:3 NLT

My soul wakes early and turns to You, O God, for the light. Your light is better than life; therefore my lips shall praise You. Take my hand in Yours, and make the crooked places straight and the rough places plain, that Your name may be glorified in my daily walk and conversation.

F. B. MEYER

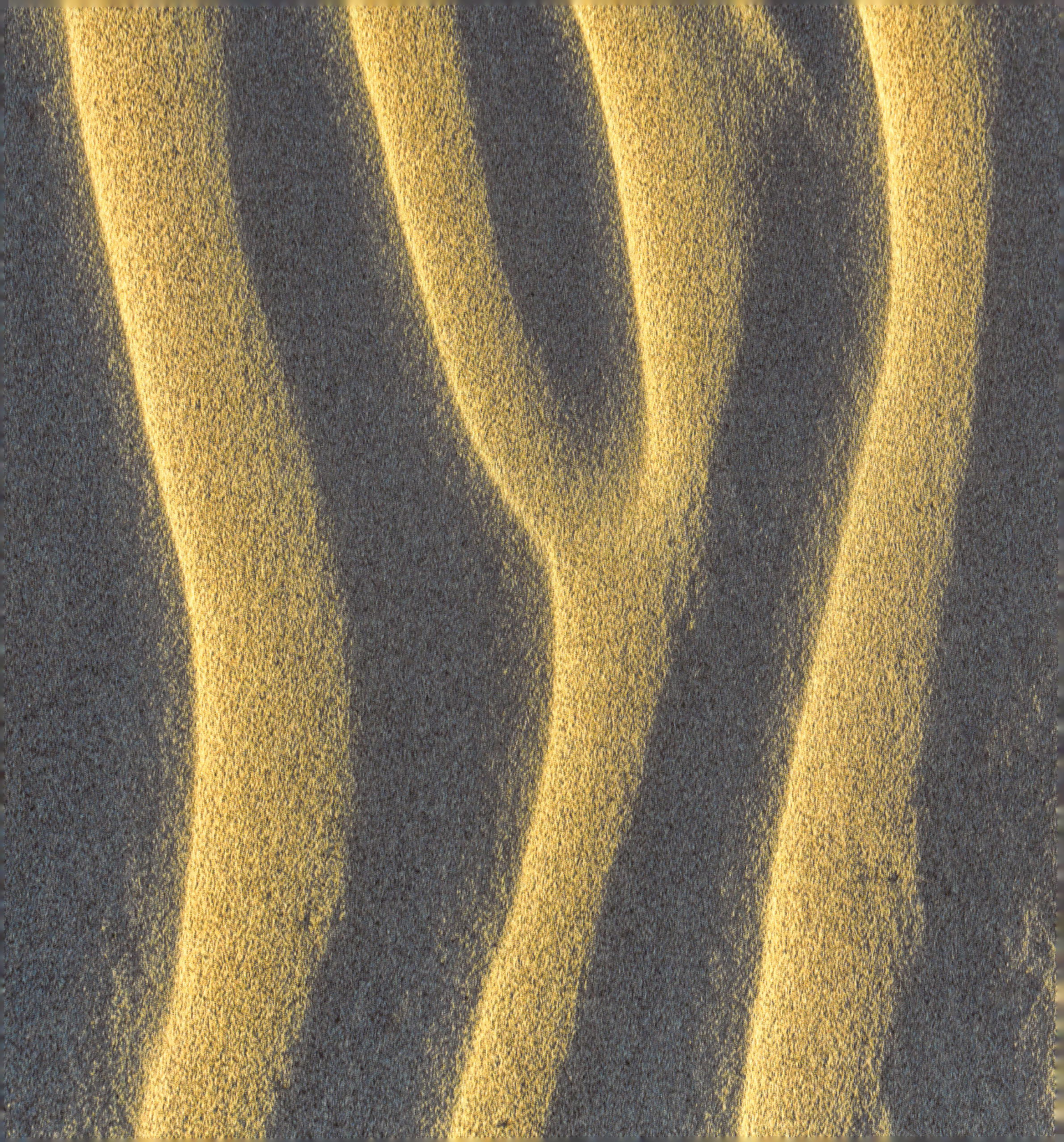

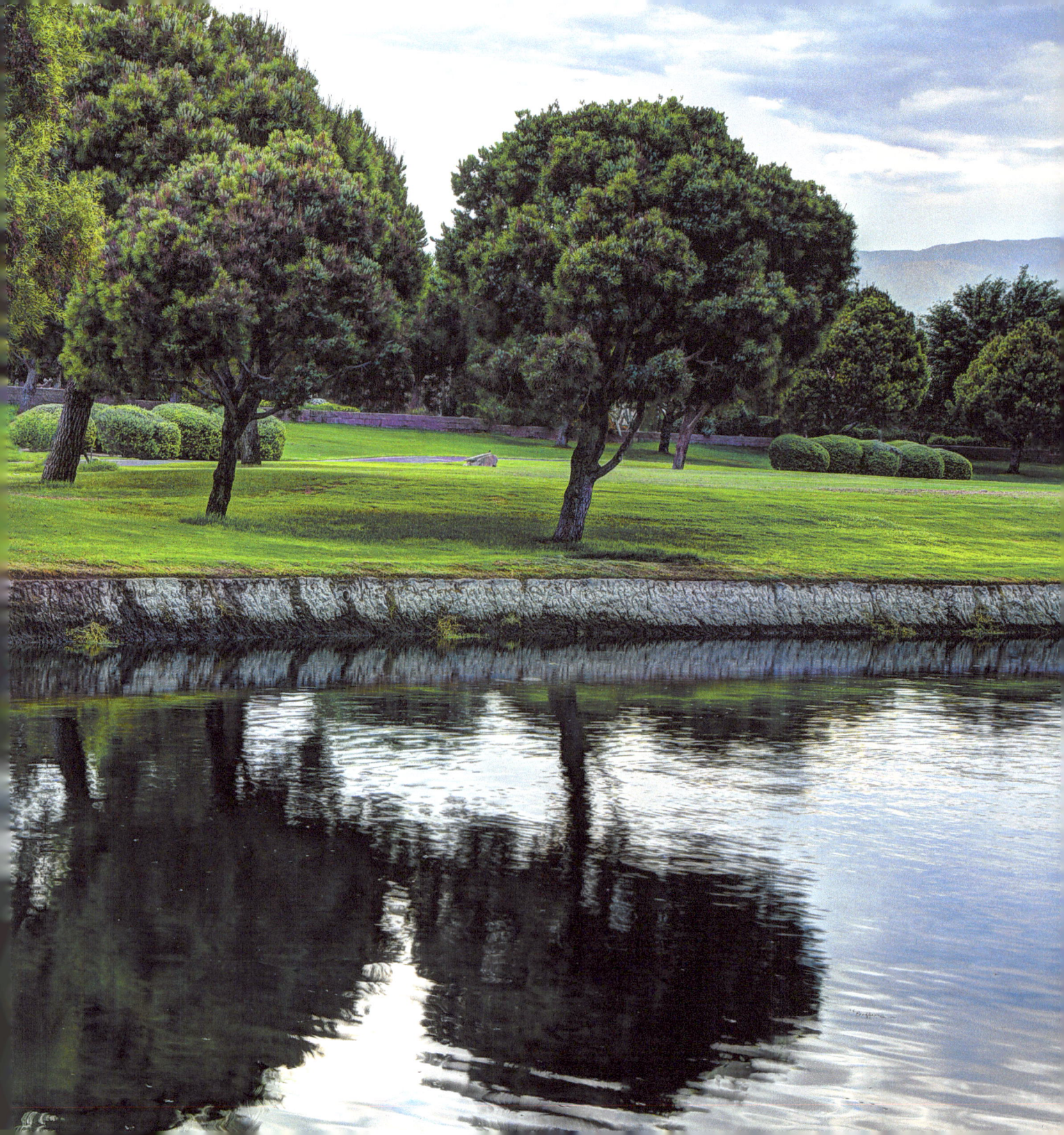

INTERLUDE
REFLECTIONS

KNOWING AND TRUSTING GOD

In the beginning was the Word, and the Word was with God, and the Word was God…
And the Word became flesh and dwelt among us, and we saw His glory…
JOHN 1:1, 14

How well do you know your God? He has revealed Himself in His creation and in Jesus as His One and Only Son. Just think—more than two thousand years ago, God Himself came and lived among us. In fact, John 1:18 tells us that Jesus explained God. Jesus is "the exact representation of His [God's] nature" (Hebrews 1:3). If you want to know what God is like, look at Jesus. If you want to know God, you can—through Jesus. Jesus said, "I am the way, the truth, and the life; No one comes to the Father, but through Me" (John 14:6). Will you come to Jesus today to begin the great adventure of knowing and trusting God?

Lord, thank You for making Yourself known to me.
I draw near to You now and desire a relationship with You.
Thank you for the promise of forgiveness of sins and eternal life. In Jesus' name, Amen.

FIRST DAY

In the first chapter of the Bible, Genesis 1, we are introduced to God, the Creator, and learn His name, Elohim. We discover His creation is laid out in the form and pattern of "days," and we see what He does in a first, second, third, fourth, fifth, sixth, and seventh day. Now we turn our attention to all Elohim can create in a day. On the first day, "God said, 'Let there be light,' and there was light." These are the first recorded words of God in the Bible. God is turning on the light to begin His story, the true story of time's beginning, and His creation of everything in heaven and earth, including us.

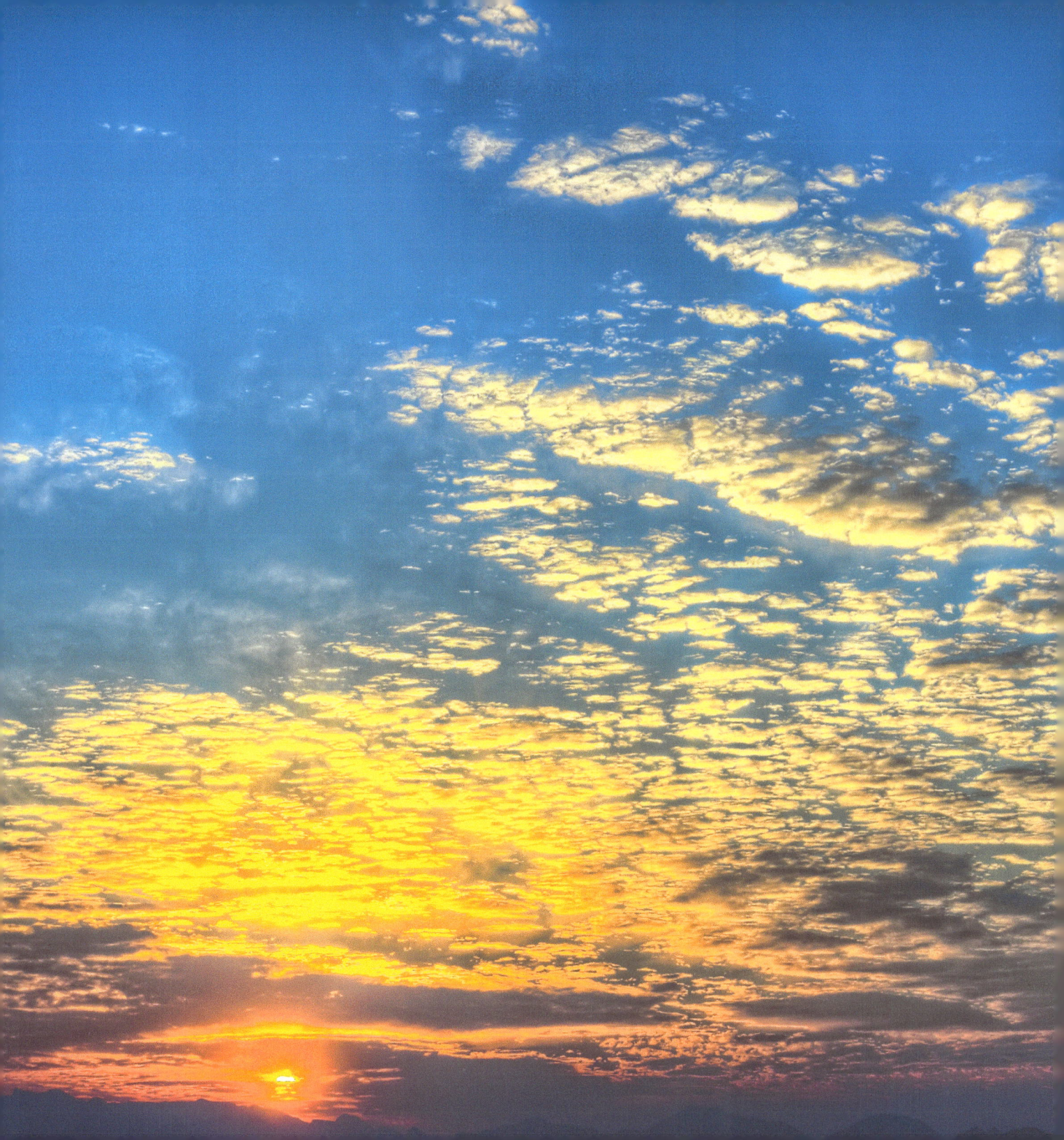

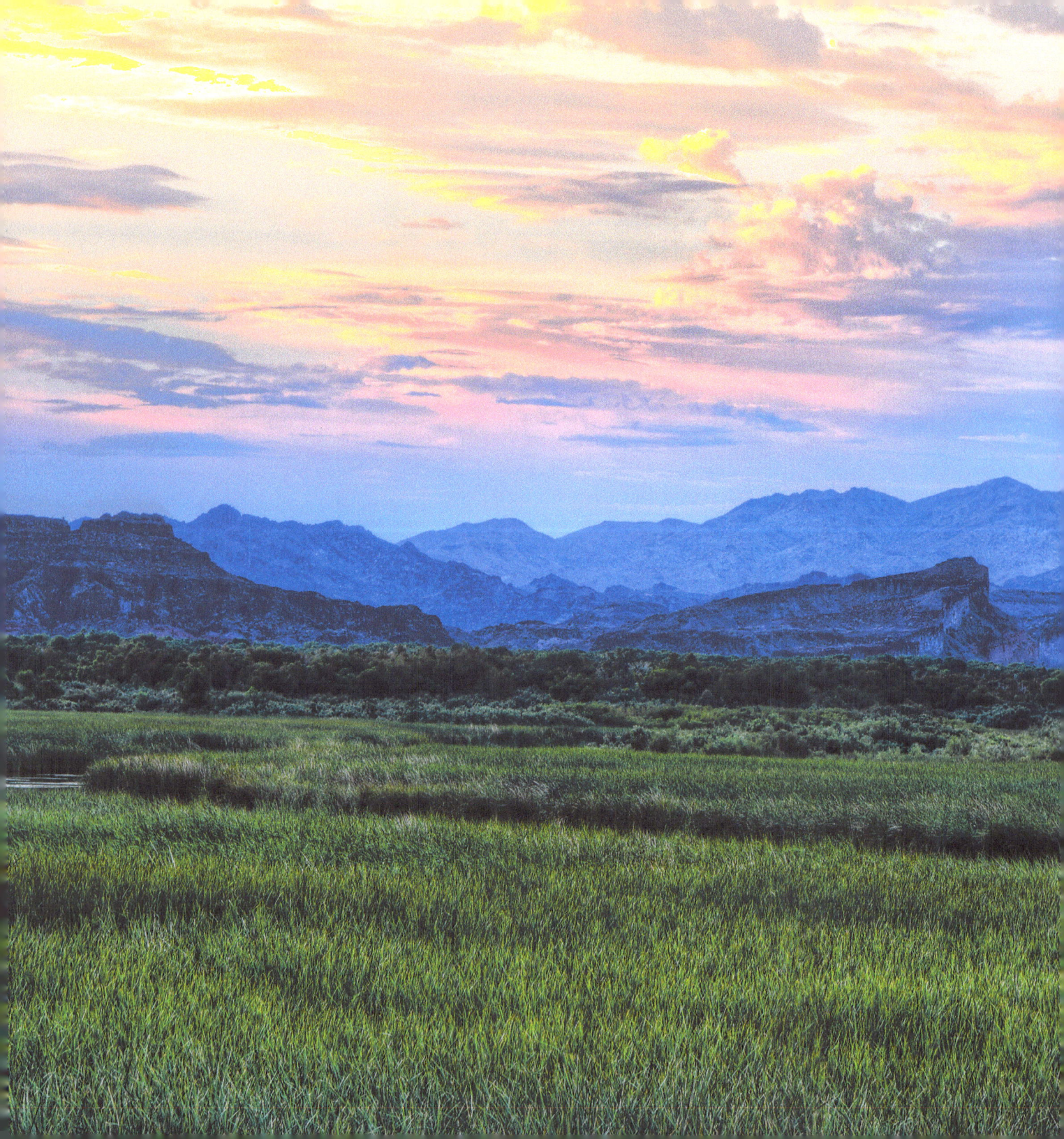

4
THE POWER OF GOD'S WORD

Then God said, "Let there be light," and there was light.

GENESIS 1:3 NLT

Where is your trust? Is it in God and His Word or is it in feelings and the world? What commands your beliefs and actions? Your response will determine your steadfastness in the storms of life. A reporter roamed the streets of a large city and asked people what truth is and whether you can know truth. Some responded that you couldn't know what is true. Others said that truth is how you feel or whatever you want it to be. In Genesis 1:3 we discover the Word of God in action: "Then God said, 'Let there be light,' and there was light." John 1:3 tells us Jesus is the Word and all things came into being through Him. So in Genesis 1:3 we are seeing Jesus, the Word, at work as Elohim commanded light into existence. God is the measure of truth, and the fact that Elohim, the Creator, has spoken, reveals that He is the authority for our belief. God determines truth, and we discover it. When we trust God and His Word, we become like trees firmly planted and steadfast (Jeremiah 17:8). So today, will you open the pages of His Word, discover all God says, and trust in Him?

Blessed are those who trust in the LORD… they are like trees planted along a riverbank with roots that go deep into the water.

JEREMIAH 17:8 NLT

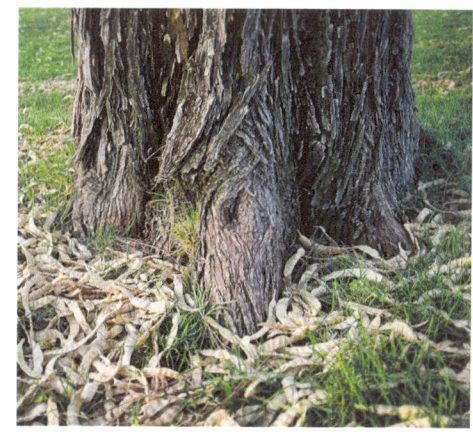

For you have been born again, but not to a life that will quickly end. Your new life will last forever because it comes from the eternal living word of God. As the Scriptures say, "People are like grass; their beauty is like a flower in the field. The grass withers and the flower fades. But the word of the Lord remains forever."

1 Peter 1:23-25 NLT

Heaven and earth will pass away, but God's Word will not. This means that no matter how I feel or what I experience, I can choose to depend on the Word of God as the unchanging reality in my life…The Lord is concerned about what we go through, but I believe He is more concerned about how we respond to what we go through. That response is a matter of our wills. He allows the trials, temptations, and pressures of life to come so that we have the opportunity to respond either by trusting our feelings and life experiences, or by taking Him at His Word. I have learned to get into the habit of taking God at His Word…I have made a lifetime commitment to bank my life on the Word of God, and God has honored that commitment.

Faith Is Not A Feeling — Ney Bailey

Everyone who hears these words of Mine, and acts on them, may be compared to a wise man who built his house on the rock. And the rain fell, and the floods came, and the winds blew and slammed against that house; and yet it did not fall, for it had been founded on the rock.

Matthew 7:24-25

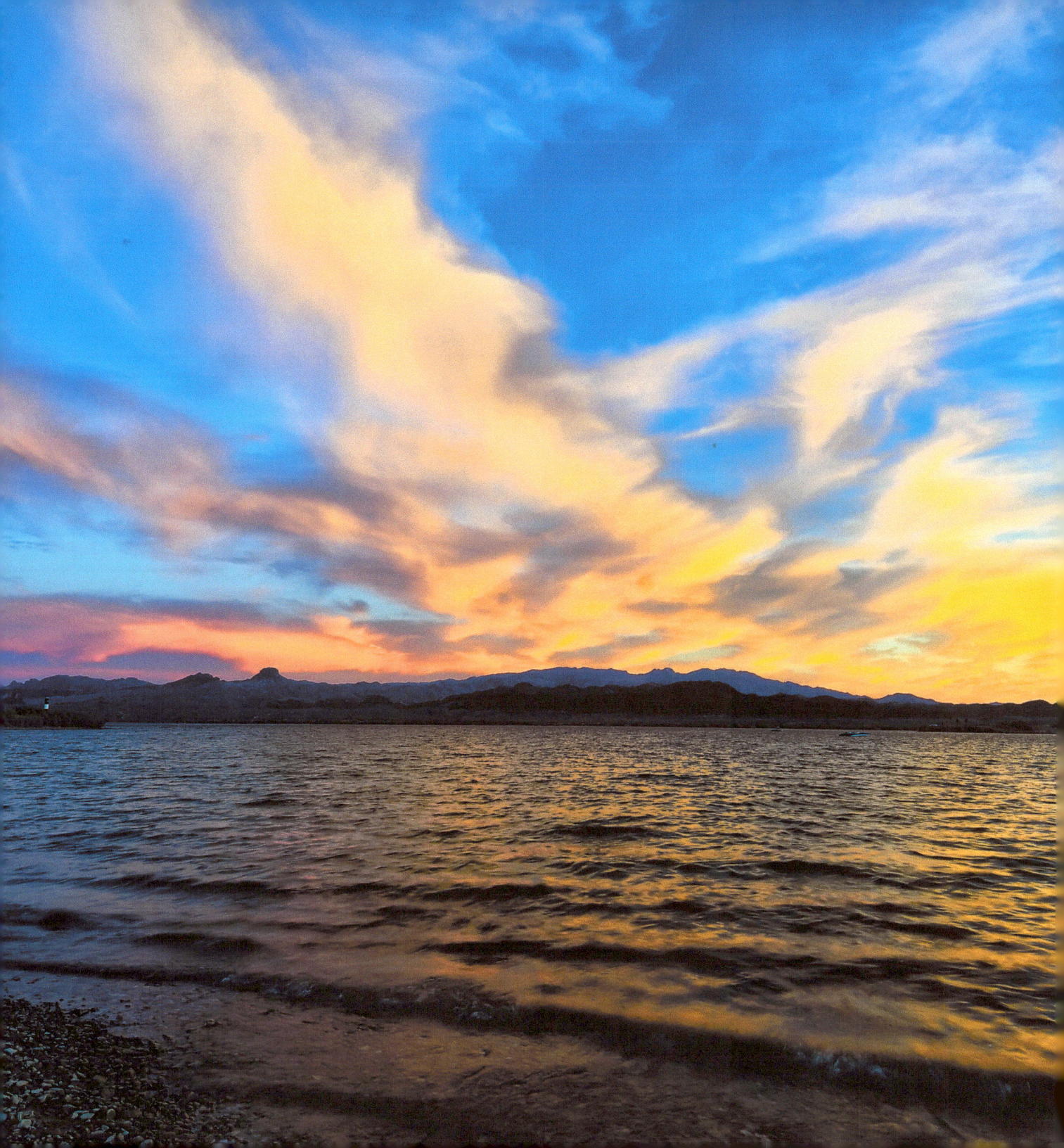

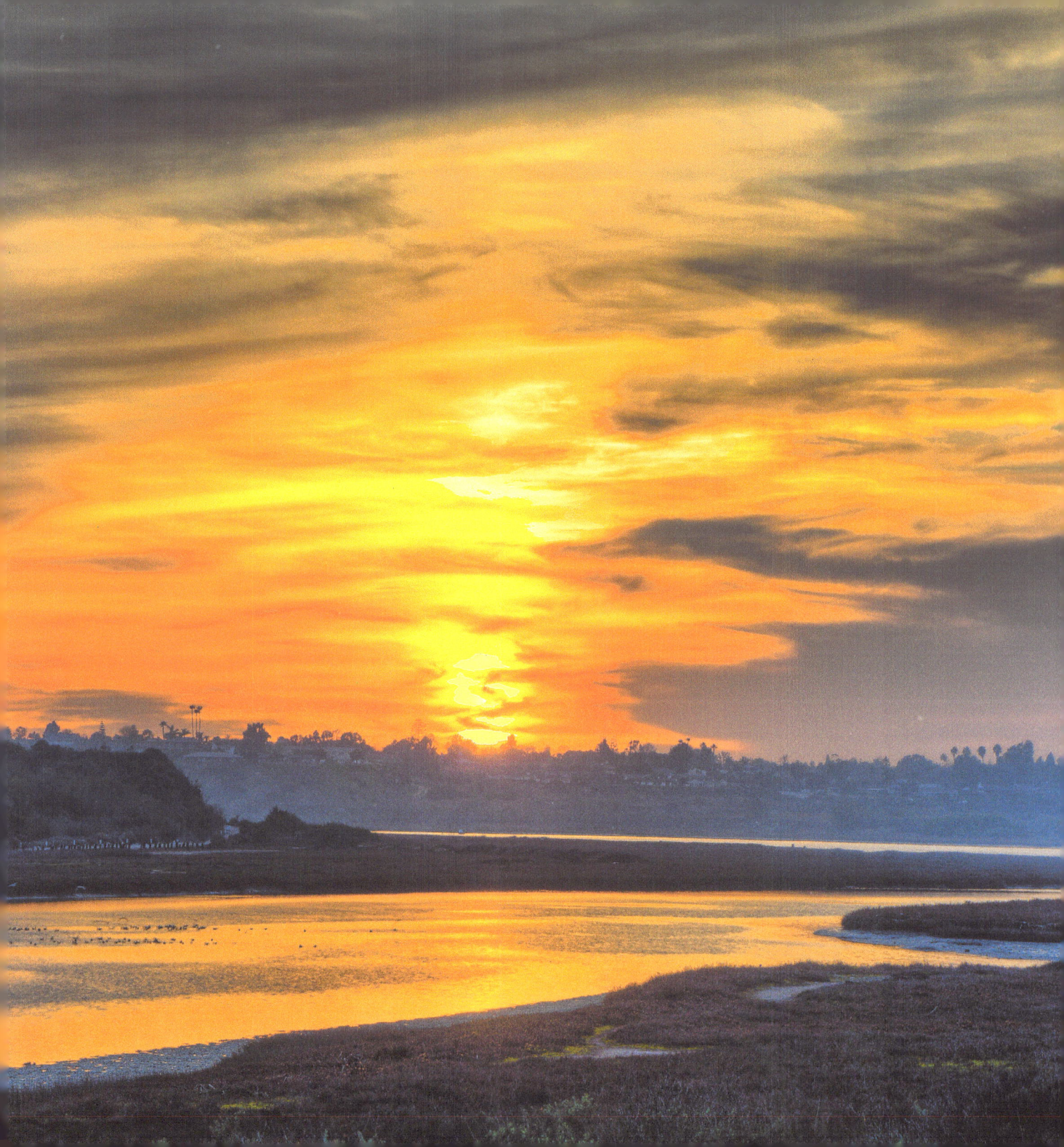

5 Painting The Empty Canvas

Then He separated the light from the darkness. God called the light "day" and the darkness "night." And evening passed and morning came, marking the first day.

Genesis 1:4-5 NLT

Artists who paint or draw have said that the most daunting moment is facing the empty canvas. Lifting the brush and dipping it in the paint and then touching the chosen surface to make the first mark is always a brave and adventurous move. Imagine the Triune God, Elohim, "in the beginning," as He made His first mark on the canvas, so to speak, by saying "Let there be light." God's ability to create in the biblical sense is unique and entirely different than the human activity we describe as creativity. Dr. Ronald Youngblood, in his book, *How It All Began*, describes the Old Testament use of the word, *create*. He writes: "It always has God as its subject; it is never used of human activity. We may make or form or fashion, but only God creates." The psalmist writes: "On the glorious splendor of Your majesty and on Your wonderful works, I will meditate" (Psalm 145:7). As a result, the psalmist tells all who will listen of the greatness of God. Those who hear remember God's abundant goodness. "God saw that the light was good." May you trust in His goodness and beauty today.

God saw that the light was good.

Genesis 1:4 NLT

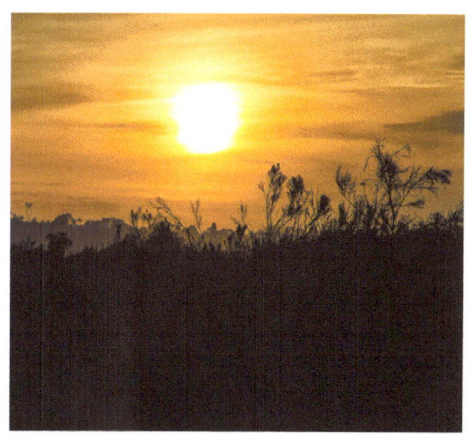

Nothing in the created order is equal to the remarkable essence God assigns to light. It establishes the speed limit for the entire universe. Its speed is the only constant in the universe. It is outside of time. It never ages. It anchors the laws of relativity. It is both a wave and particle. It allows us to see. It comforts us with its presence and depresses us by its absence. It conveys the energy and warmth that allows us to live. It consumes darkness but itself is never consumed by darkness. It is mentioned as the first thing God created after the heavens and the earth. It apparently has a divine aspect to its nature.

More Than Meets The Eye — Richard A. Swenson, M.D.

"The new is in the old concealed; the old is in the new revealed." This famous statement by Saint Augustine expresses the remarkable way in which the two testaments of the Bible are so closely interrelated with each other. The key to understanding the New Testament in its fullest is to see in it the fulfillment of those things that were revealed in the background of the Old Testament. The Old Testament points forward in time, preparing God's people for the work of Christ in the New Testament.

Dr. R.C. Sproul

Christ is the visible image of the invisible God. He existed before anything was created and is supreme over all creation, for through Him God created everything in the heavenly realms and on earth. He made the things we can see and the things we can't see…Everything was created through Him and for Him. He existed before anything else, and He holds all creation together.

Colossians 1:15-17 nlt

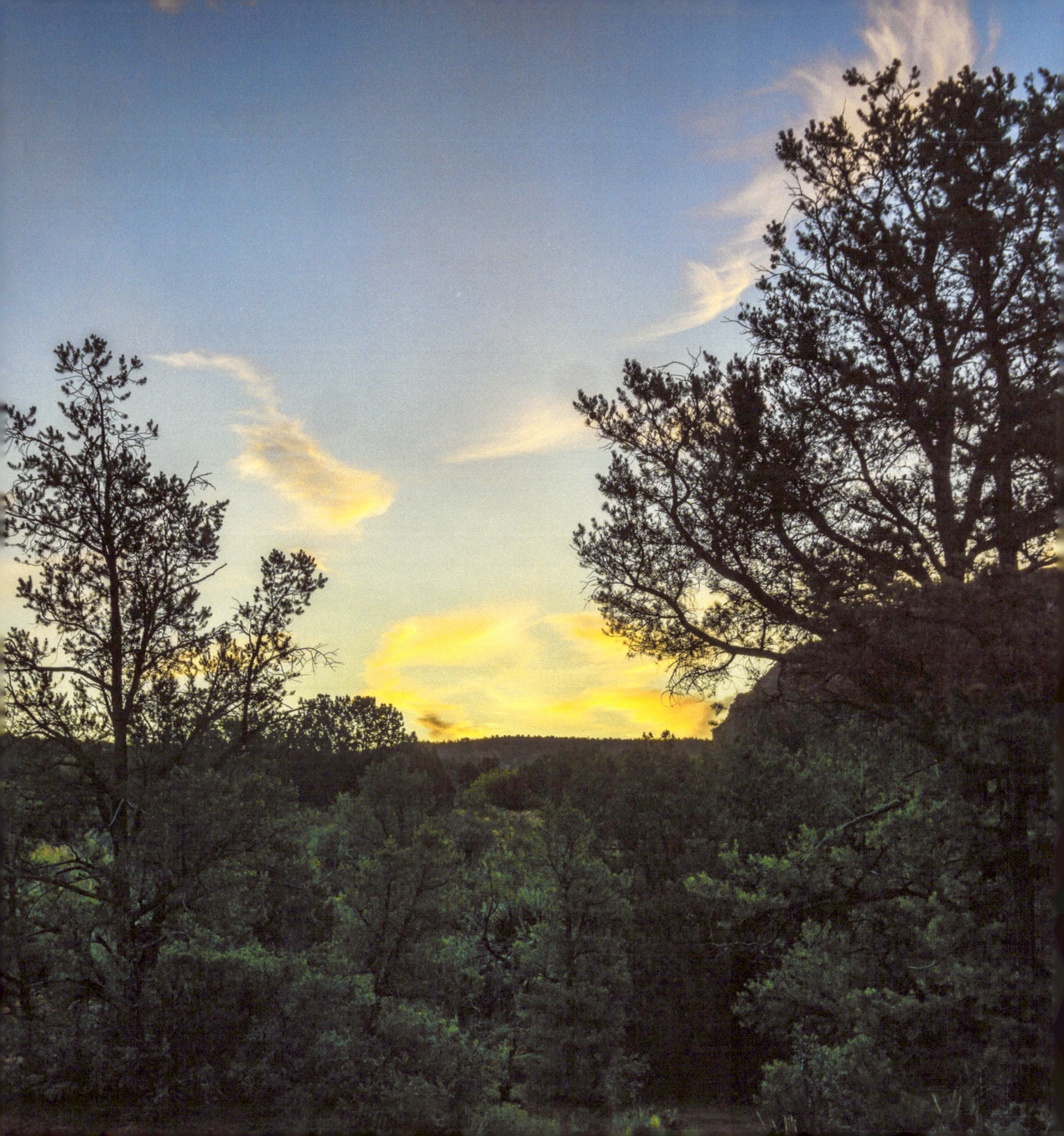

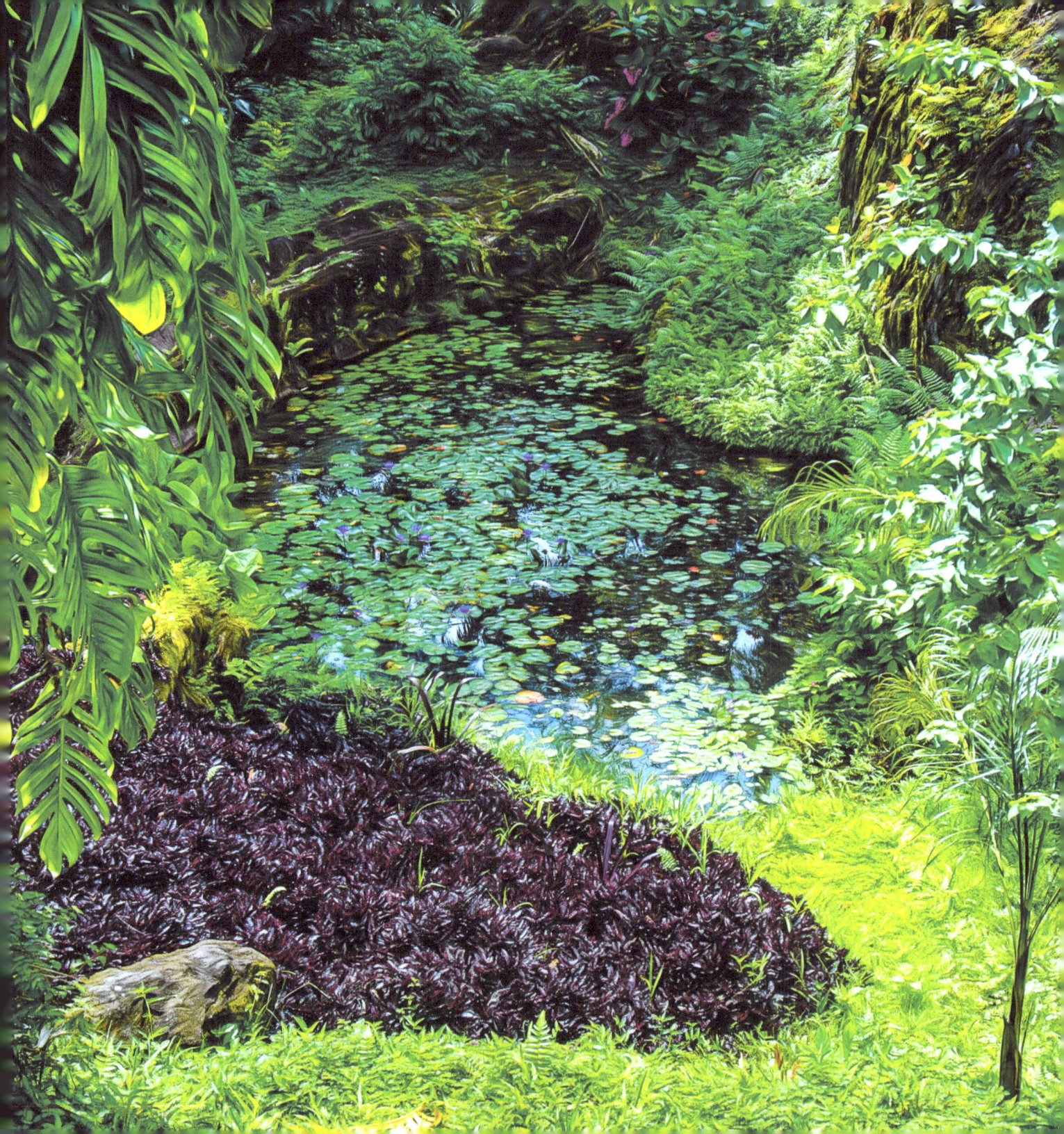

6
From Darkness To Light

The Word gave life to everything that was created, and his life brought light to everyone. The light shines in the darkness, and the darkness can never extinguish it.

John 1:4-5

John described himself in the gospel he wrote as "the disciple Jesus loved" (John 21:20). He clearly enjoyed an intimate relationship with Jesus. In John's gospel, he opens up the true identity of Jesus as "the Word" and clearly demonstrates Jesus is God. John writes, "In the beginning the Word already existed. The Word was with God, and the Word was God. God created everything through Him" (John 1:1-3). John reveals that the Word gives light and life (John 1:4-5). Light is necessary for growth. We know in the process of photosynthesis plants use sunlight and other essentials to grow. Jesus said, "I am the light of the world. If you follow Me, you won't have to walk in darkness, because you will have the light that leads to life" (John 8:12). No wonder on the first day of creation, God said, "Let there be light." We learn in 1 John 1:5 that "God is light, and in Him there is no darkness at all." At the end of God's book, the Bible, we see that in heaven there is no need for lamps or the sun, because God Himself will shine (Revelation 22:5). Trust in Jesus today and enjoy His light and life.

This is the message we have heard from Him, and announce to you, that God is light, and in Him there is no darkness at all.

1 John 1:5

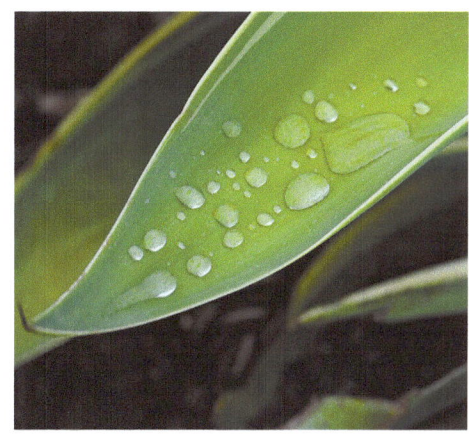

Christ is the light of life; not merely a teacher of truth in the abstract, but a practical and personal Guide. The light He gives is the light of life, that is, the light that men can live by, shining on the path of duty, perplexity and trial, illuminating and cheering every step of the Christian life.

THE CHRIST IN THE BIBLE COMMENTARY — A.B. SIMPSON

The Word of God brings light! The Father is the source of all things (Genesis 1:1), the Spirit is the energizer of all things (Genesis 1:2), and the Word is the revealer of all things (Genesis 1:3)…When light appeared, "God divided the light from the darkness." Darkness was not removed completely, so far as the earth was concerned, but only separated from the light…The very first time He used the word "day" (Hebrew yom), He defined it as the "light," to distinguish it from the darkness called "night." Having separated day and night, God had completed his first day's work.

THE GENESIS RECORD — DR. HENRY M. MORRIS

And there will no longer be any night; and they will not have the need of the light of a lamp nor the light of the sun, because the Lord God will illumine them; and they will reign forever and ever.

REVELATION 22:5

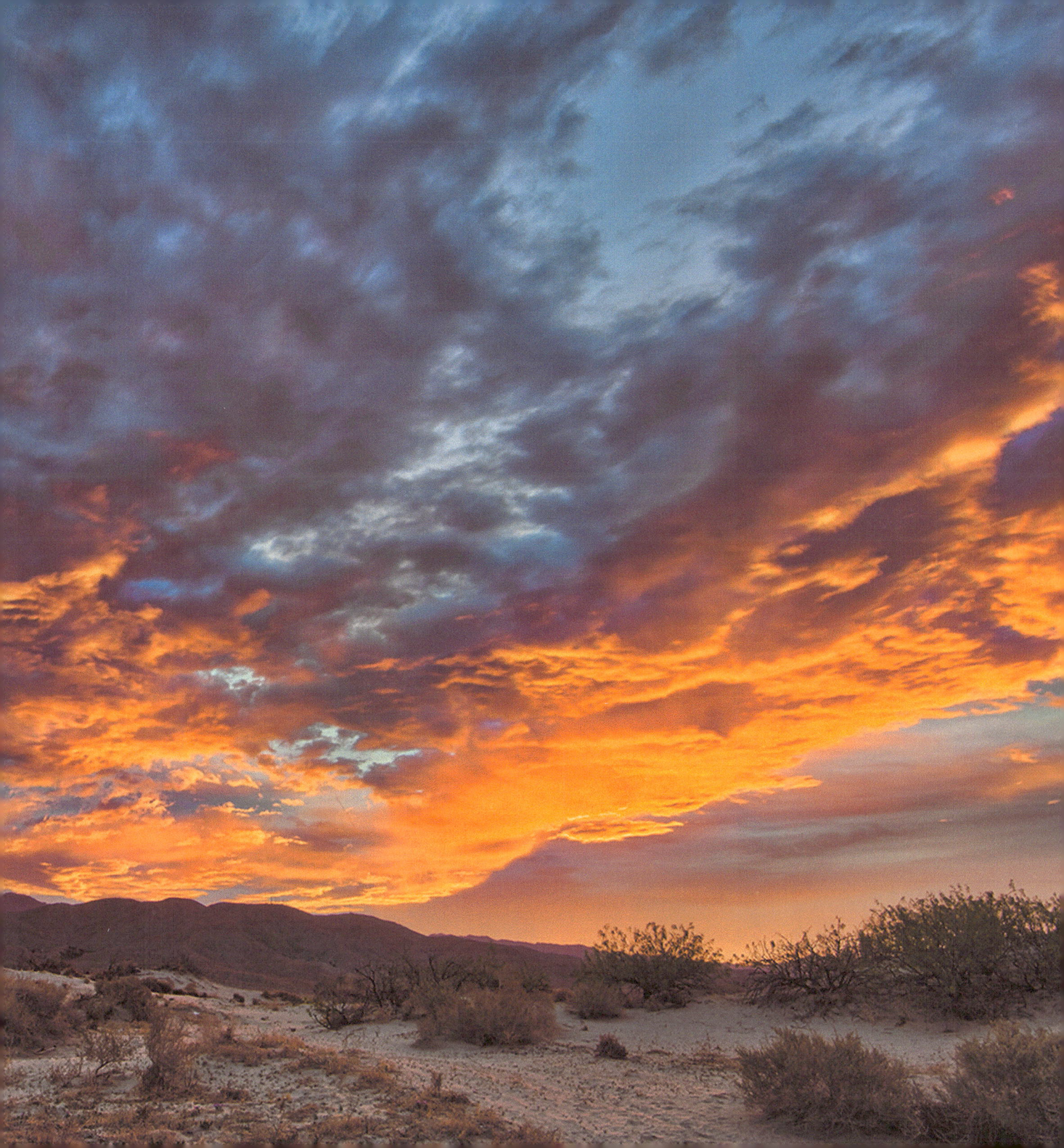

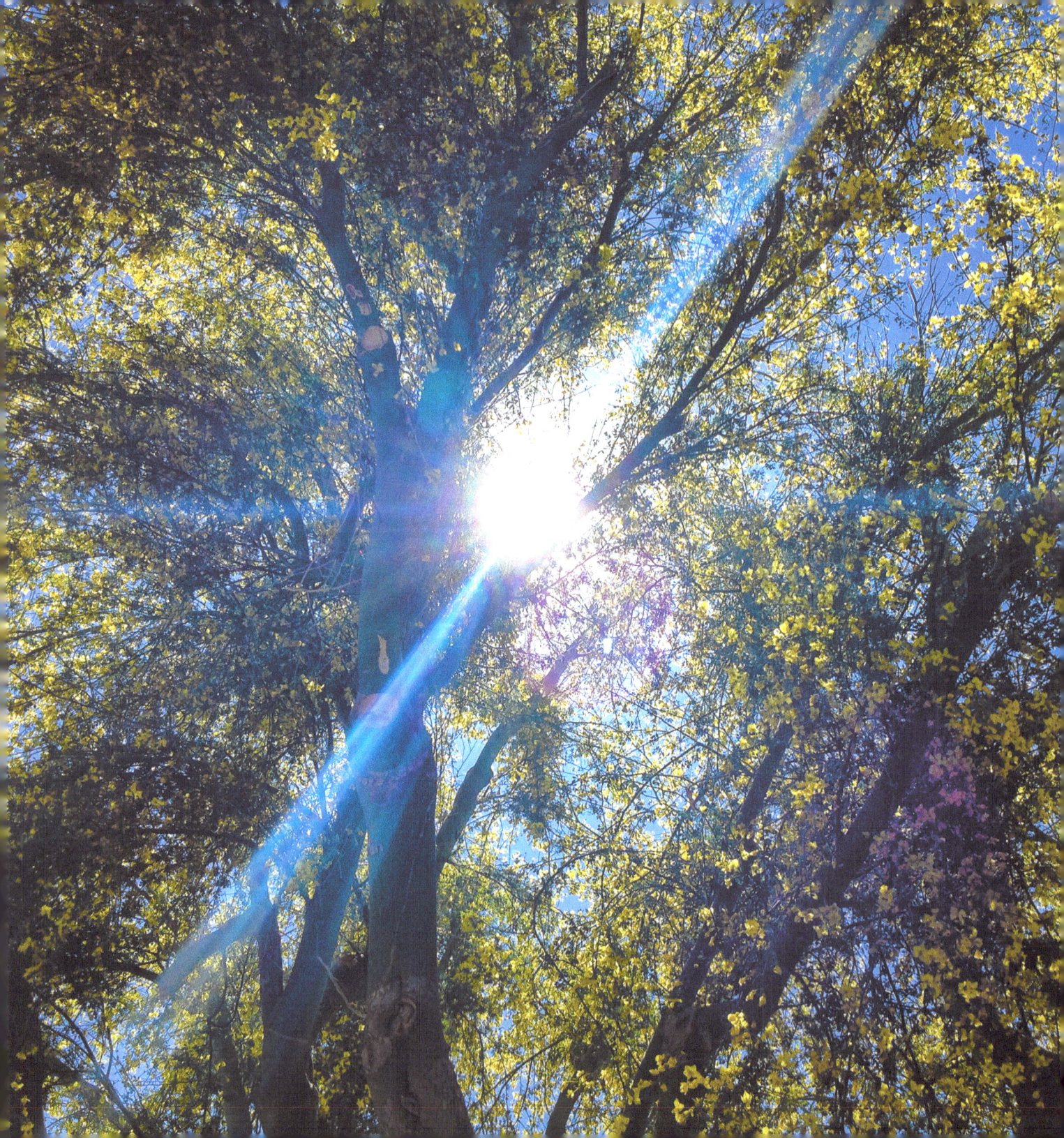

FIRST DAY
REFLECTIONS

FOLLOW THE LIGHT

*The people who were sitting in darkness saw a great Light, and those who were
sitting in the land and shadow of death, upon them, a Light dawned.*
MATTHEW 4:16

The prophet Isaiah told the people of his day words from God about a future time when a great light would shine on people who were walking in darkness and living in a dark land (Isaiah 9:2). Matthew, a tax collector who left everything to follow Jesus, confirmed that Jesus was that great Light spoken of by Isaiah (Matthew 4:16). Jesus made a life-changing promise while on earth: "I am the Light of the world; he who follows Me will not walk in darkness, but will have the light of life" (John 8:12). Will you follow the light today? Will you follow Jesus? If you will, you will not walk in darkness, but will have the light of life.

*Lord, thank You for being the Light of the world.
Today I choose to follow You and Your light. May I experience a sunrise in my heart, and
the dawn of a new day as You, the great Light, shine on me. In Jesus' name, Amen.*

SECOND DAY

And now, on the second day, God continued commanding creation into existence. He said, "Let there be a space between the waters, to separate the waters of the heavens from the waters of the earth. And that is what happened…God called the space 'sky'" (Genesis 1:7-8 NLT). He is preparing the way for what He will create in other days including birds and animals and humans. The expanse or space that God created is the atmosphere and sky, perfect for life on earth. Think about all God did on the second day and trust Him with your care and concerns today.

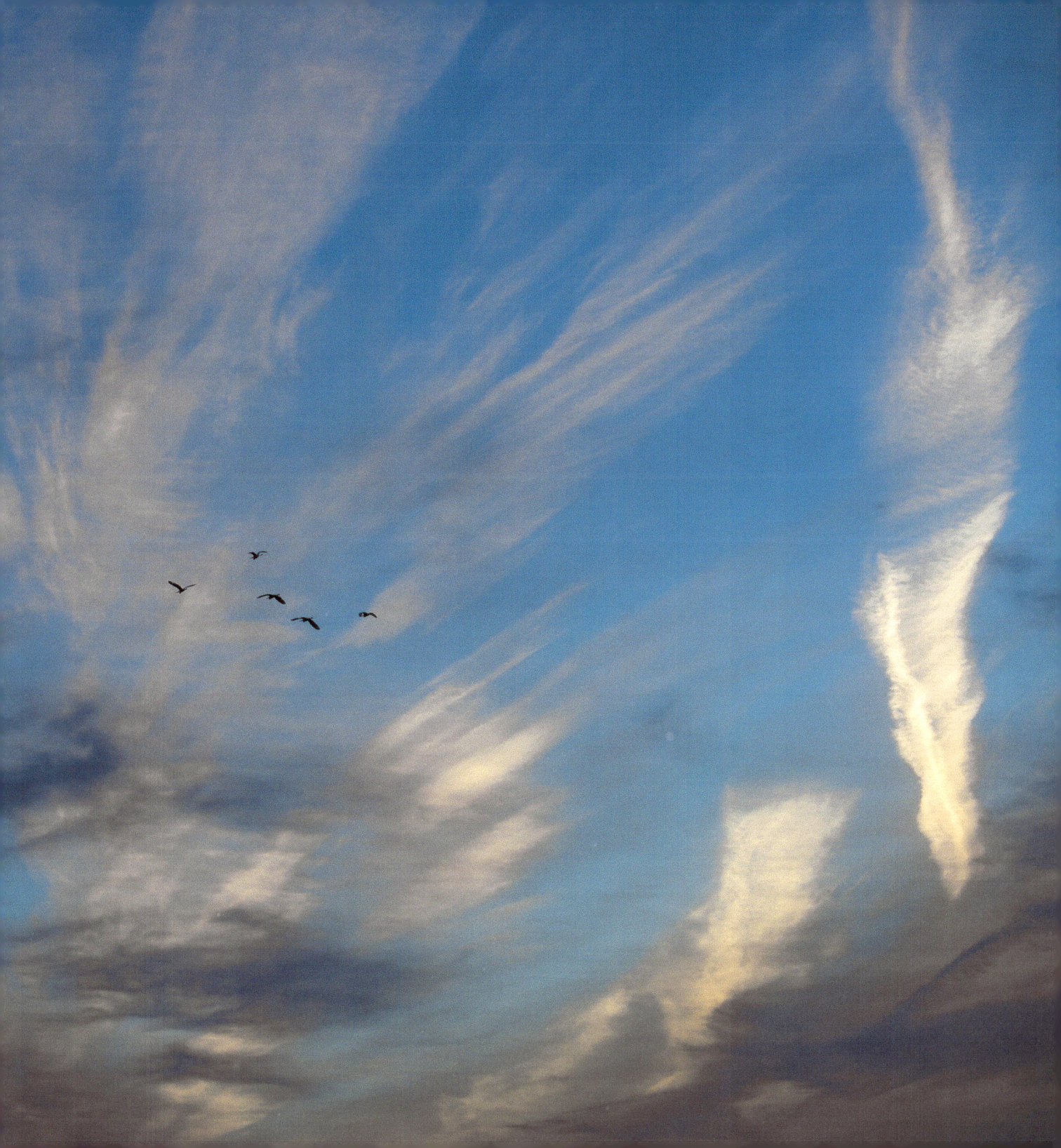

7
Looking Up

Then God said, "Let there be a space between the waters"…God called the space "sky." And evening passed and morning came, marking the second day.

GENESIS 1:6-8 NLT

When I was a little girl, I used to lie in the grass on my back to look up at the sky. The expanse was awesome to me and when it was filled with clouds, I was often overwhelmed with the glorious beauty. As we grow up to be adults, we sometimes lose that sense of wonder we had when we were children. Let's stop for a moment and regain the view of a child. Maybe we need to find a grassy area in our back yard, lie on our backs and look up. Much of what we see is invisible to the naked eye, yet nevertheless real. When God created the expanse of the heavens, He created atmosphere and sky. Atmosphere is composed of gases that are found in layers—troposphere, stratosphere, mesosphere, thermosphere, and exosphere containing unique features including temperature and pressure. Earth's atmosphere is perfectly designed to protect life on earth. Only God can command the atmosphere and sky into existence. He did it with you and me in mind so we could actually live here on planet earth. Lift up your eyes to your God in heaven and trust Him with every detail of your life today.

I lift my eyes to You, O God, enthroned in heaven.

PSALM 123:1 NLT

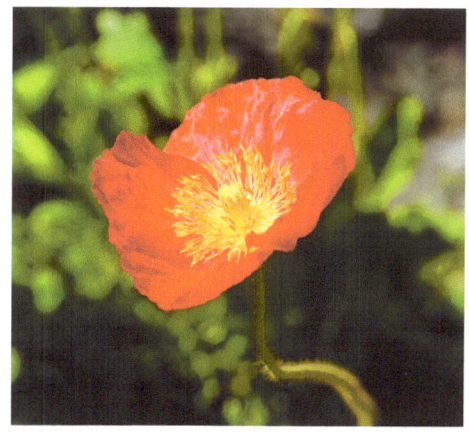

He spoke the universe into existence. Nothingness obeys His voice. He controls time, space, matter, and light. He monitors the position of every elementary particle. He is sufficient unto Himself. He does not need anybody or anything to accomplish His purposes. He answers to no one. He obeys only His own counsel.

More Than Meets The Eye — Richard A. Swenson, M.D.

Since He has at His command all the power in the universe, the Lord God omnipotent can do anything as easily as anything else. All His acts are done without effort. He expends no energy that must be replenished… All the power required to do all that He wills to do lies in undiminished fullness in His own infinite being.

The Knowledge Of The Holy — A.W. Tozer

I am convinced that no one can ever begin to live supernaturally and have the faith to believe God for impossible things, if he does not know what God is like…You start by getting to know God, who He is, what He is like, and the benefits which we enjoy when we belong to Him…Our view of God determines the quality of our faith. A small view of God results in a small faith. But great faith is the result of a correct biblical view of God as one who is great and worthy of our trust.

Believing God For The Impossible — Dr. Bill Bright

Yours, O LORD, is the greatness, the power, the glory, the victory, and the majesty. Everything in the heavens and on the earth is Yours, O LORD, and this is Your kingdom. We adore You as the one who is over all things.

1 Chronicles 29:11 NLT

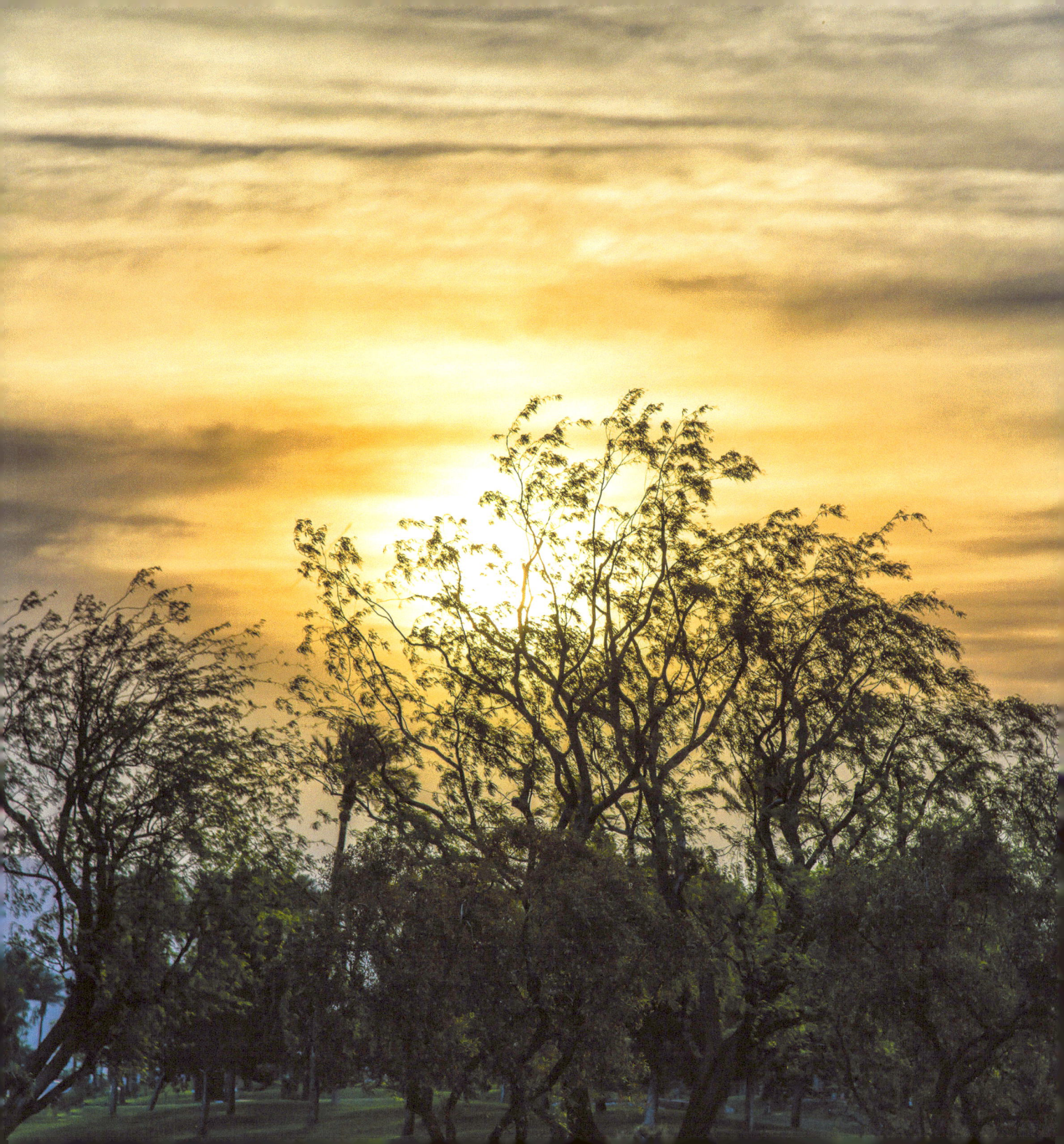

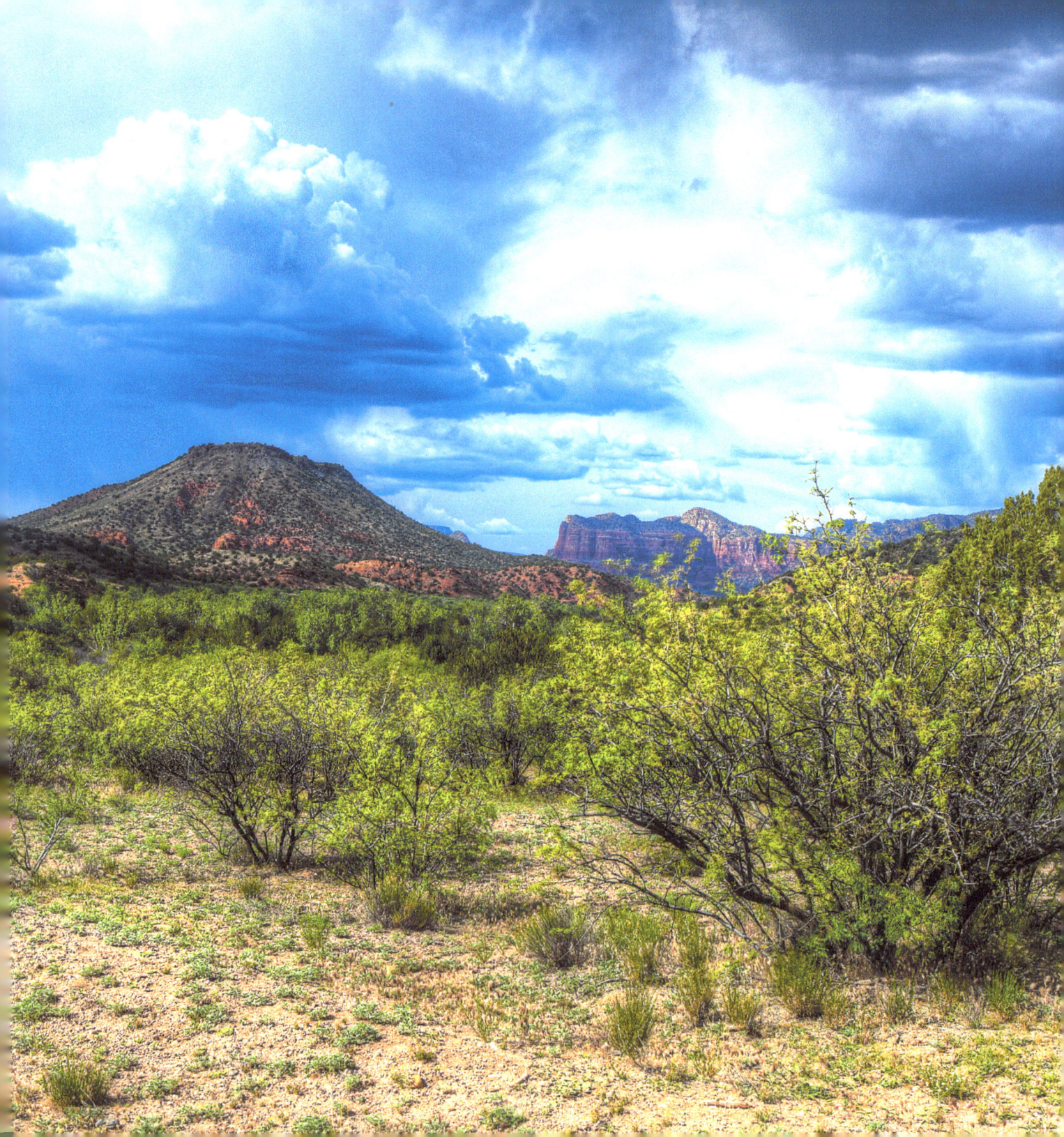

8
God's Chariot Of Clouds

You make the clouds Your chariot; You ride upon the wings of the wind.

Psalm 104:3 NLT

God's voice is heard in all that He has created. When you see His creation in the skies, You are witnessing Triune God's glory and His artistry. David, the man after God's own heart, wrote: "The heavens proclaim the glory of God. The skies display His craftsmanship. Day after day they continue to speak; night after night they make Him known" (Psalm 19:1-2 NLT). As you read on in the Psalms, you discover more about God than you may have ever known. He makes the clouds His chariot and He rides upon the wings of the wind. George Wood, in *A Psalm In Your Heart*, says that we are being given a glimpse of God at His workbench as He builds "His master work of earth and sky." Just think about the glory of God seen in His chariot of clouds. There are more than a hundred types of clouds with three general categories—cirrus, stratus, and cumulus—and ten types within those categories. No cloud is ever the same. Only God can make a cloud and once designed, it is His chariot. So the next time you look up at the clouds in the sky, "be still and know" that He is God (Psalm 46:10).

The heavens proclaim the glory of God. The skies display His crafsmanship.

Psalm 19:1 NLT

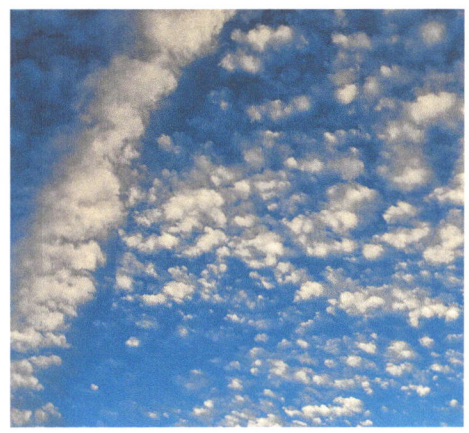

Immortal, invisible, God only wise, in light inaccessible hid from our eyes;
most blessed, most glorious, the Ancient of Days, almighty, victorious, thy great name we praise.
Unresting, unhasting, and silent as light, nor wanting, nor wasting, thou rulest in might;
thy justice like mountains high soaring above thy clouds, which are fountains of goodness and love.
To all life thou givest, to both great and small; in all life thou livest, the true life of all;
we blossom and flourish as leaves on the tree, and wither and perish but naught changeth thee.
Great Father of glory, pure Father of light, thine angels adore thee, all veiling their sight;
all praise we would render, O help us to see 'tis only the splendor of light hideth thee.

IMMORTAL, INVISIBLE, GOD ONLY WISE — WALTER C. SMITH

"Let all that I am praise the LORD. O LORD my God, how great you are! You are robed with honor and majesty. You are dressed in a robe of light. You stretch out the starry curtain of the heavens; you lay out the rafters of your home in the rain clouds. You make the clouds your chariot; you ride upon the wings of the wind." (Psalm 104:1-3 NLT). The Psalmist in Psalm 104 takes us by the hand and walks us back in time when all was fresh and pure. He draws open the shutters of heaven and lets us look in on God at His workbench—designing and building His master work of earth and sky. In such a setting you become still and hushed, reverent again…You are now outside of your own pain-filled world of sorrow and loss, caught up in God's activity, recognizing that He who creates also desires to make all things bright and beautiful for you. If He does such wonders in hanging universes and worlds in place—will He not also perform His creative work in living flesh like yours…Turn your focus heavenward and in your inward self of emotions, will, and intellect, consciously praise Him. Elect not to wallow in despair nor complain against His ways. Don't demean His providence toward you. Acquiesce and say, "O Lord, my God, You are very great, You are clothed with splendor and majesty" (Psalm 104:1).

A PSALM IN YOUR HEART — DR. GEORGE O. WOOD

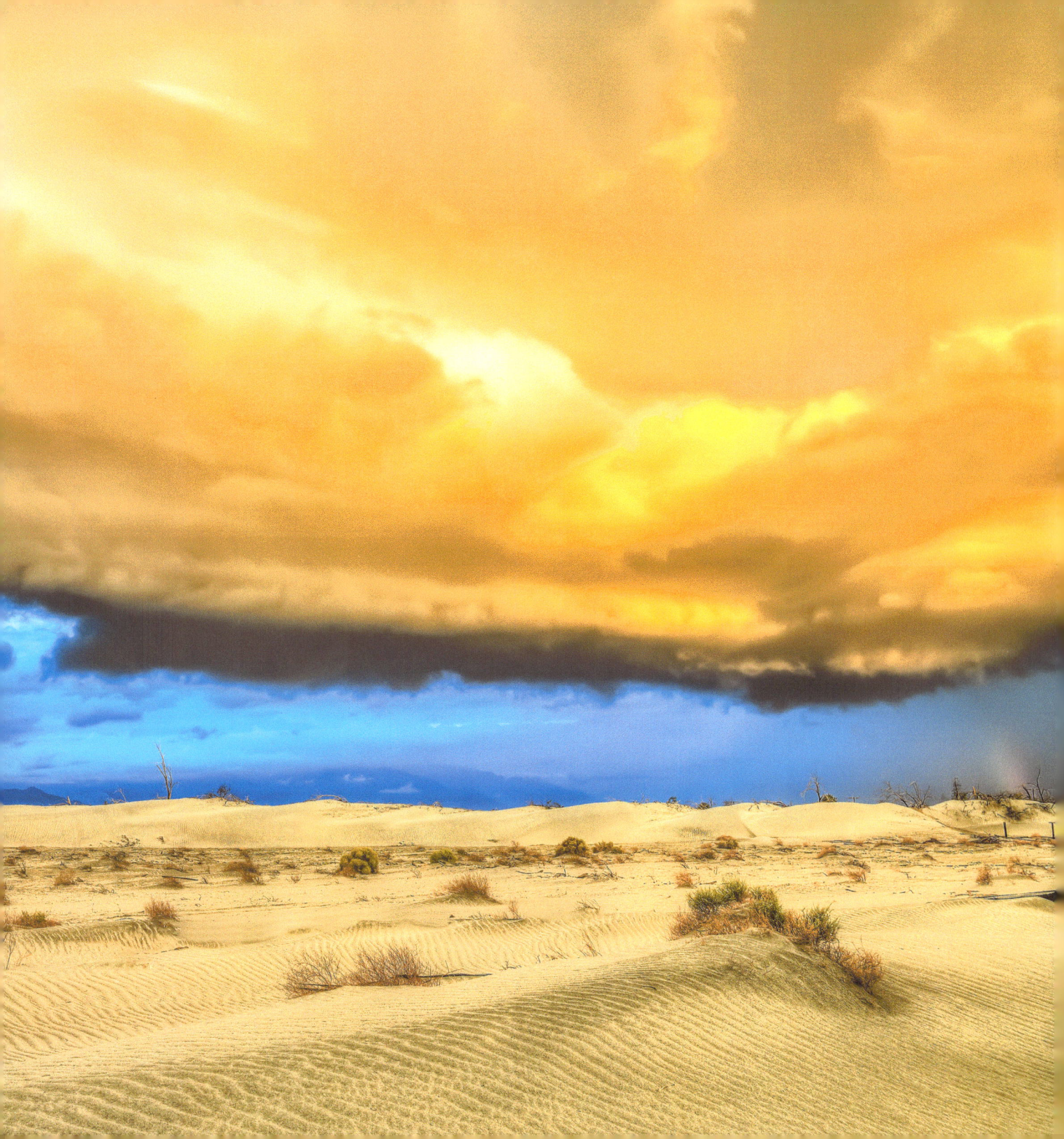

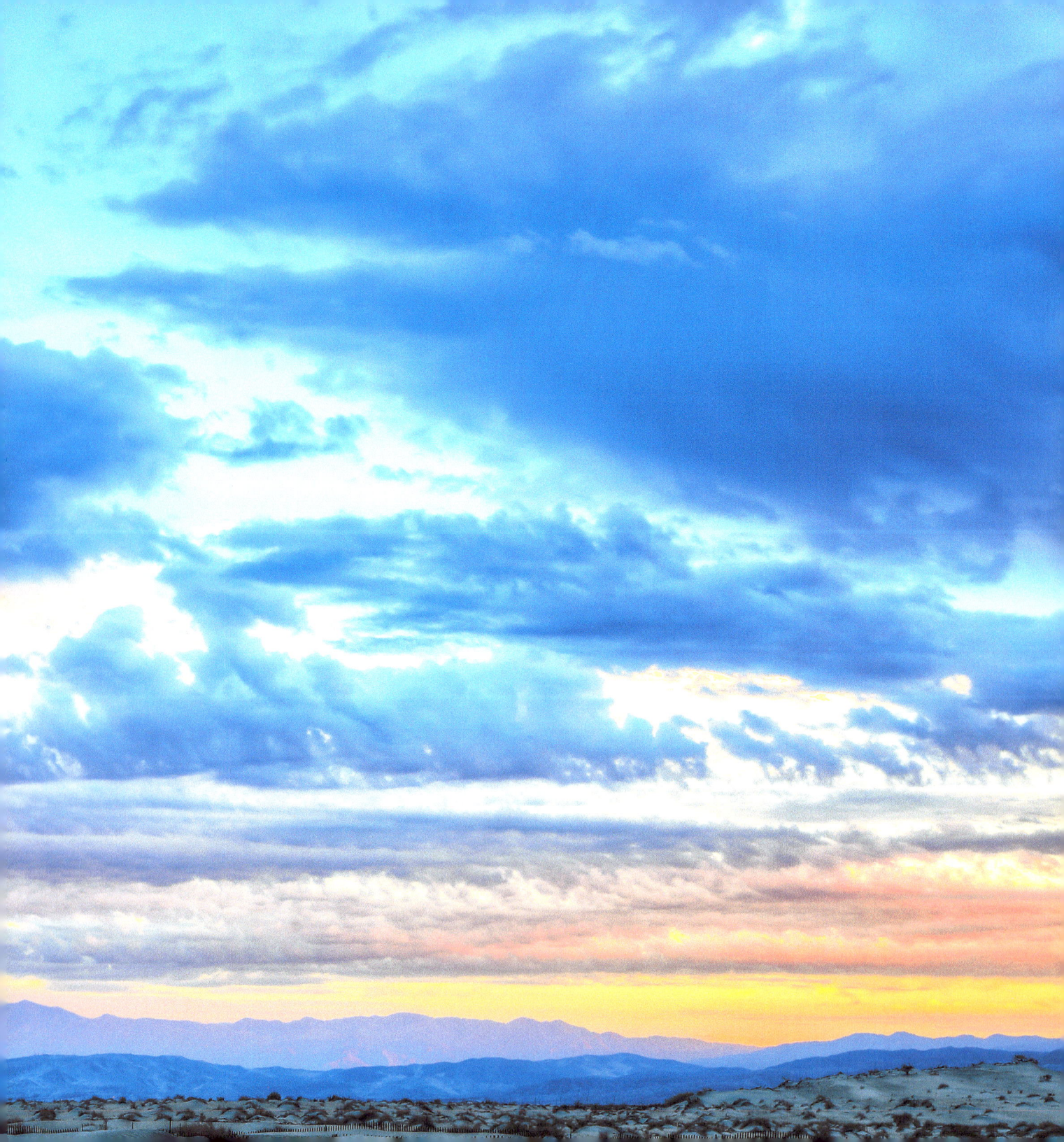

SECOND DAY
REFLECTIONS

THE MESSAGE OF GOD'S CREATION

Their message has gone throughout the earth, and their words to all the world.
PSALM 19:3

God speaks His message in creation. The words His creation proclaims are everywhere for all to hear. That's what David, the man after God's own heart, said when he wrote Psalm 19. He talked about the proclamation of God's glory in the heavens and the display of God's craftsmanship in the skies (Psalm 19:1). I like to think of God's general revelation in creation as His multimedia to show us in living color who He is, what He does, and what He says. How shall we respond? First, we need to be still and know that He is God (Psalm 46:10). And then, surrender your life to Him and trust Him in every circumstance you face today.

Lord, I gaze at all You have created and behold Your glory. You are all-powerful and all-sufficient. If you can handle the details of creation, then I trust You today to handle the circumstances of my life. In Jesus' name, Amen.

THIRD DAY

On the third day, God commanded the dry land, seas, vegetation including plants, flowers, and trees into existence. The visible beauty of the earth began to appear. "God called the dry land earth, and the gathering of the waters He called seas; and God saw that it was good…Then God said, 'Let the earth sprout vegetation'…and it was so" (Genesis 1:10-12). As you take time to give a long look at the details of each of God's designs, may you be filled with awe and wonder at the hand of the Grand Artist at work. The more you know Him, the more you will trust Him.

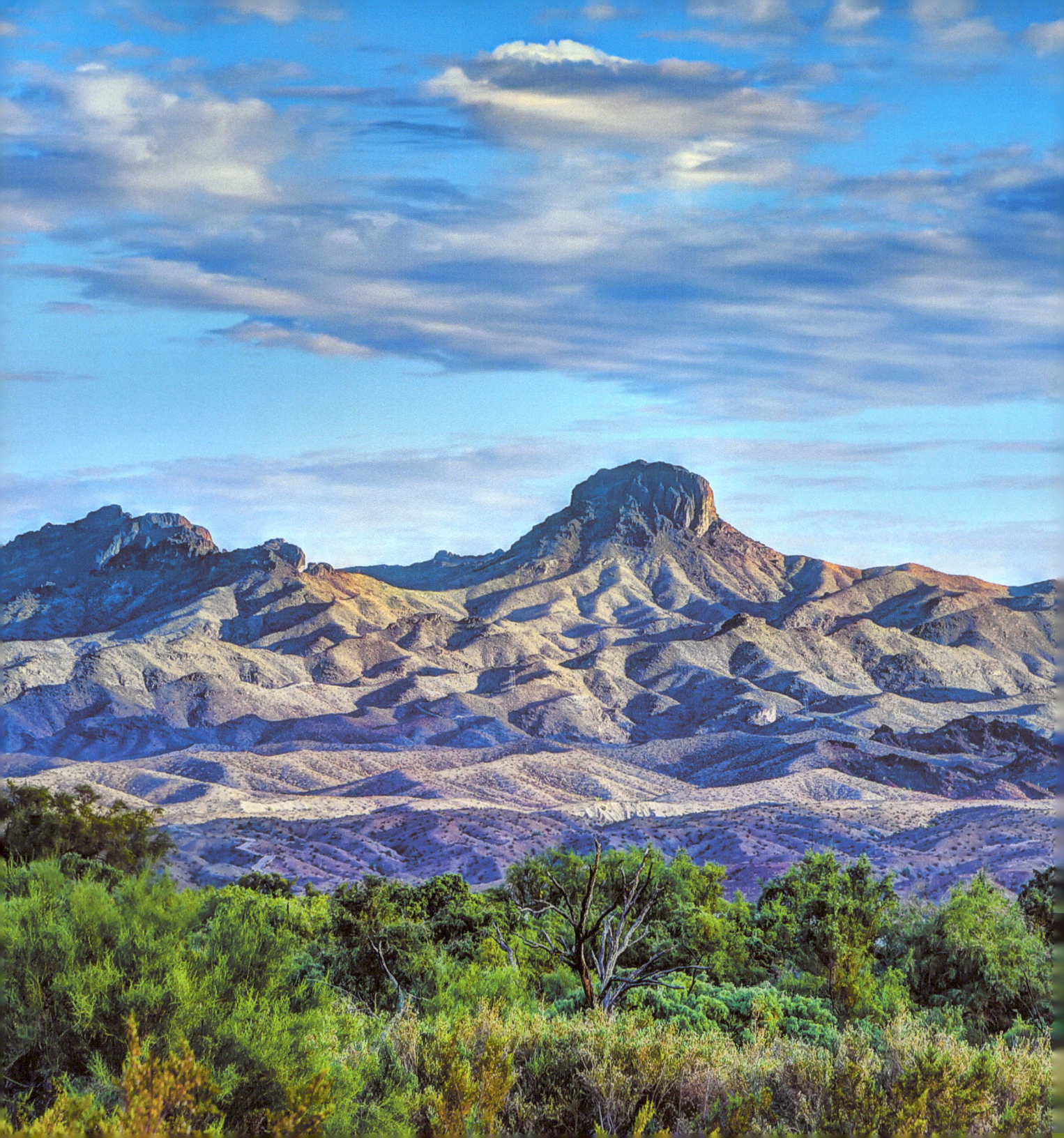

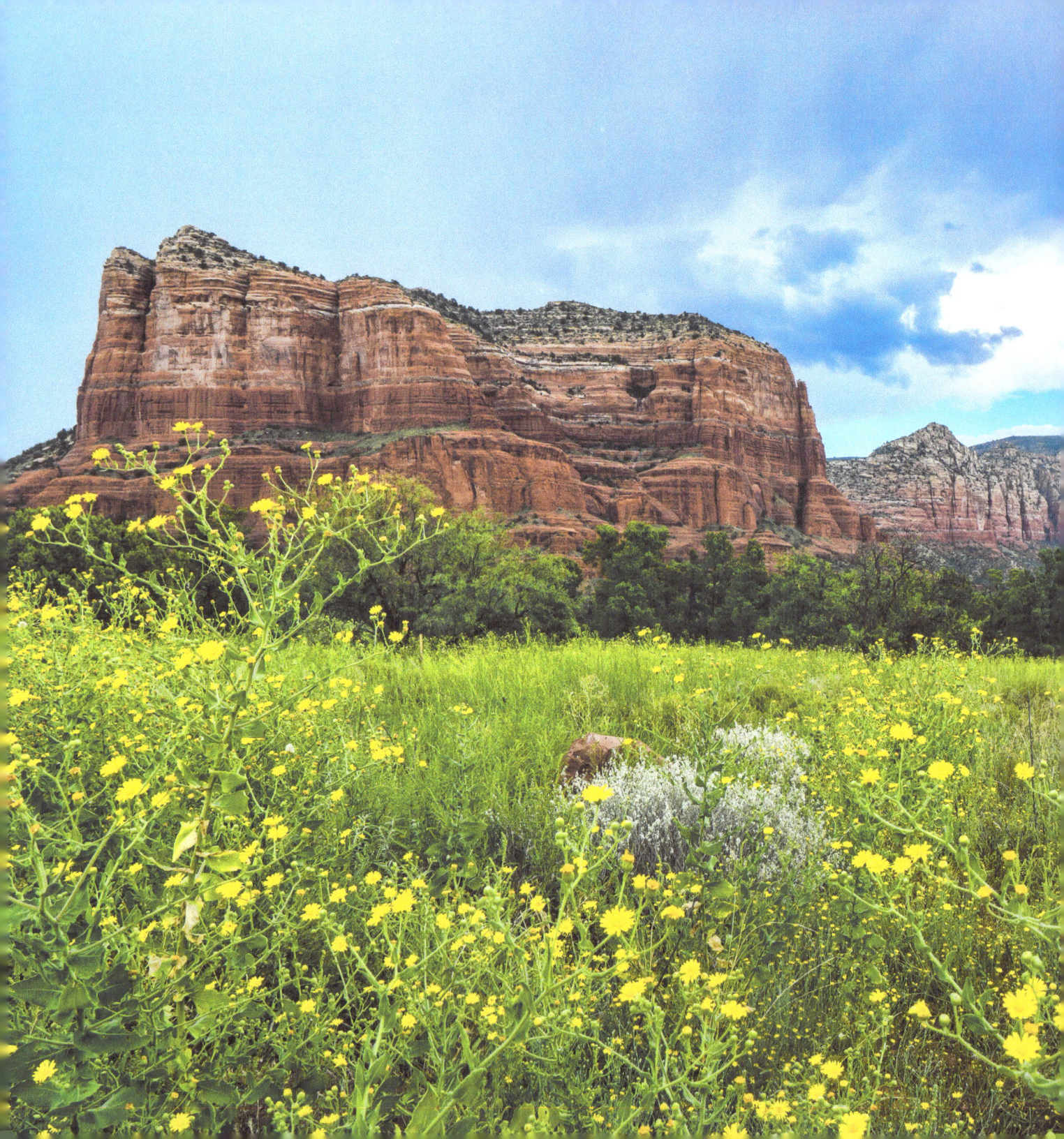

9
THE BEAUTY OF THE EARTH

God called the dry land earth.

GENESIS 1:10

When God began the third day, He commanded earth into existence by saying, "Let the waters below the heavens be gathered into one place, and let the dry land appear; and it was so" (Genesis 1:7). Those words *it was so* speak volumes for us, informing us that when God commands creation, even the waters, heavens, and dry land jump into action, obeying His every word. This fact is fuel for your trust today. When you look at the beauty around you in God's creation, stop for a moment, and remember you are looking at God's handiwork, the result of His very Word at work. If the Triune God can sculpt mountains with His Word, imagine what He can and will do in your life as you trust in Him. There is so much more to the making of the earth than we can even imagine. The structure of the earth has distinct layers—the outer crust, the mantle, and the core. The internal heat of the earth is located in the mantle, and it is thought that earth's magnetic field is controlled by the liquid core. Just think—God not only understands the structure, He designed it Himself!

O LORD, our Lord, Your majestic name fills the earth!

PSALM 8:1 NLT

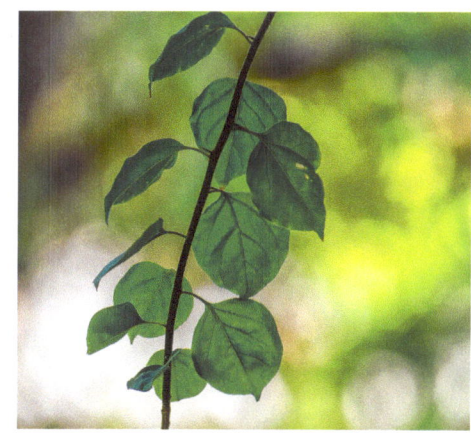

For the beauty of the earth,
for the glory of the skies,
for the love which from our birth
over and around us lies.
Refrain
*Christ, our Lord, to You we raise
this, our hymn of grateful praise.*
For the wonder of each hour
of the day and of the night,
hill and vale and tree and flower,
sun and moon and stars of light.
For Yourself, best gift divine,
to the world so freely given,
agent of God's grand design;
peace on earth and joy in heaven.

FOR THE BEAUTY OF THE EARTH — FOLLIOTT SANDFORD PIERPOINT

Oh Lord, how many are Your works! In wisdom You have made them all; The earth is full of Your possessions…Let my meditation be pleasing to Him; As for me, I shall be glad in the Lord.

PSALM 104:24, 34

This is the day the LORD has made. We will rejoice and be glad in it.

PSALM 118:24 NLT

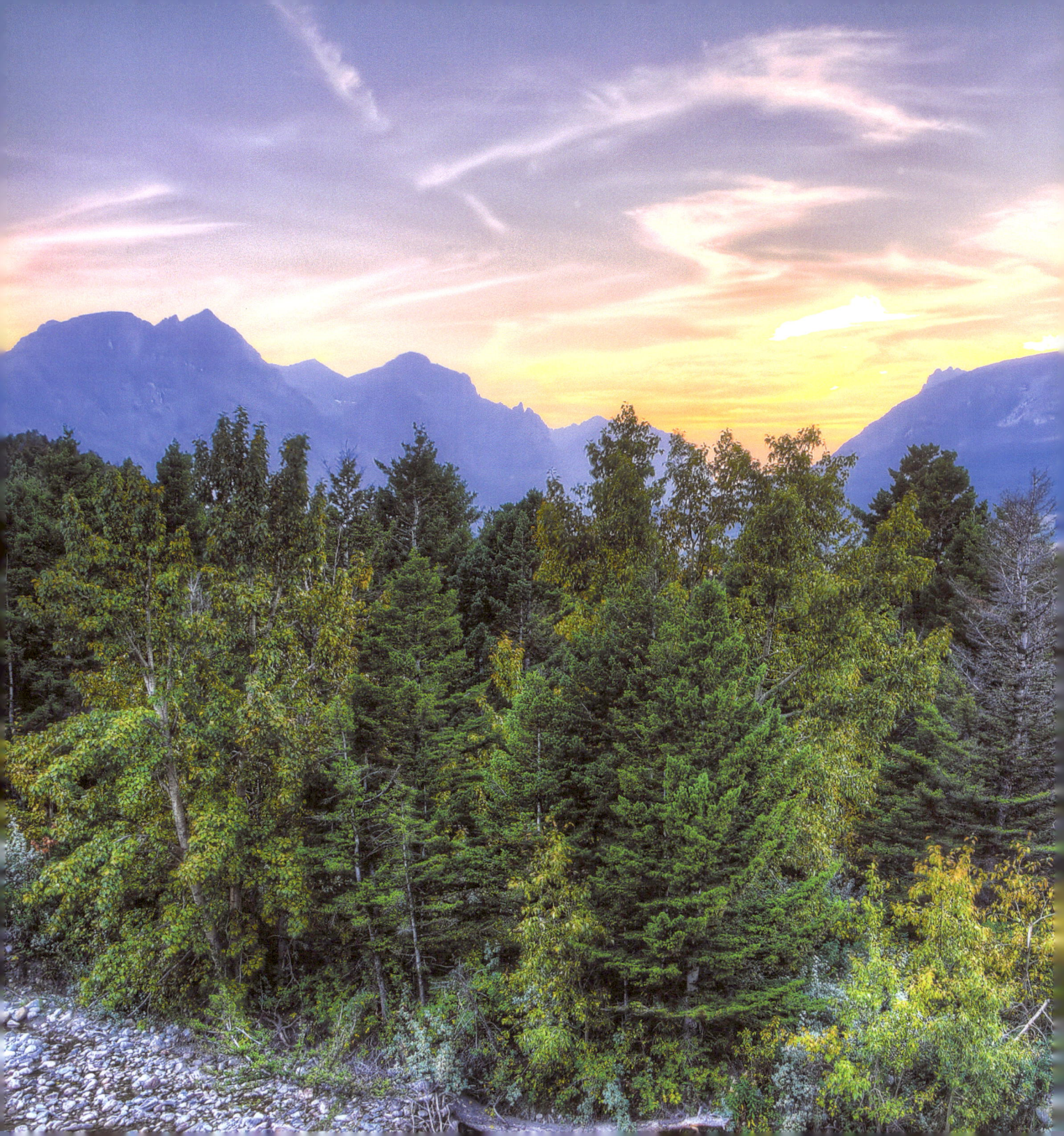

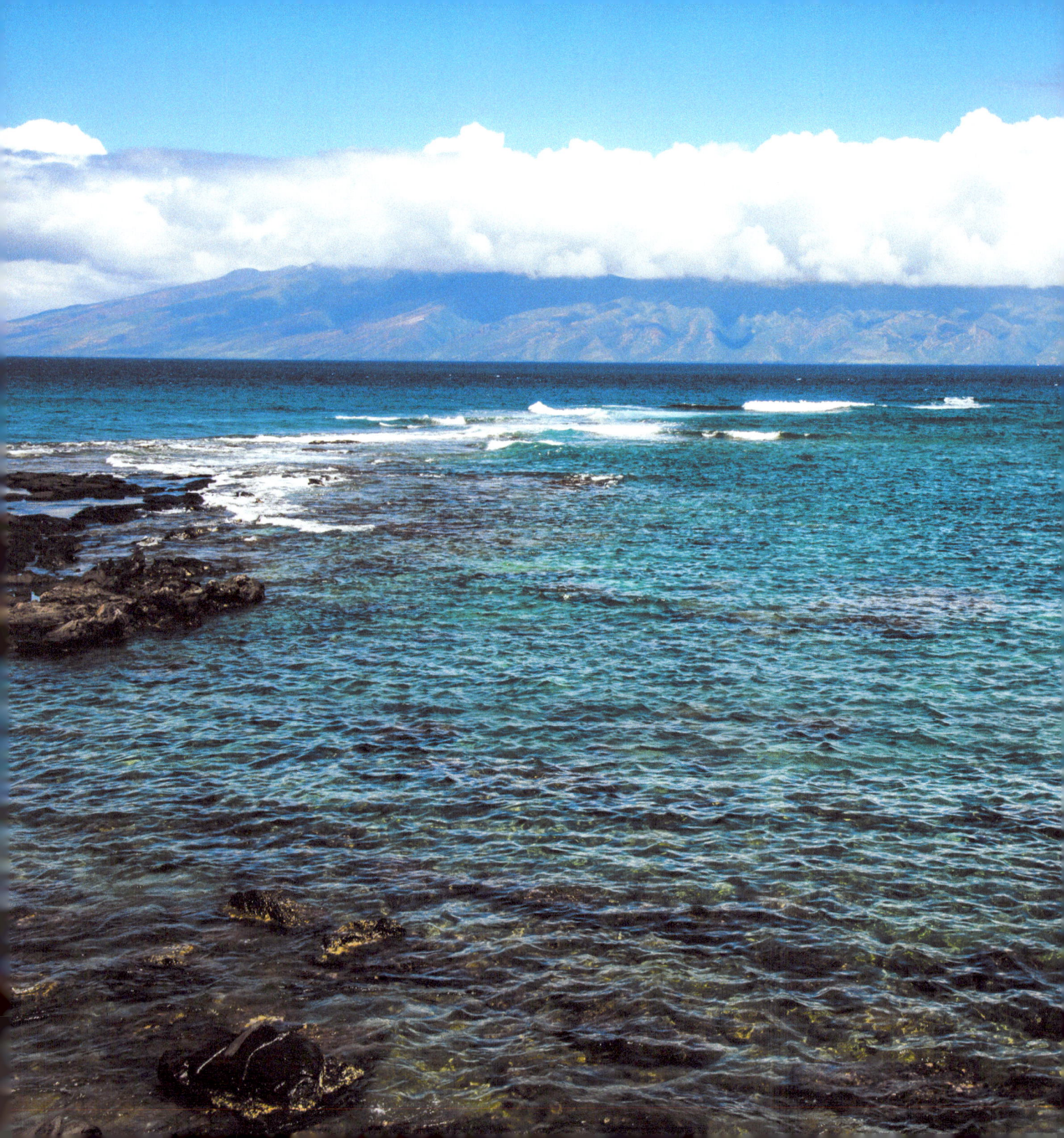

10
WHEN GOD MADE THE OCEAN

The gathering of the waters He called seas.

GENESIS 1:10

Can you remember the first time you ever saw the ocean? When my niece Kayla saw it for the first time, she threw off her shoes, ran across the beach toward the ocean waves crashing along the shore, and shouted at the top of her lungs, "I'm living the dream!" I laughed and cried at the same time to witness the awe and wonder in a little 8-year-old girl seeing something that no words can adequately describe. The ocean is magnificent and spectacular with multiple layers of color. And that is only the view from the surface. There is so much more life below all the way to the ocean floor. Just imagine what it was like for God, on the same day He created earth, to then command the ocean into existence. There was more in His mind than just the earth in all of its beauty. He also envisioned, designed, and created the ocean in all of its glory. Some of the most beautiful views of the ocean are found on the big island of Hawaii where you catch a glimpse of its beauty with the azure blue waters rolling across lava rocks. You find yourself basking in the Lord's beauty and giving glory and praise to God.

He made heaven and earth, the sea, and everything in them. He keeps every promise forever.

PSALM 146:6 NLT

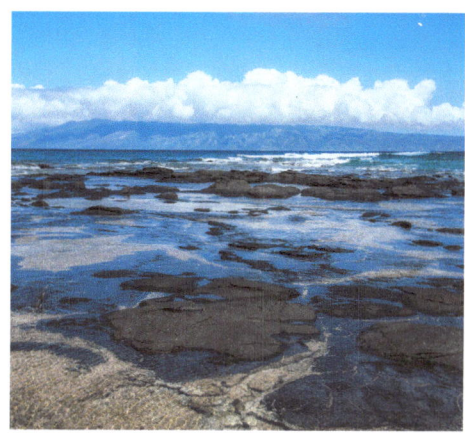

Then the LORD answered Job from the whirlwind…
Where were you when I laid the foundations of the earth?
Tell me, if you know so much.
Who determined its dimensions
and stretched out the surveying line?
What supports its foundations,
and who laid its cornerstone
as the morning stars sang together
and all the angels shouted for joy?
Who kept the sea inside its boundaries
as it burst from the womb,
and as I clothed it with clouds
and wrapped it in thick darkness?
For I locked it behind barred gates, limiting its shores.
I said, "This far and no farther will you come.
Here your proud waves must stop!"
Have you ever commanded the morning to appear
and caused the dawn to rise in the east?
Have you made daylight spread to the ends of the earth,
to bring an end to the night's wickedness? As the light approaches,
The earth takes shape like clay pressed beneath a seal;
It is robed in brilliant colors…
Have you explored the springs from which the seas come?
Have you explored their depths?

THE DAY GOD SPOKE TO JOB WITH AN EXPANDED VIEW OF HIS CREATION — JOB 38:1-16

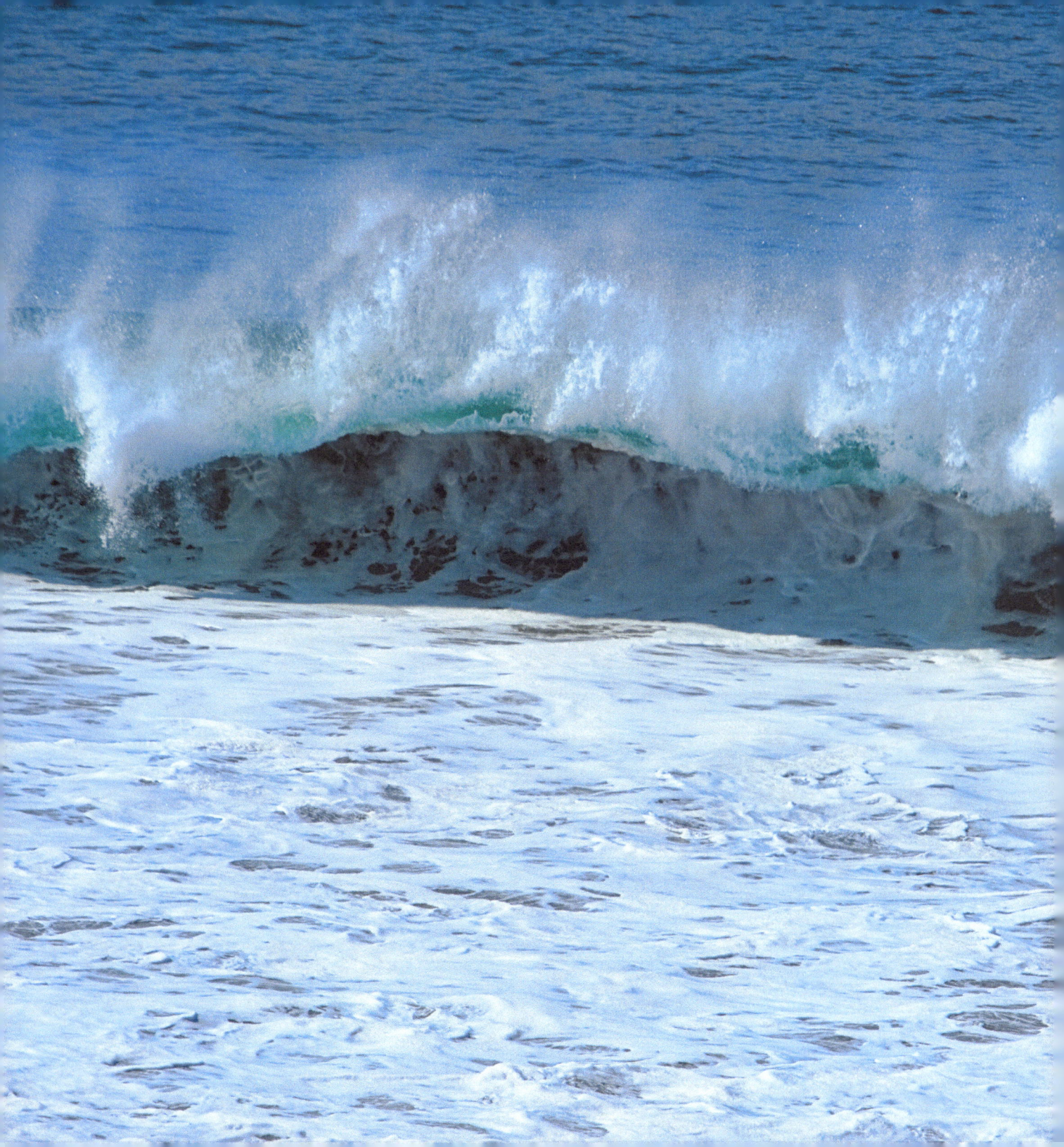

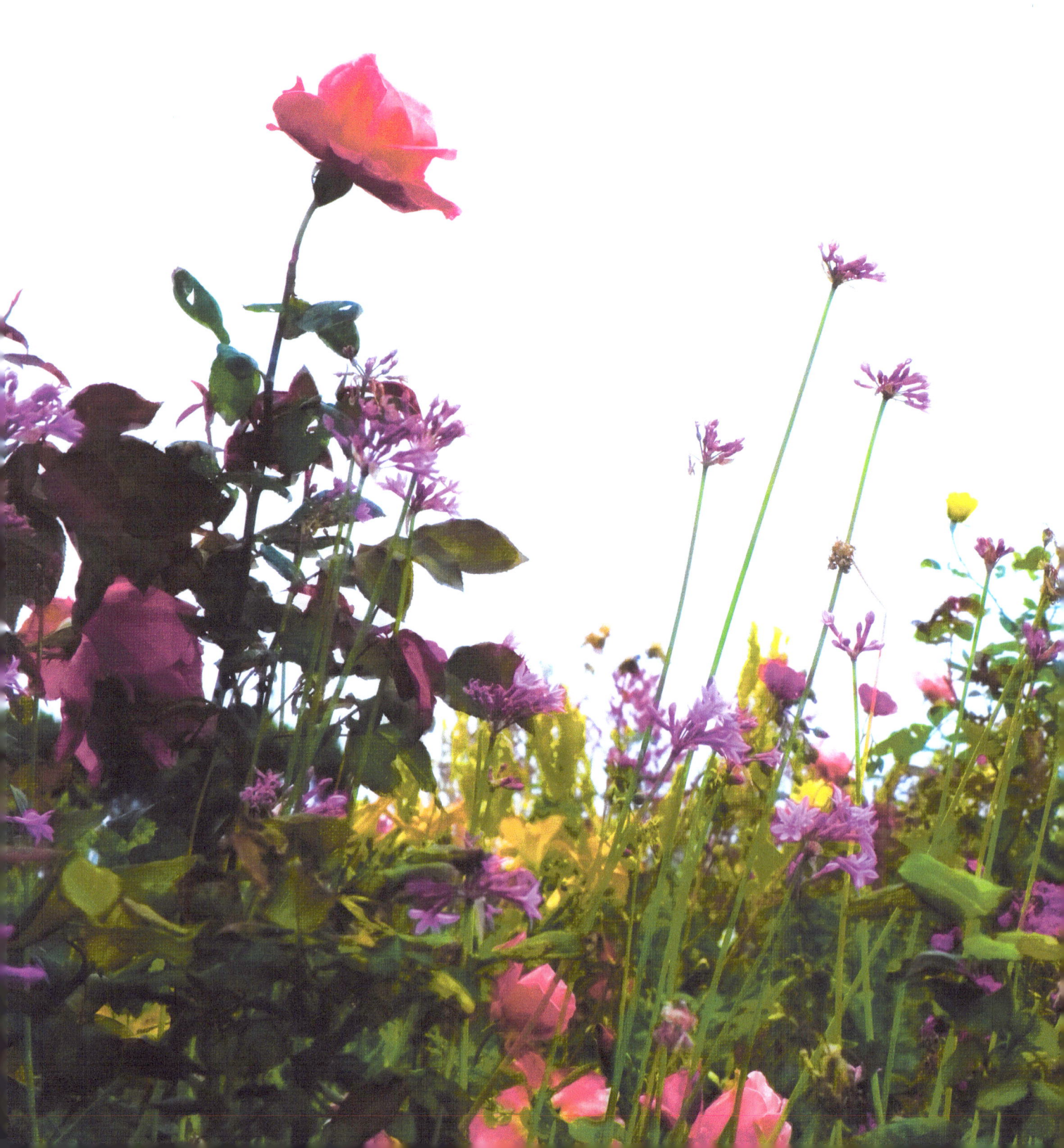

II
A New Kind Of Beauty

Then God said, "Let the land sprout with vegetation—every sort of seed-bearing plant, and trees that grow seed-bearing fruit."

GENESIS 1:11 NLT

God created the earth and the ocean on the third day. You might have thought that was enough for one day. However, God still had more in mind. He sent forth His word again with a brand new kind of beauty filled with brilliant color and vibrant growth. Then God said, "Let the land sprout with vegetation—every sort of seed-bearing plant, and trees that grow seed-bearing fruit. And that is what happened" (Genesis 1:11). Once again we see all of creation standing at attention and obeying God when He spoke. "The land produced vegetation—all sorts of seed-bearing plants and trees with seed-bearing fruit" (Genesis 1:12). This one command from God resulted in at least 391,000 known plant species according to the Royal Botanic Gardens Kew in the United Kingdom. Think about the many kinds of trees: birch, maple, oak, pine, magnolia, apple, orange, lemon, dogwood, walnut, fig, mulberry, and more. Jesus often referred to plants in His parables signifying just how meaningful His creation is to Him. The details in God's designs inspire a new and deeper trust in Him.

You can identify them by their fruit…a good tree produces good fruit…yes, just as you can identify a tree by its fruit, so you can identify people by their actions.

MATTHEW 7:16-20 NLT

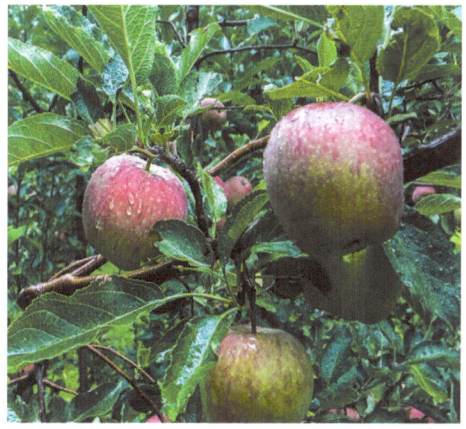

To see a world in a grain of sand and a heaven in a wildflower,
Hold infinity in the palm of your hand and eternity in an hour.

WILLIAM BLAKE

If he can exercise control over nature and nations, can He not rule over the difficult circumstances in your own life? If He has the whole world in His hands, cannot He hold you also?

A PSALM IN YOUR HEART — DR. GEORGE O. WOOD

Those who live at the ends of the earth stand in awe of Your wonders. From where the sun rises to where it sets, You inspire shouts of joy. You take care of the earth and water it, making it rich and fertile. The river of God has plenty of water; it provides a bountiful harvest of grain, for You have ordered it so. You drench the plowed ground with rain, melting the clods and leveling the ridges. You soften the earth with showers and bless its abundant crops. You crown the year with a bountiful harvest; even the hard pathways overflow with abundance. The grasslands of the wilderness become a lush pasture, and the hillsides blossom with joy…they all shout and sing for joy!

PSALM 65:8-13 NLT

Be still, and know that I am God!

PSALM 46:10 NLT

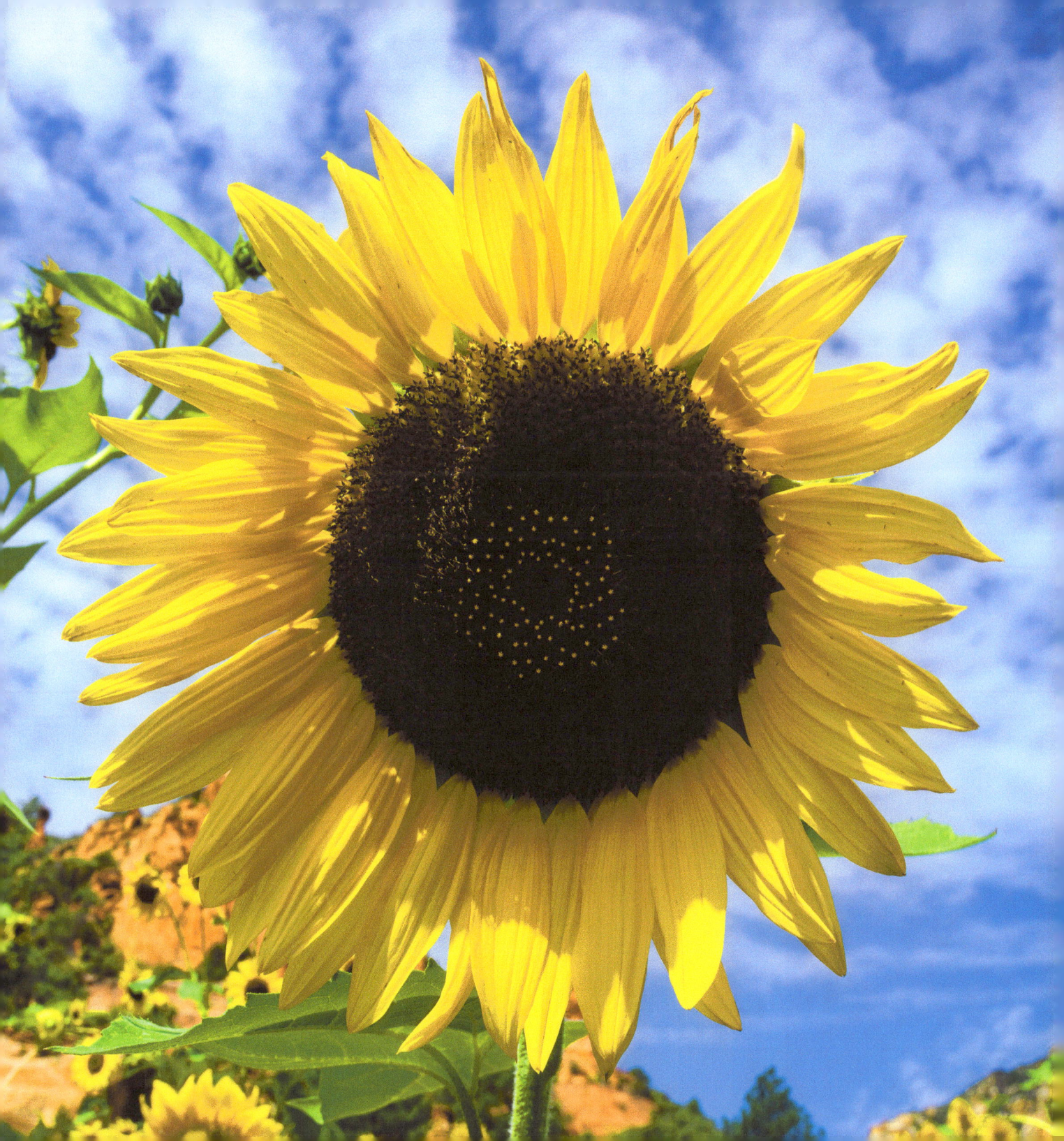

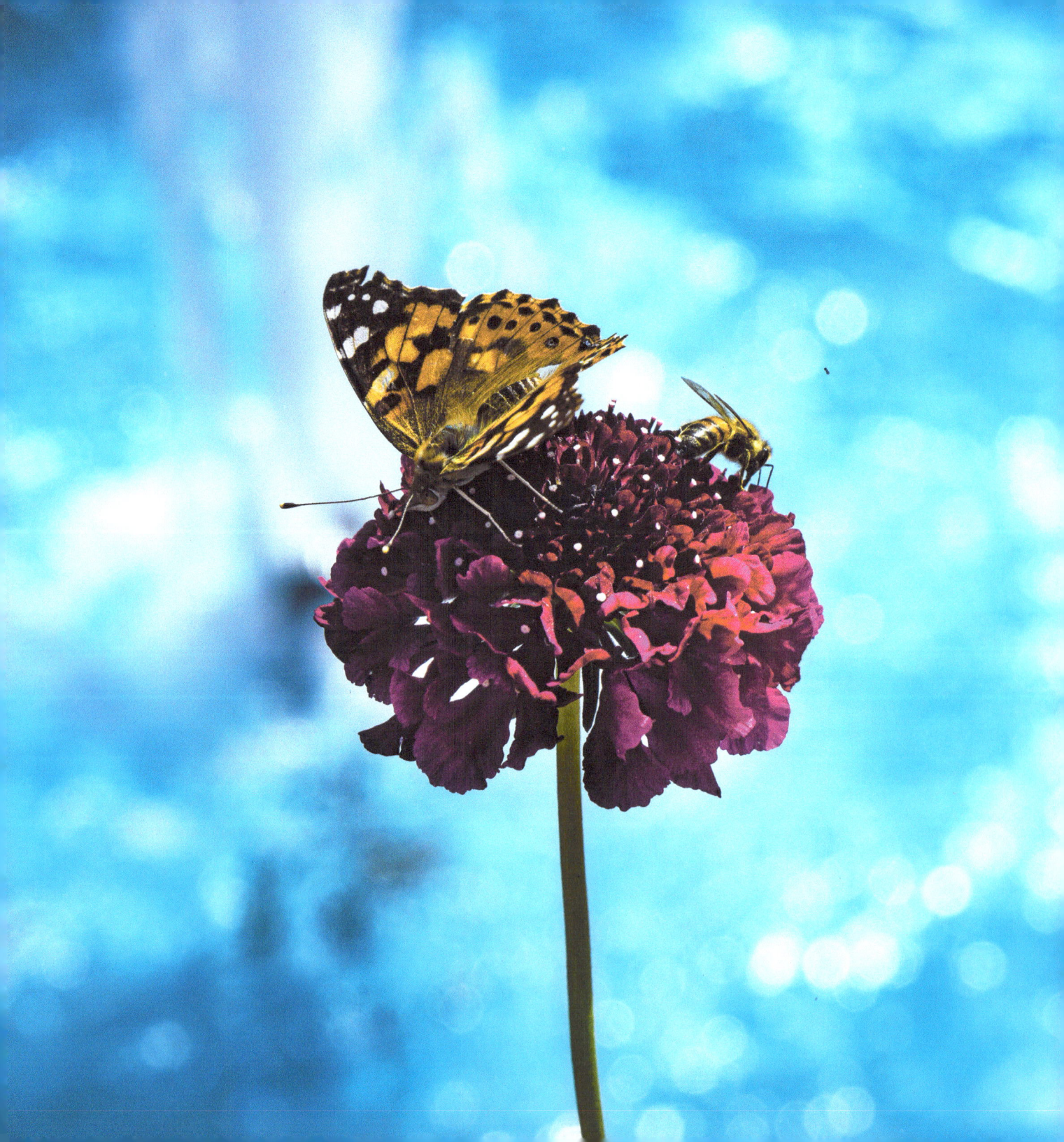

12
God Saw That It Was Good

And God saw that it was good. And evening passed and morning came, marking the third day.

Genesis 1:12-13 NLT

Once God created, He did not move on to the next day quite yet. There is something more. We learn that "God saw that it was good" (Genesis 1:12). In fact, again and again throughout these days, He sees that His creation is good. God is looking upon His work making it perfect and complete. When He saw that it was good, He was pronouncing His work beautiful and perfect in every way, and He was pleased. We learn here that God is omniscient (all-knowing) and He is omnipresent (everywhere at all times). What does this mean for you today? Throughout Scripture you discover that the Lord's eye is always on you. God is looking, always looking, deep into our hearts. We may try to run, but we cannot hide. Do you realize His eye is on you today? He knows all about You, all the way to your deepest thoughts and feelings. He knows what you are facing in your present circumstances, whether peaceful or turbulent. This realization of the presence and personal attention of your God is a call to come near and respond to His overtures and invitations in your life.

I will instruct you and teach you in the way which you should go. I will counsel you with My eye upon you.

Psalm 32:8

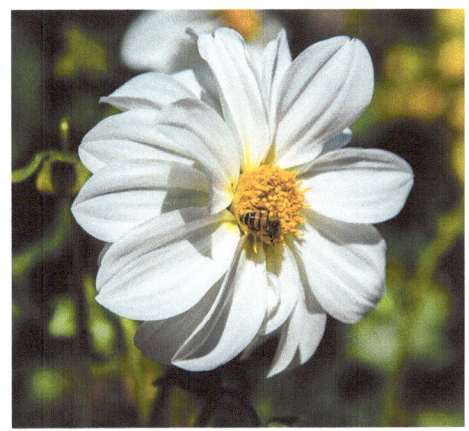

For the eyes of the Lord move to and fro throughout the earth that He
may strongly support those whose heart is completly His.

2 CHRONICLES 16:9

When we lift our inward eyes to gaze upon God we are sure to meet friendly eyes gazing back at us, for it is written that the eyes of the Lord run to and fro throughout all the earth. The sweet language of experience is *Thou God seest me* (Genesis 16:13). When the eyes of the soul looking out meet the eyes of God looking in, heaven has begun right here on this earth.… When the habit of inwardly gazing Godward becomes fixed within us, we shall be ushered onto a new level of spiritual life more in keeping with the promises of God and the mood of the New Testament. The Triune God will be our dwelling place even while our feet walk the low road of simple duty here among men.

THE PURSUIT OF GOD — A.W. TOZER

One day while reading the Bible, I came across the words, *O taste and see that the Lord is good* (Psalm 34:8). Suddenly, they meant something…Since God is omniscient, He must know what is the best and highest good of all; therefore, His goodness must necessarily be beyond question…I felt nothing could go wrong under His care. It seemed to me that no one could ever be anxious again…He always, under every circumstance, acts in the highest ideal of goodness.

THE GOD OF ALL COMFORT — HANNAH WHITALL SMITH

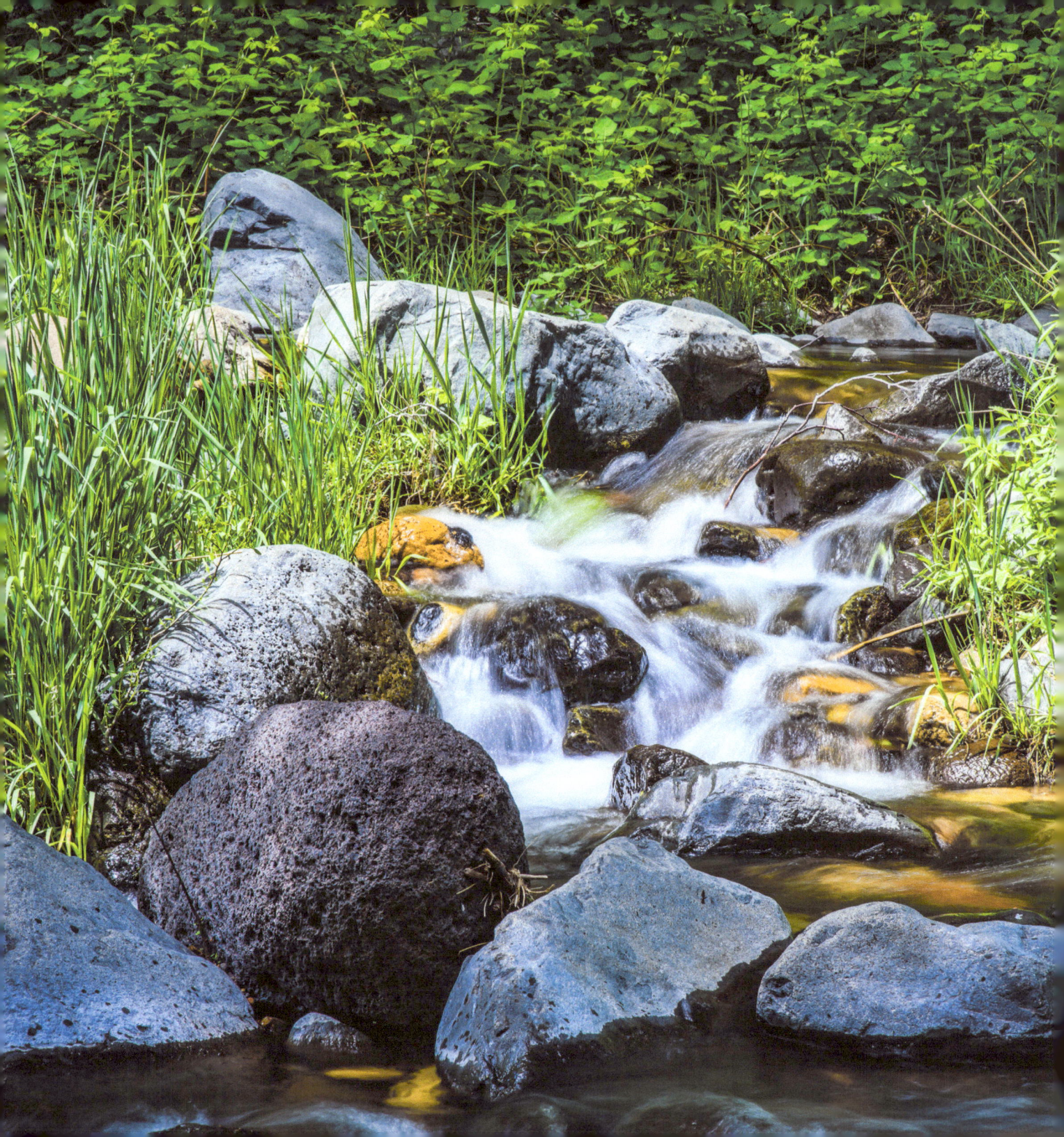

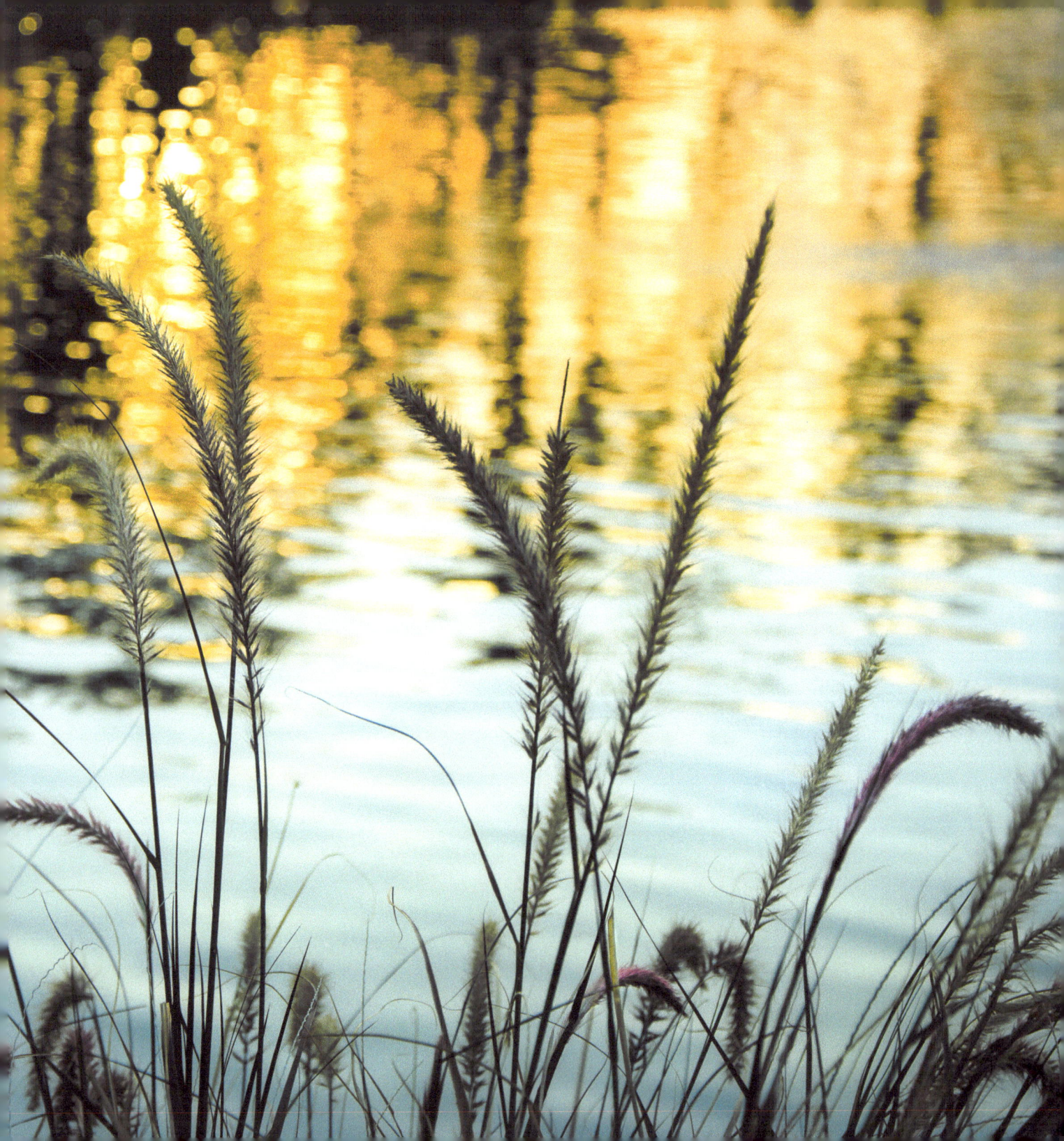

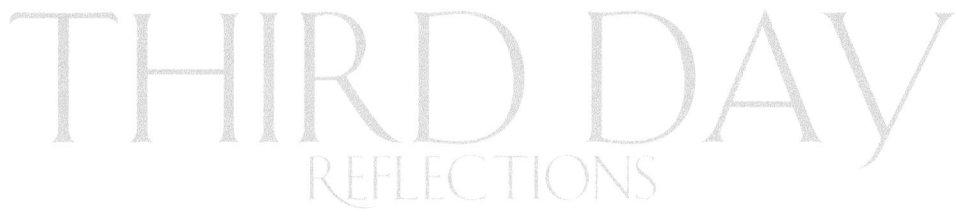

BEHOLD YOUR GOD

For since the creation of the world His invisible attributes, His eternal power and divine nature, have been clearly seen, being understood through what has been made.
ROMANS 1:20

God's creation reveals His character. When you look with purpose and intention, to discover the nature of the One who created, you will have a whole new world open up to you. You realize at once that you are truly beholding your God. According to Paul in Romans 1:20, you are clearly seeing His "eternal power and divine nature." Looking at God's creation on the third day, you realize that only God can do this. And then, you bow the knee in worship and adoration, praising your Creator for His wondrous and beautiful creation.

Lord, thank You for Your creation to help me know You and see You more clearly. In all I see, I behold Your eternal power and divine nature. I worship and adore You today. In Jesus' name, Amen.

FOURTH DAY

There is no limit to what God can do in a day. On the fourth day, we watch as God commanded billions of galaxies to fill the universe. Within these galaxies, He painted into existence with His Word the sun, moon, and billions of stars. Imagine the creative thought in His infinite mind when He said, "'Let lights appear in the sky to separate the day from the night. Let them be signs to mark the seasons, days, and years. Let these lights in the sky shine down on the earth.' And that is what happened" (Genesis 1:14-15 NLT). Look up at the lights He created and worship the Lord.

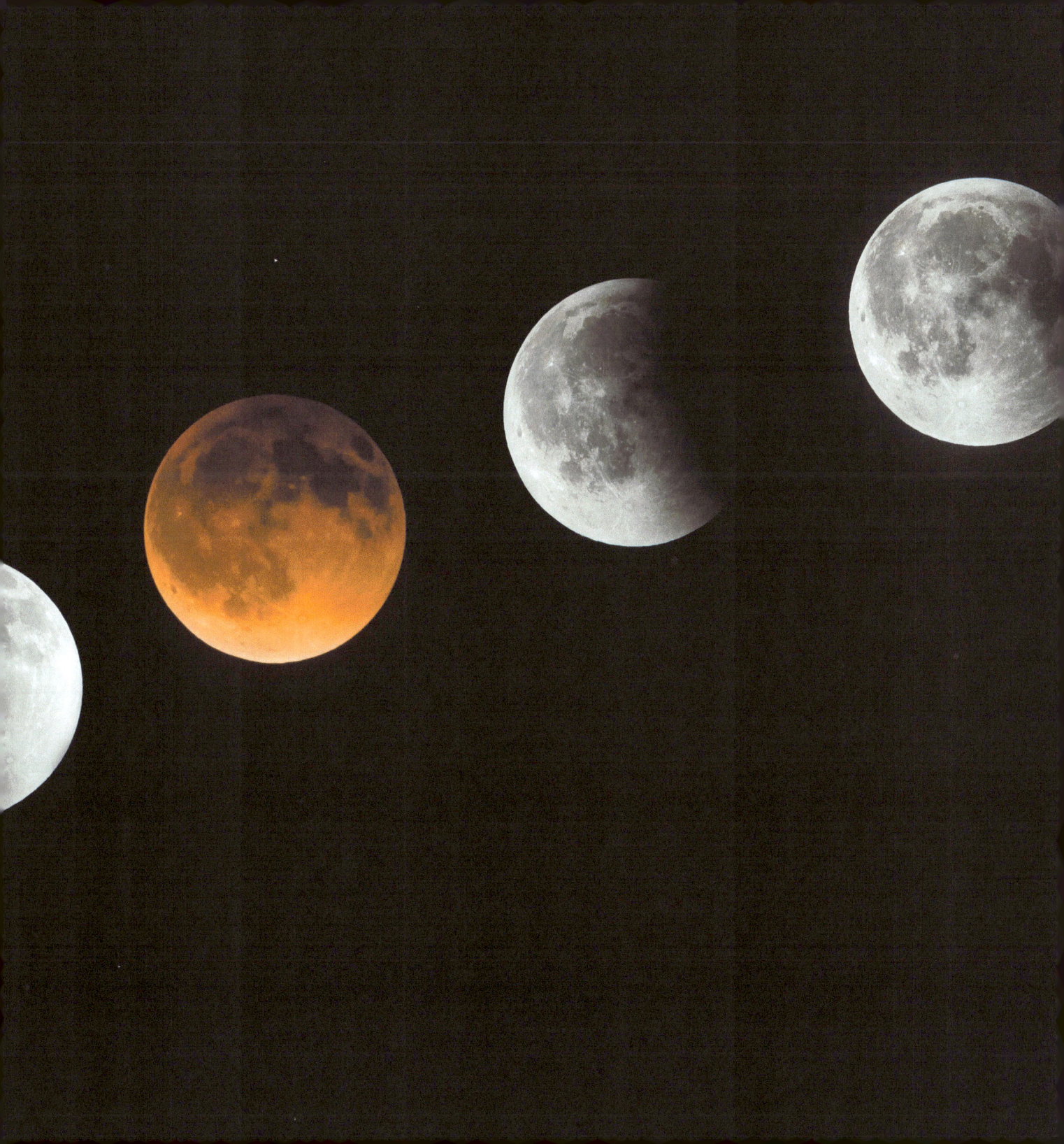

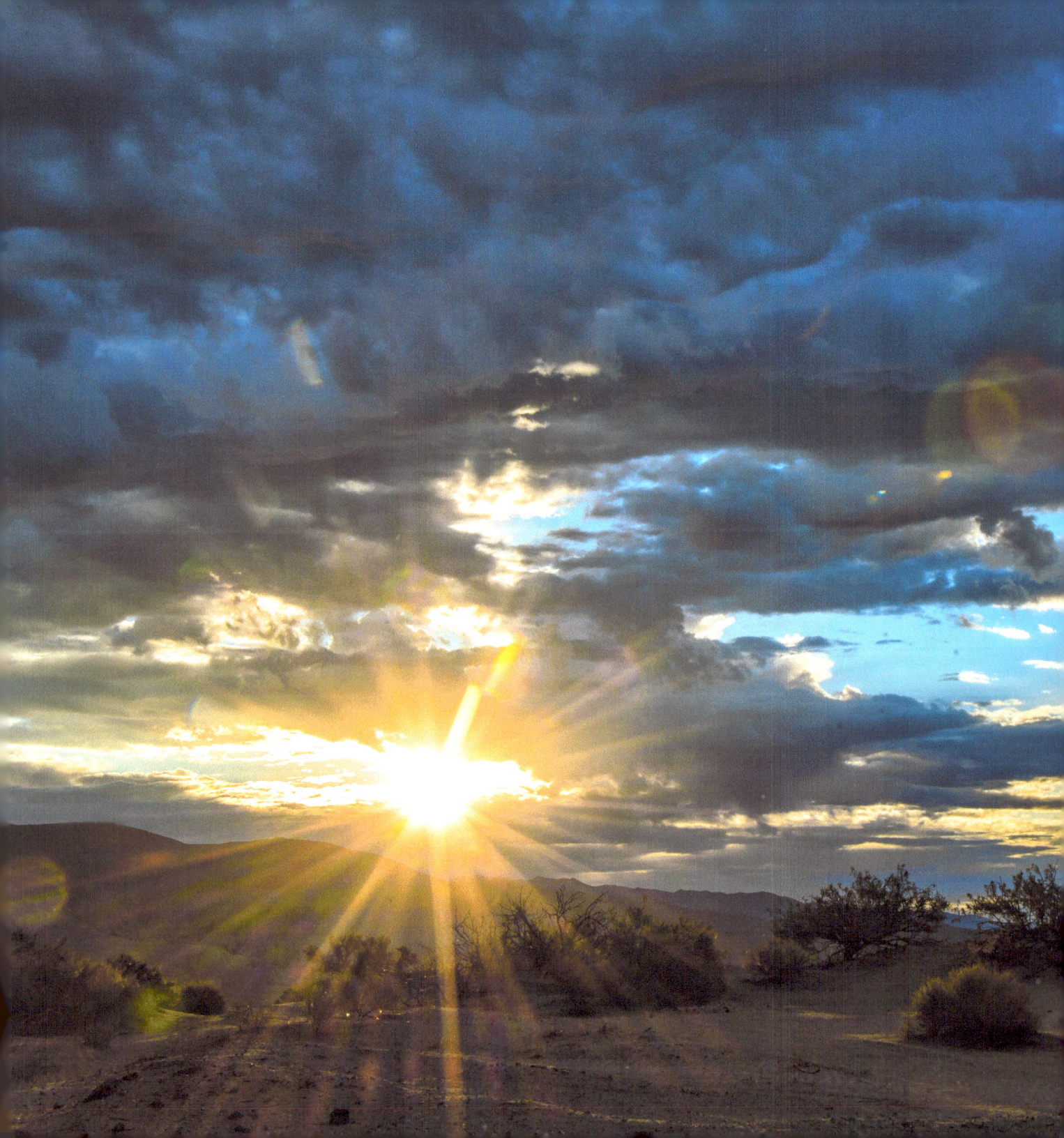

13 A STANDING OVATION

God made two great lights—the larger one to govern the day…God set these lights in the sky to light the earth…

GENESIS 1:16-17 NLT

At the beginning of the day, with the first light, as the sun begins to rise, I find myself faced with a choice. *Will I focus on the Lord and walk and talk with Him? Will He be the highlight of my day? Will my life show Him off in His greatness and glory? Will I celebrate Jesus today?* I pull out my Bible, journal, devotionals and spend quiet time with the Lord. Then I look outside with the first light to see how the Lord may paint the sky at sunrise. It's different every day. And often, I grab my Nikon camera, and go to a special place in the desert where I can capture God's handiwork in action. And when I see God paint light and color in the sky through magnificent bursts of clouds, I stop, look up to heaven, clap my hands with a standing ovation, and say: *Good job Lord! That was amazing and magnificent!* The sun rising is used by the writer of Proverbs to describe the life of those who are righteous: "The way of the righteous is like the first gleam of dawn, which shines brighter until the full light of day" (Proverbs 4:18 NLT). Living in the light of the Lord each day, you will thrive, like a beautiful flower.

The way of the righteous is like the first gleam of dawn, which shines brighter until the full light of day.

PROVERBS 4:18 NLT

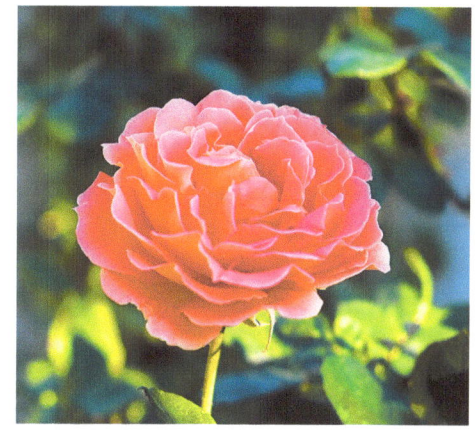

Do you not know? Have you not heard? Has it not been declared to you from the beginning? Have you not understood from the foundations of the earth? It is He who sits above the circle of the earth, and its inhabitants are like grasshoppers, who stretches out the heavens like a curtain and spreads them out like a tent to dwell in.

Isaiah 40:21-22

We live on a grand estate called Earth. As we look at the beauty and intricacies of our residence, we marvel at the genius of the design. When we gaze up into the heavens, we are overcome with awe at the vastness of what our Creator has brought into being…To get just a small idea of God's creative power, let us consider our universe. We live on one of the nine planets that revolve around the sun. As the dominant light of our solar system, our sun gives off far more energy in one second than all mankind has produced since creation. With a diameter of approximately 860,000 miles, the sun could hold one million planets the size of the Earth. Yet our sun is only an average-size star. Our sun is just one among 100 billion stars in our galaxy, the Milky Way…The Andromeda Spiral galaxy is 2 million light-years away and contains about 400 billion stars. No one knows how many galaxies there are in the universe, but scientists estimate that there are billions of them.

God—Discover His Character — Dr. Bill Bright

God made a home in the heavens for the sun. It bursts forth like a radiant bridegroom after his wedding. It rejoices like a great athlete eager to run the race. The sun rises at one end of the heavens and follows its course to the other end. Nothing can hide from its heat.

Psalm 19:4-6 NLT

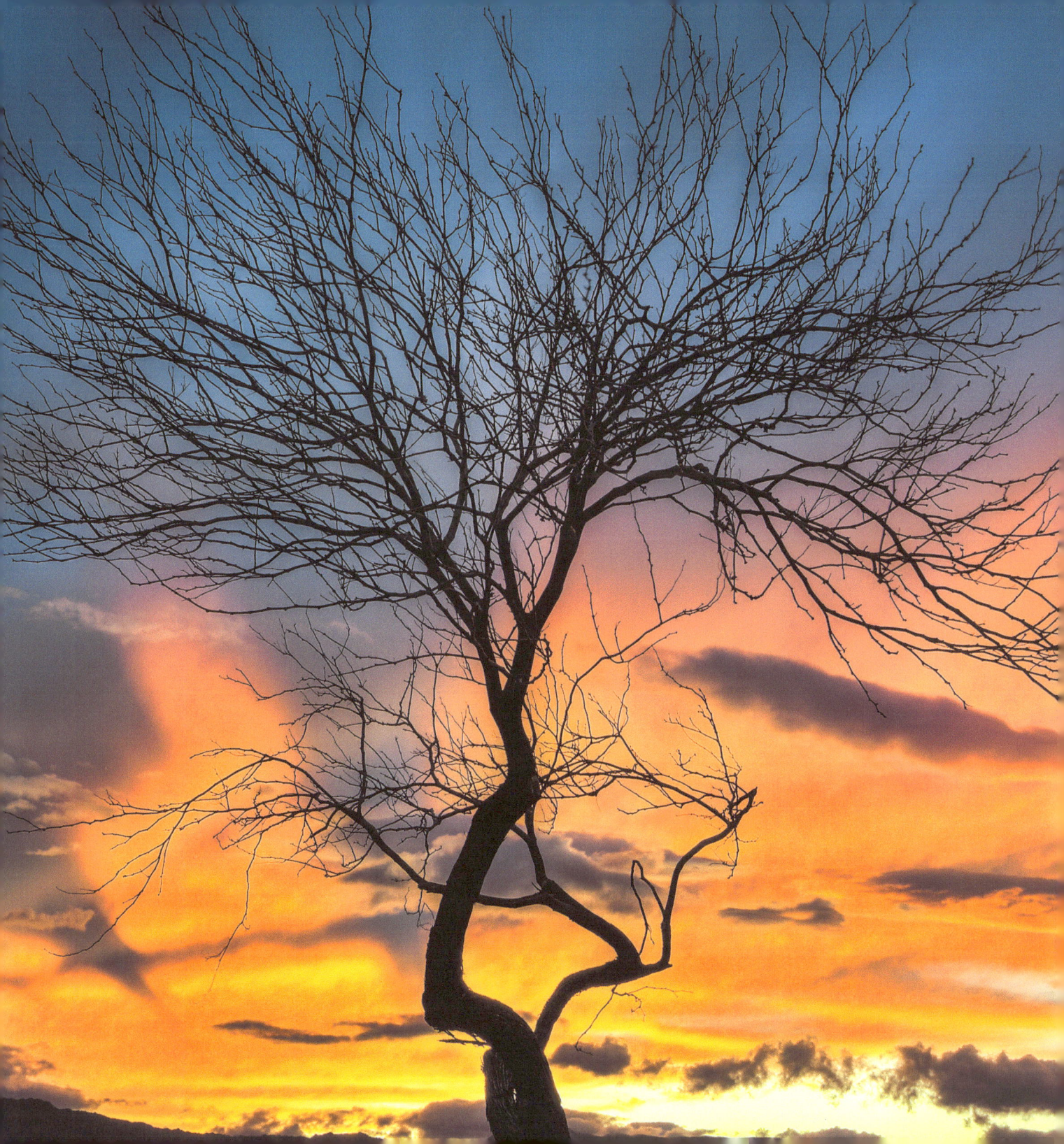

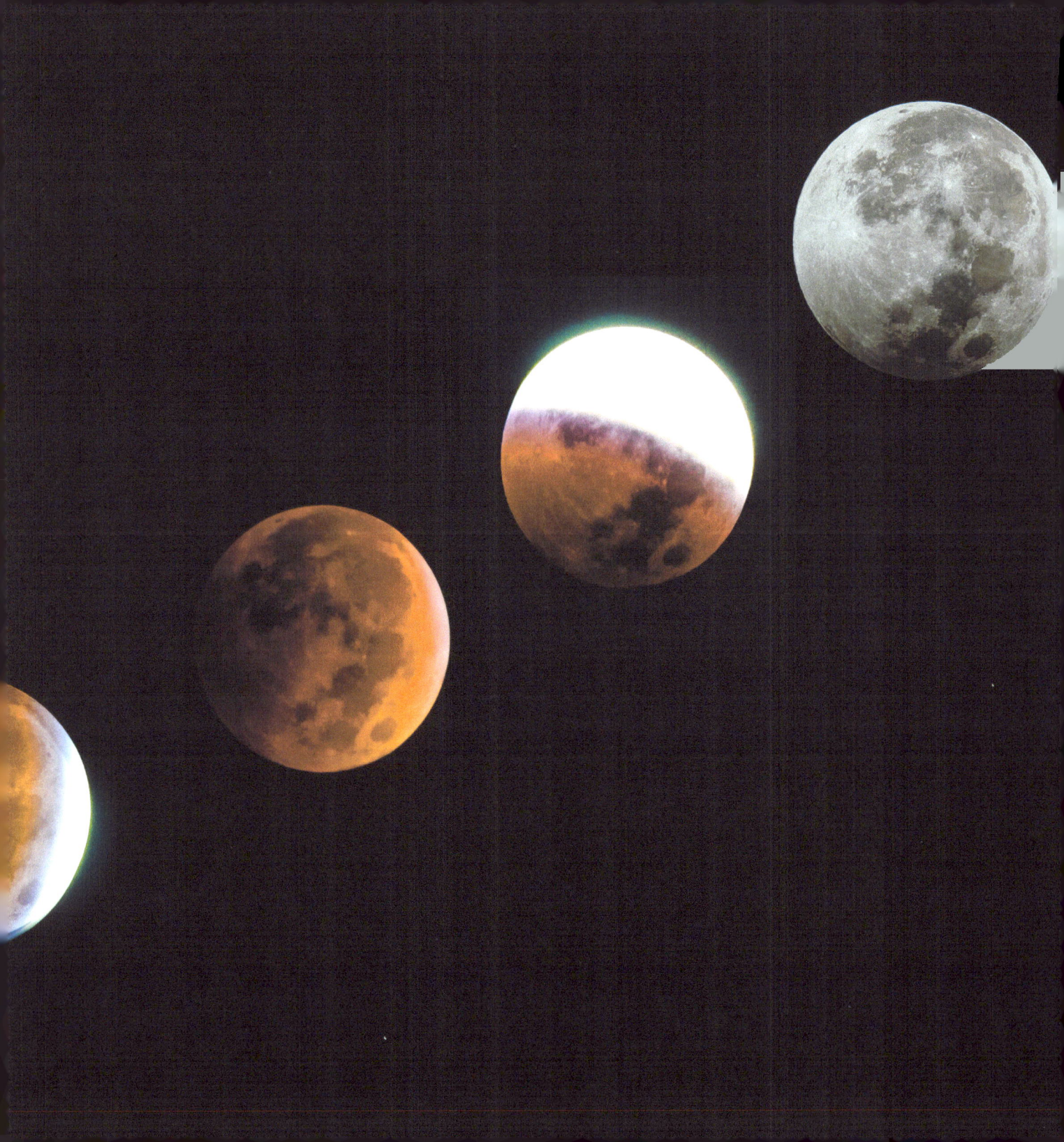

14
The Blood Red Moon

...the lesser light to rule the night...And God set them in the expanse of the heavens to give light on the earth, to rule over the day and over the night.

Genesis 1:16-18 ESV

I learned that there was going to be a lunar eclipse with a blood red moon. I had always wanted to shoot the moon, and this was the perfect opportunity. The red moon is possible because while the moon is in total shadow cast by the earth, some light from the sun passes through Earth's atmosphere and is bent toward the moon. The effect is to cast all the planet's sunrises and sunsets on the moon. The night of the eclipse I had a surprisingly clear sky in the Coachella valley desert of California. I stood still in the silence, waiting patiently, drinking in the moment. I had my Nikon D7000 camera set up on a tripod with my 80-400mm lens, hands poised on my camera trigger, desperate to catch these amazing images as they progressed relentlessly in panorama. And oh, what glory I witnessed! It was an amazing sight to watch the moon in all of its phases in a lunar eclipse, especially when the moon seemingly caught on fire in a glowing red vibrance. And then it was over, perhaps a once in a lifetime event for me. I sat for some time in awe and wonder at the power of our great God.

Thus says the Lord, Who gives the sun for light by day and the fixed order of the moon and the stars for light by night...the Lord of hosts is His name.

Jeremiah 31:35

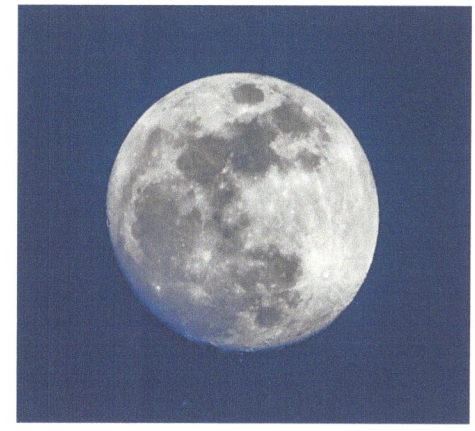

God will take care of you, be not afraid;
He is your safeguard thro' sunshine and shade;
Tenderly watching and keeping His own,
He will not leave you to wander alone.
Chorus
God will take care of you still to the end;
Oh, what a Father, Redeemer and Friend!
Jesus will answer whenever you call,
He will take care of you, trust Him for all.

God will take care of you, thro' all the day,
Shielding your footsteps, directing your way;
He is your Shepherd, Protector and Guide,
Leading His children where still waters glide.

God will take care of you, long as you live,
Granting you blessings no other can give;
He will take care of you when time is past,
Safe to His kingdom will bring you at last.

God Will Take Care Of You — Fanny Crosby

Trust in the LORD with all your heart; do not depend on your own understanding. Seek His will in all you do, and He will show you which path to take.

Proverbs 3:5-6 NLT

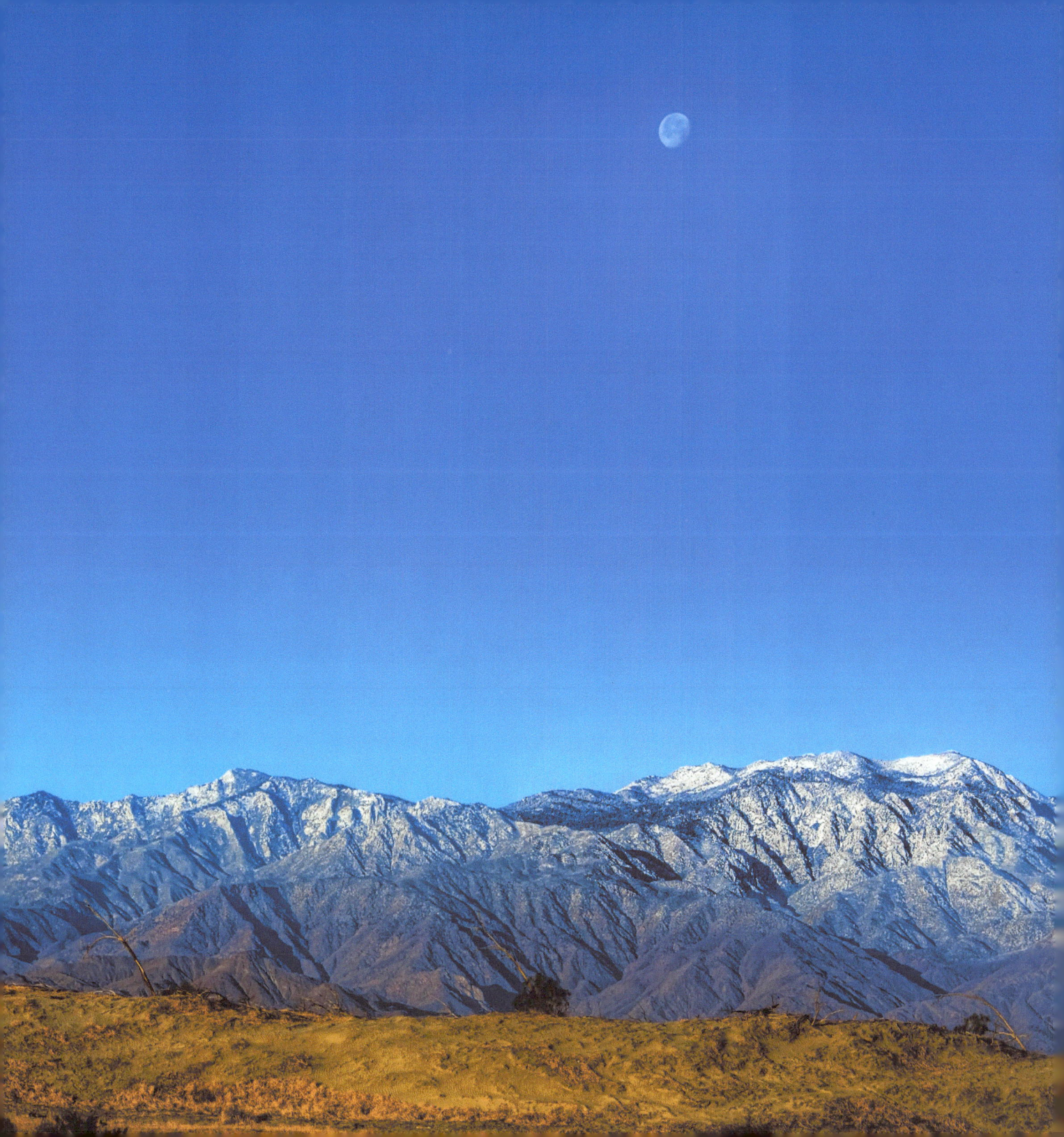

15 Painting The Sky

He also made the stars…And evening passed and morning came, marking the fourth day.

Genesis 1:16-,19 NLT

God is the Master Artist and when He paints the sky, it's not with pigment, oil, or gum arabic. He paints with stars, planets, galaxies, light, and clouds in all array of colors. His brush is His Word and His canvas is the sky. All who live on the earth can experience His Masterpieces of creation. The beauty of all He paints in the sky speaks volumes about who He is, what He does and what He says. Makoto Fujimura, a young gifted artist, at the age of 27, came to the realization that he didn't have what he calls "a shelf in his heart to hold that beauty—the very beauty he was creating." He was searching and filled with deep questions about God. He came to understand, through a poem by William Blake, that God is love and Jesus died on the cross for him. In this realization he found the answers to his questions, and began to "run with Jesus," as he describes his defining moment. He saw the beauty he created in his own art in a whole new way. He discovered that beauty is not just self-expression, but is an offering. Art became for him an intimate exchange with Jesus.

Lift up your eyes on high and see who has created these stars, the One who leads forth their host by number, He calls them all by name.

Isaiah 40:26

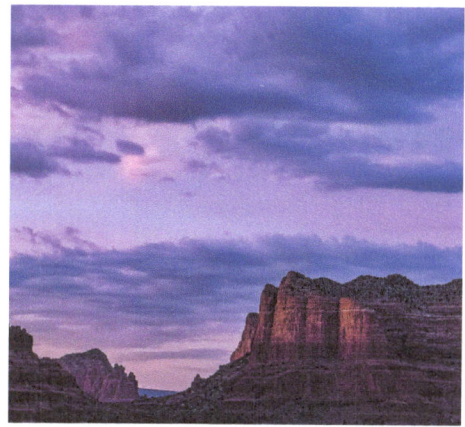

The Bible begins with Creation and ends with New Creation. Everywhere in between, Creator God (the grand Artist) beckons the broken, but creative, creatures (the little- 'a' artists) to create shalom/peace in the face of our "Ground Zero" reality all around us. God sent God's Son, Jesus to be the reconciler and redeemer—to set the world right, and to exhibit God's love to the world. Jesus, God incarnate, spoke in parables and exhibited artistic qualities that inspire me as an artist. We are created to be creative…God does not just mend, repair, and restore; God renews and generates, transcending our expectations of even what we desire, beyond what we dare to ask or imagine.

Art And Faith — Makoto Fujimura

Poetry, painting, photography, film, and other forms of art can help us see the revelation of God that is evident in the world around us…the beauties of nature, whether seen in their native state or captured by a work of art, aren't just beautiful—they are trying to tell us something…They help us pay attention to what we ordinarily would have missed…If we are really paying attention, we will often find ourselves gasping at the beauty and mystery of life…The sense of of overpowering awe, of your own smallness in the larger scheme of things, the ever-changing visual exuberance before you, and the silent stillness of awe are just something that must be experienced. What you are experiencing is wonder.…Wonder is a way of talking about our response both to the mystery of life and to our experience of God in the context of His creation. Wonder is that which takes our breath away.

Discovering God Through The Arts — Dr. Terry Glaspey

Thus says the Lord, your Redeemer, and the one who formed you from the womb, "I, the Lord, am the maker of all things, stretching out the heavens by Myself and spreading out the earth all alone."

Isaiah 44:24

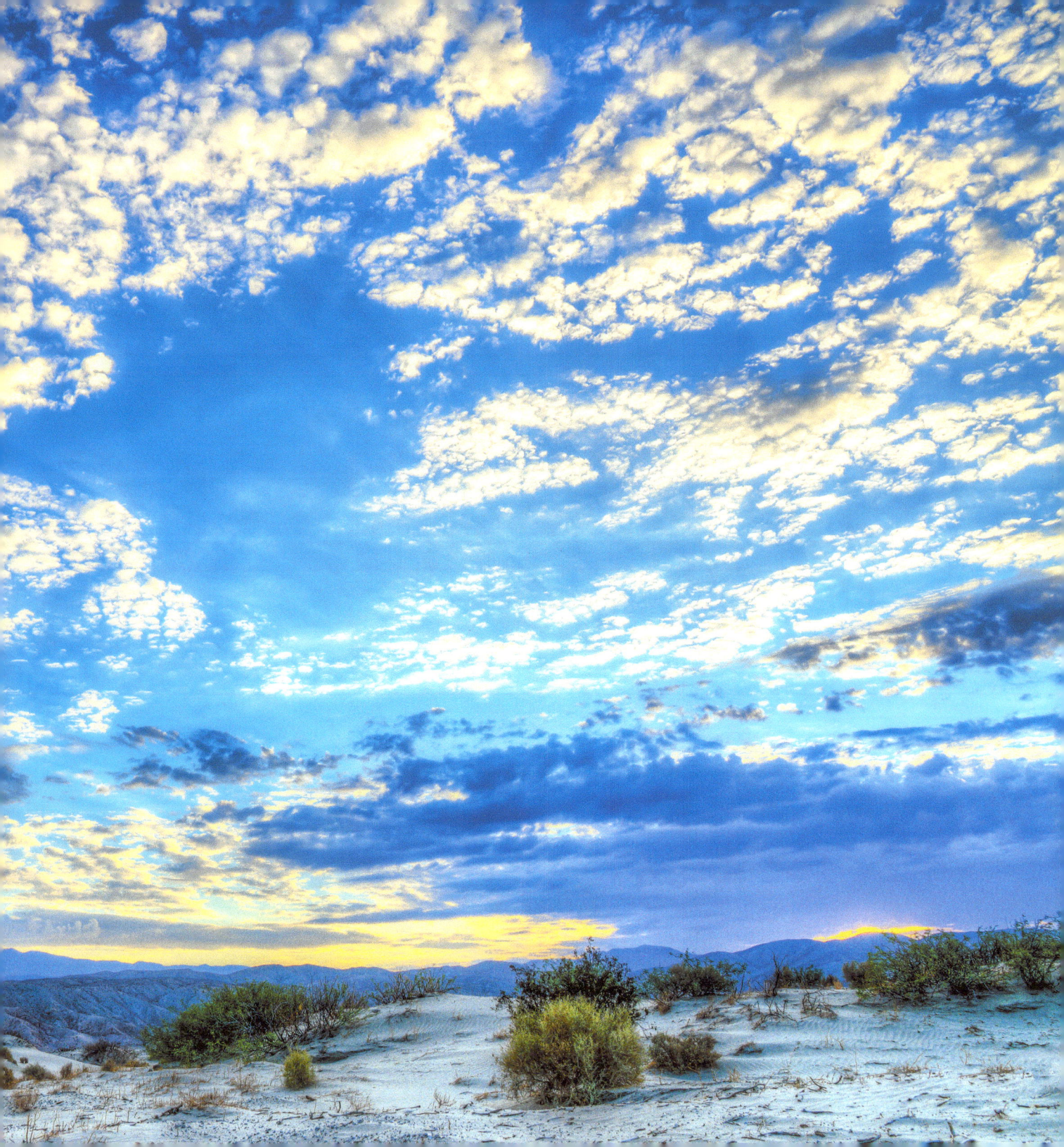

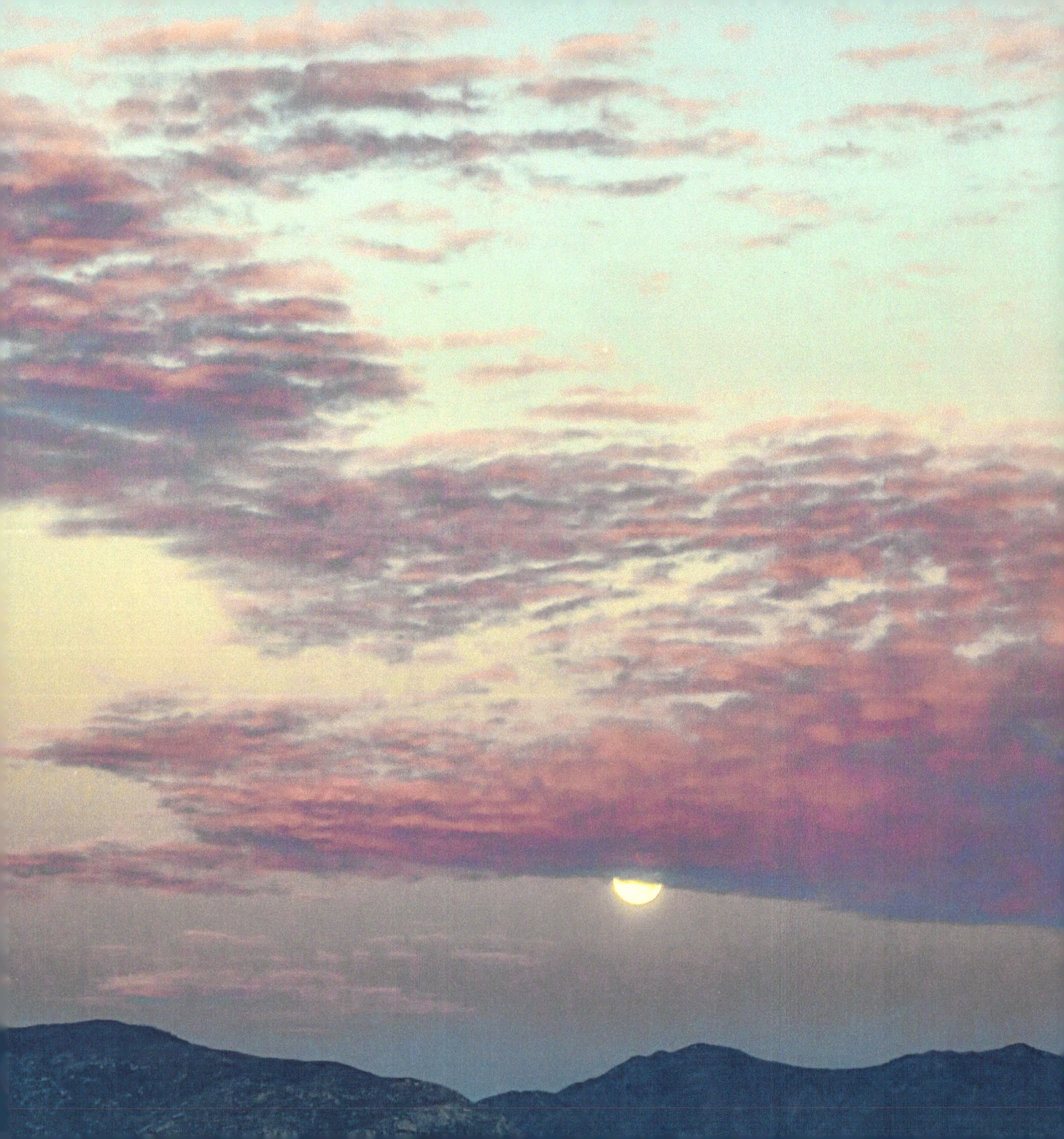

FOURTH DAY REFLECTIONS

RESPONDING TO THE EDGES OF HIS WAYS

Indeed these are the mere edges of His ways...
Job 26:14 NKJV

How shall we respond to all we see of the Lord in creation? We have come a long way when we recognize that God is the Creator and we are beginning to discover all He has created. When we gaze at all His hand has created, the greatness and glory of His creation help us realize the truth Job realized. "Indeed these are the mere edges of His ways" (Job 26:14 NKJV). We arrive at this overwhelming thought as we discover we are only catching a glimpse of what God can do. He is more than we know Him to be and He has created infinitely more than we see right now. And then, we discover He is personal, revealing Himself to us in and through all He has created. This is when we draw near to Him, to know and love Him with our heart and soul.

Lord, we are humbled to see that Your creation is the mere edges of Your ways. You are infinite and incomprehensible. Thank you for encouraging us to draw near that we might know and love You. In Jesus' name, Amen.

FIFTH DAY

As you watch God's handiwork day after day in creation, just think about what each day's work is like for Him. Now, on the fifth day, you are going to see more of God's brilliance and even His sense of humor as you look at the fish and birds commanded into existence with His Word. "Let the waters swarm with fish and other life. Let the skies be filled with birds of every kind" (Genesis 1:20 NLT). Just another day in the office of heaven. All in a day's work for God. As you slow down and look at the details of God's creation, cultivate a new sense of wonder and awe at His majesty.

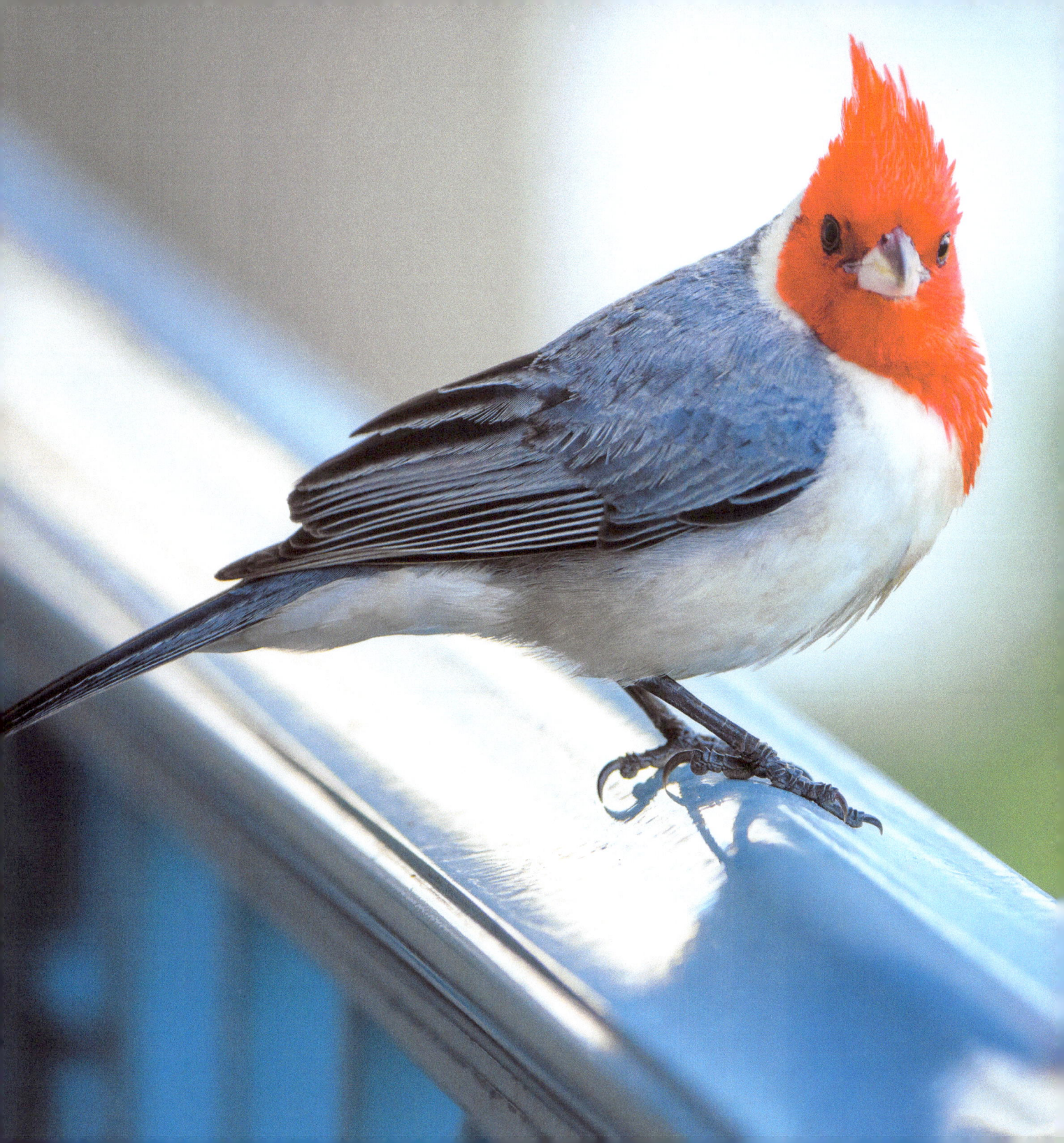

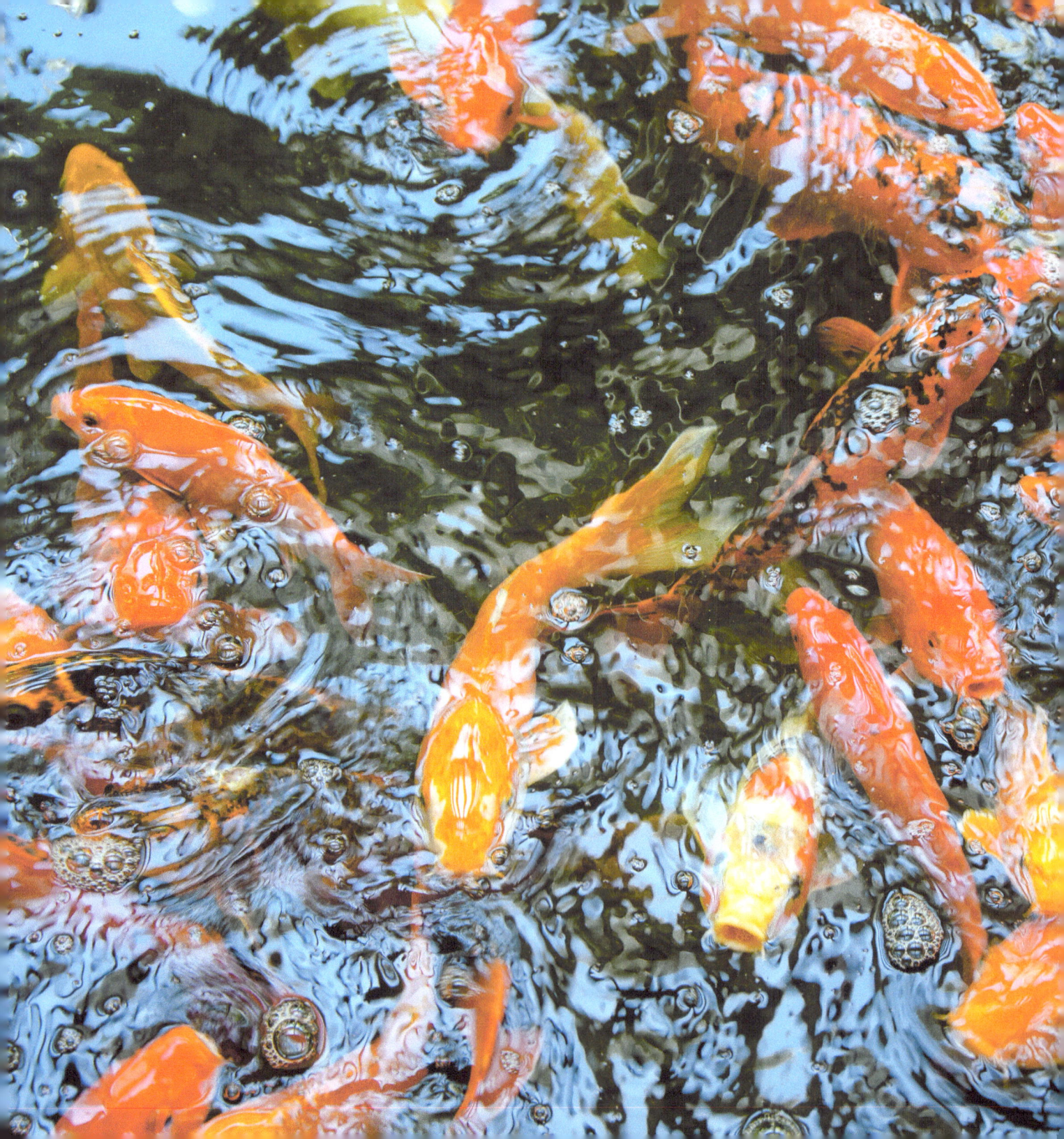

16
Life In The Water

Then God said, "Let the waters swarm with fish and other life"…

Genesis 1:20 NLT

God had more in mind for His creation once the earth and sky had light, atmosphere, and growing plants. He created it to be inhabited. In Isaiah 45:18, we learn from God Himself what was in His mind when He created the heavens and earth: "For thus says the Lord—Who created the heavens, God Himself, Who formed the earth and made it, Who established it and did not create it to be a worthless waste; He formed it to be inhabited—'I am the Lord, and there is no one else.'" On the fifth day, God began inhabiting the earth with the command, "Let the waters swarm with fish and other life…" (Genesis 1:20 NLT). This is the first time the word "life" occurs in Genesis. He created all kinds of marine animals including invertebrates, vertebrates, and reptiles. There are at least 33,000 known fish species and hundreds of thousands of unknown marine life forms. One scientist has said that the oceans are basically unexplored and little is known about the life they support. But God knows because He created every single one—sharks, dolphins, whales, and even the giant squid.

Then God blessed them, saying, "Be fruitful and multiply. Let the fish fill the seas"…

Genesis 1:22 NLT

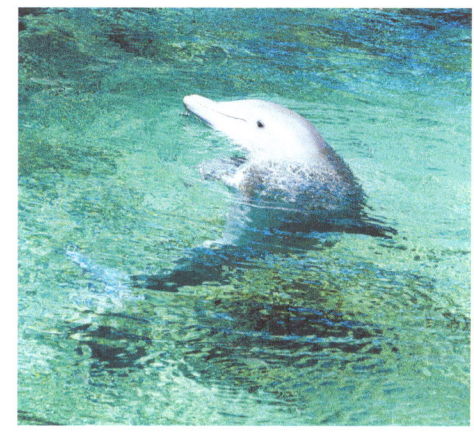

What would creation have been without his design? Is there a fish in the sea, or a fowl in the air, which was left to chance for its formation? No, in every bone, joint, and muscle, sinew, gland, and blood-vessel, you mark the presence of a God working everything according to the design of infinite wisdom.

Morning and Evening — Charles Haddon Spurgeon

We sing the mighty power of God that made the mountains rise,
that spread the flowing seas abroad and built the lofty skies.
We sing the wisdom that ordained the sun to rule the day;
the moon shines full at his command, and all the stars obey.
We sing the goodness of the Lord that filled the earth with food;
he formed the creatures with his word and then pronounced them good.
Lord, how your wonders are displayed, where'er we turn our eyes,
if we survey the ground we tread or gaze upon the skies.
There's not a plant or flower below but makes your glories known,
and clouds arise and tempests blow by order from your throne;
while all that borrows life from you is ever in your care,
and everywhere that we can be, you, God, are present there.

I Sing the Almighty Power of God — Isaac Watts

The LORD merely spoke, and the heavens were created. He breathed the word, and all the stars were born. He assigned the sea its boundaries and locked the oceans in vast reservoirs. Let the whole world fear the LORD, and let everyone stand in awe of Him. For when He spoke, the world began! It appeared at His command.

Psalm 33:6-9 nlt

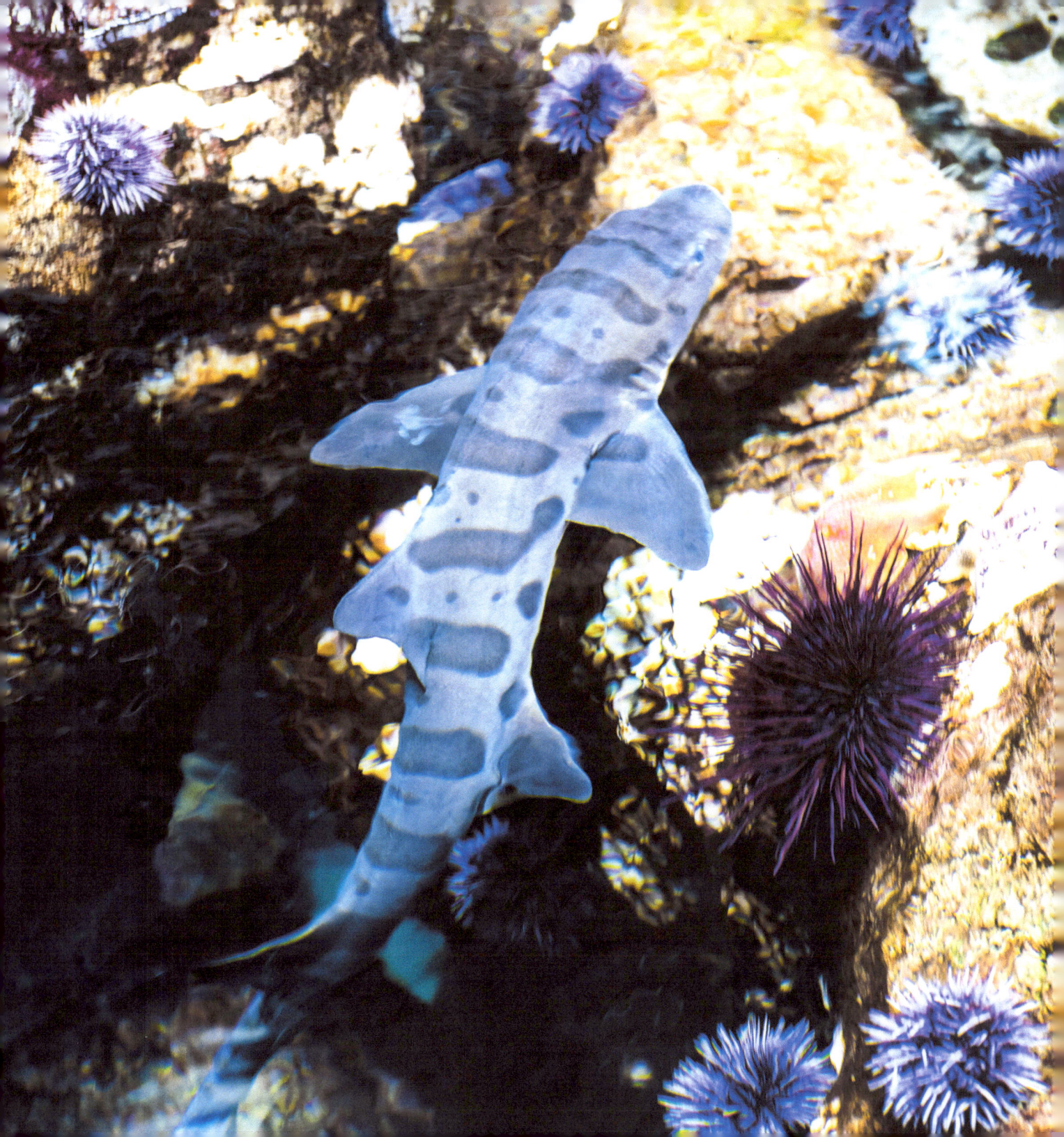

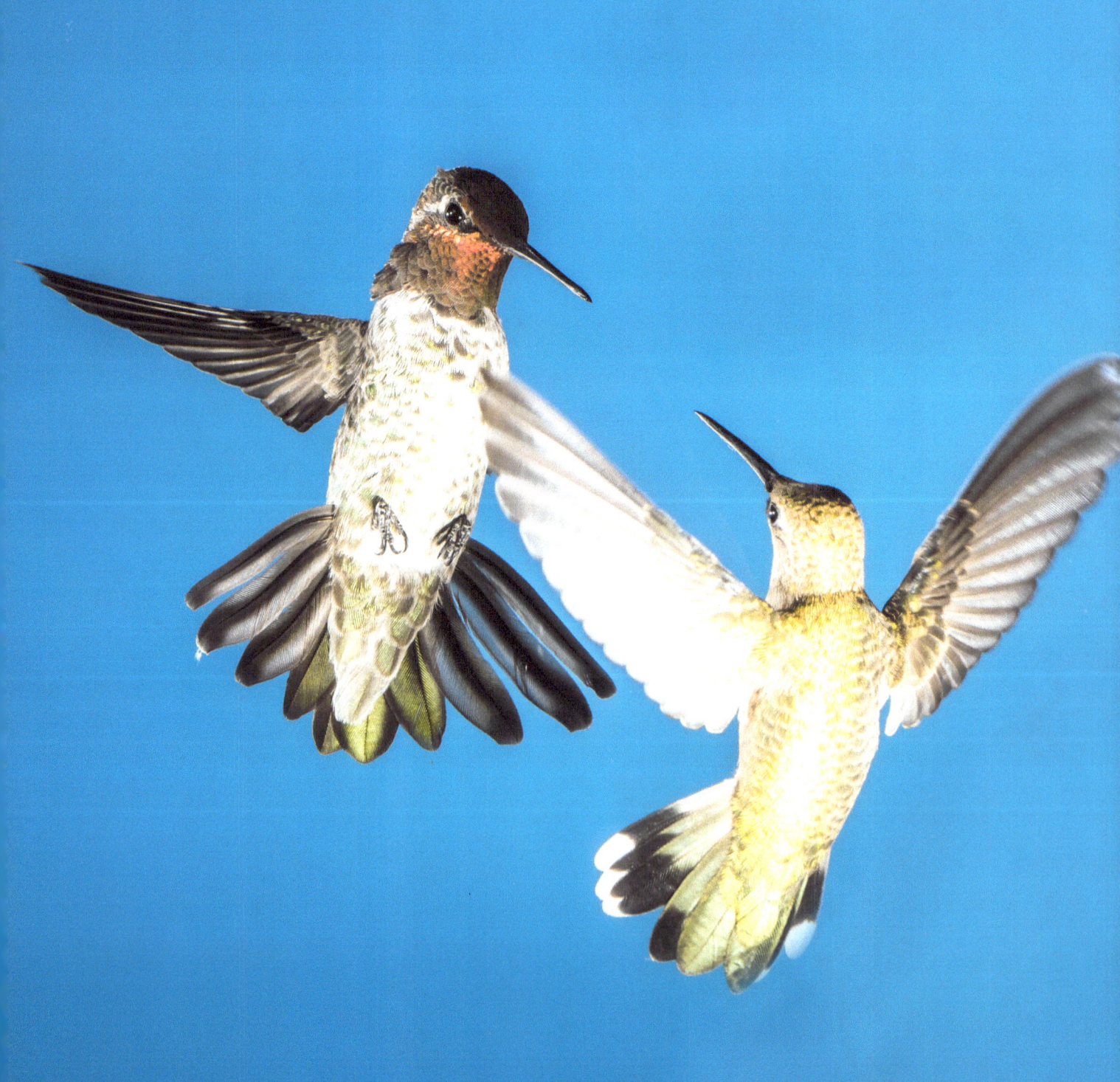

17
When Birds Dance

"Let the skies be filled with birds of every kind"…And evening passed and morning came, marking the fifth day.

Genesis 1:20,23

I once asked a scholar I greatly respected what it meant to see God's glory. I had been thinking about the bold and daring prayer of Moses, "I pray You, show me Your glory" (Exodus 33:18). The scholar told me that sometimes the Lord pulls down the shades in life just a bit and gives you a tiny glimpse of who He is, what He does, and what He says. I have never forgotten those words especially when I am out in God's creation and catch a glimpse of something magnificent created by God Himself. One morning I was up early and outside with my camera at a small pond just hoping to capture a duck on the water. Well, the Lord pulled down the shades and gave me quite the show—a glimpse of His glory in action with something only He sees most of the time—ten snowy white egrets dancing on the water and gliding across its shimmering surface. Another day, with camera in hand, I witnessed the migration of thousands of hummingbirds in Sedona, Arizona, and captured two of them dancing in mid-air. Keep your eyes open and you will catch a glimpse of God's glory in all He has created.

Let every created thing give praise to the LORD, for He issued His command, and they came into being.

Psalm 148:5 NLT

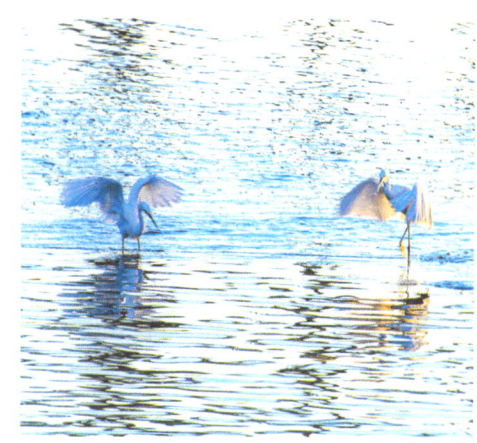

Hope is the ability to listen to the music of the future. Faith is the courage to dance to it in the present.

Dr. Peter Kuzmic

Open our eyes, dear Lord, that we may see the far vast reaches of eternity.
Help us to look beyond life's little cares so prone to fret us
And the grief that wears our courage thin.
O may we tune our hearts to Thy great harmony
That all the parts may ever be in perfect, sweet accord.
Give us Thine own clear vision, blessed Lord.

Each New Day — Corrie Ten Boom

Faith shows the reality of what we hope for; it is the evidence of things we cannot see…
And it is impossible to please God without faith. Anyone who wants to come to Him must believe that God exists and that He rewards those who sincerely seek Him.

Hebrews 11:1,6 NLT

We have the presence and the promises of God. We are meant to march to that great music.

Gold By Moonlight—Amy Carmichael

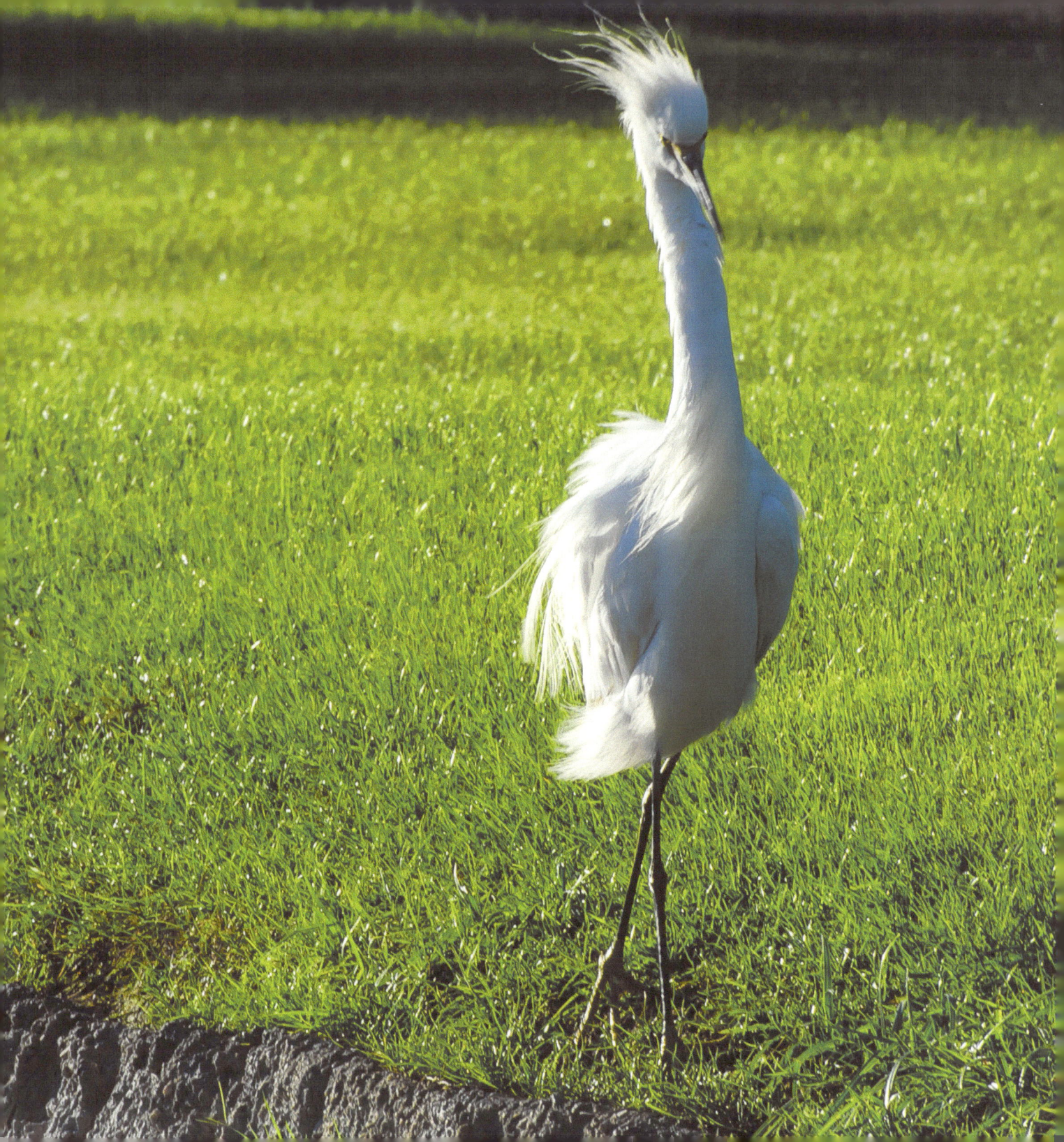

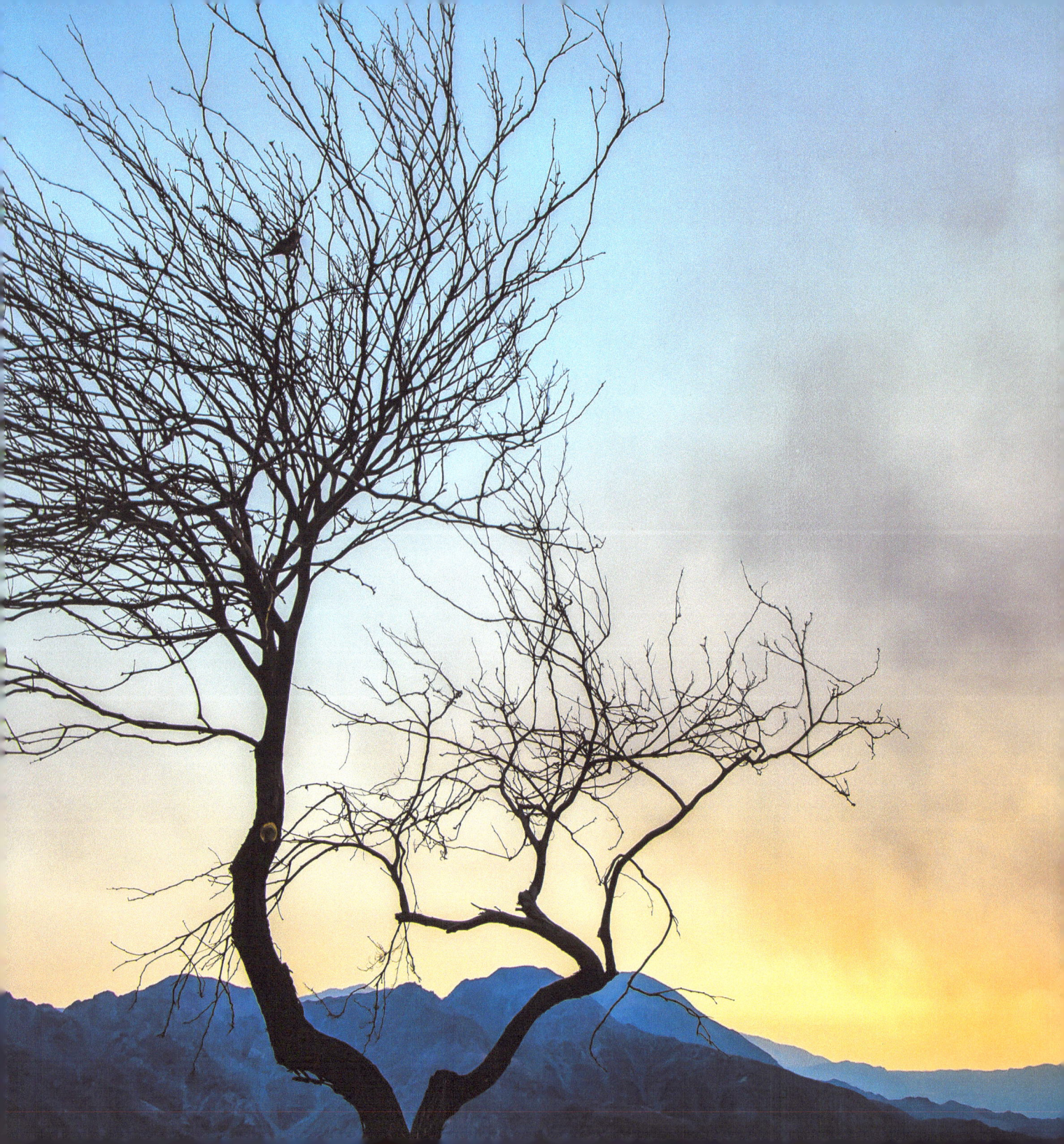

18
A Bird In A Tree

Ask the birds of the sky, and they will tell you...for the life of every living thing is in His hand and the breath of every human being.

JOB 12:7,10 NLT

When you watch the birds God created in action as they search for food, fly through the air, and seek protection from predators, you learn lessons for your own life. One day I was out capturing images as the sky was filled with smoke from a blazing fire in the mountains, and I captured a beautiful vermilion flycatcher taking refuge on a high tree branch, watching from above its perceived danger. Another day, I was in my back yard, and discovered a great-horned owl looking at me from behind a palm tree, cautiously evaluating whether or not it was in danger. These birds seem to know what it takes a lifetime for some of us to learn—the Lord is our Creator, Provider, and Protector. Job learned this when he said, "Ask the birds of the sky, and they will tell you...for the life of every living thing is in His hand and the breath of every human being" (Job 12:7,10 NLT). Jesus told us to "Look at the birds" (Matthew 6:26 NLT) to teach us not to worry, and to learn how God provides for them and for us. So today, dear friend, take a long look at these birds, and find your refuge and your help in the Lord.

God is our refuge and strength, always ready to help in times of trouble. So we will not fear...

PSALM 46:1-2 NLT

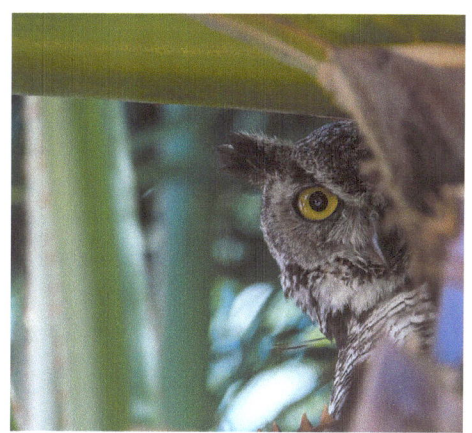

Two little girls were talking about God, and one said, "I know God does not love me. He could not care for such a tiny little girl like me." "Dear me, Sis," said the other girl, "don't you know that is just what God is for—to take care of tiny little girls who can't take care of themselves, just like us." "Is He?" said the first little girl. "I did not know that. Then I don't need to worry anymore, do I"…Our Comforter is not far-off in heaven where we cannot find Him. He is close at hand. He abides with us…He is always present and always ready to give us "joy for mourning, the garment of praise for the spirit of heaviness" (Isaiah 61:3).

THE GOD OF ALL COMFORT — HANNAH WHITALL SMITH

God surrounds His children. We dwell in Him. "There is no one like the God of Jeshurun, who rides the heavens to help you, and in His excellency on the clouds. The eternal God is your refuge, and underneath are the everlasting arms; He will thrust out the enemy from before you" (Deut. 33:26–27). These verses show that the Lord is above, around, and underneath His saints. "LORD, You have been our dwelling place in all generations" (Ps. 90:1). We are as surrounded by You as the earth is surrounded by the atmosphere: *Within Thy circling power I stand, On every side I find Thy hand; Awake, asleep, at home, abroad, I am surrounded still with God.* The eternal God is your dwelling place and your rest, and underneath are the everlasting arms…The hand of God sustains those who dwell in the secret place of the Most High and abide under the shadow of the Almighty. I will say of the Lord, "He is my refuge and my fortress; my God, in Him I will trust" (Ps. 91:1).

BESIDE STILL WATERS — CHARLES HADDON SPURGEON

What is the price of two sparrows—one copper coin? But not a single sparrow can fall to the ground without your Father knowing it. And the very hairs on your head are all numbered. So don't be afraid; you are more valuable to God than a whole flock of sparrows.

MATTHEW 10:29-31 NLT

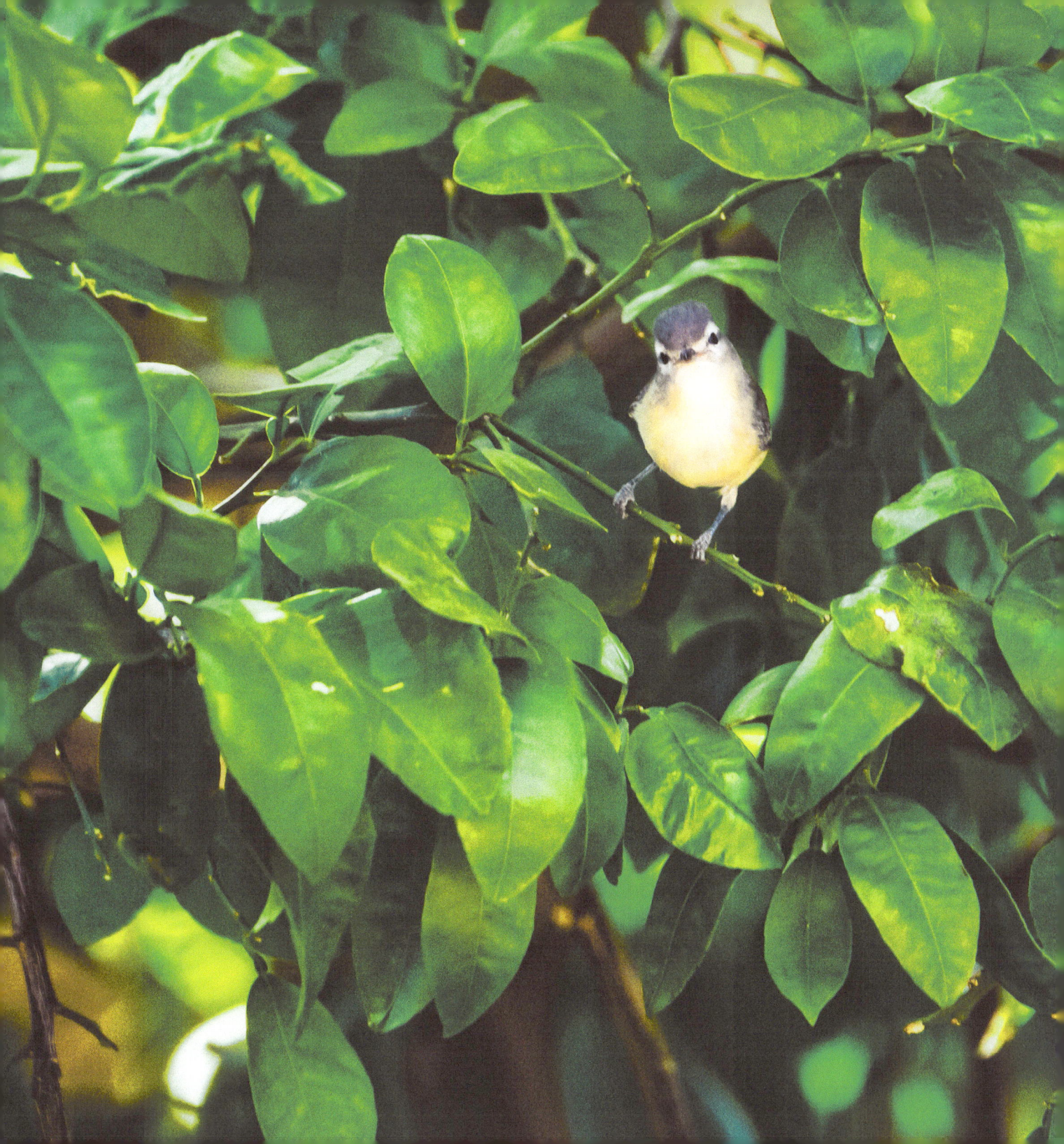

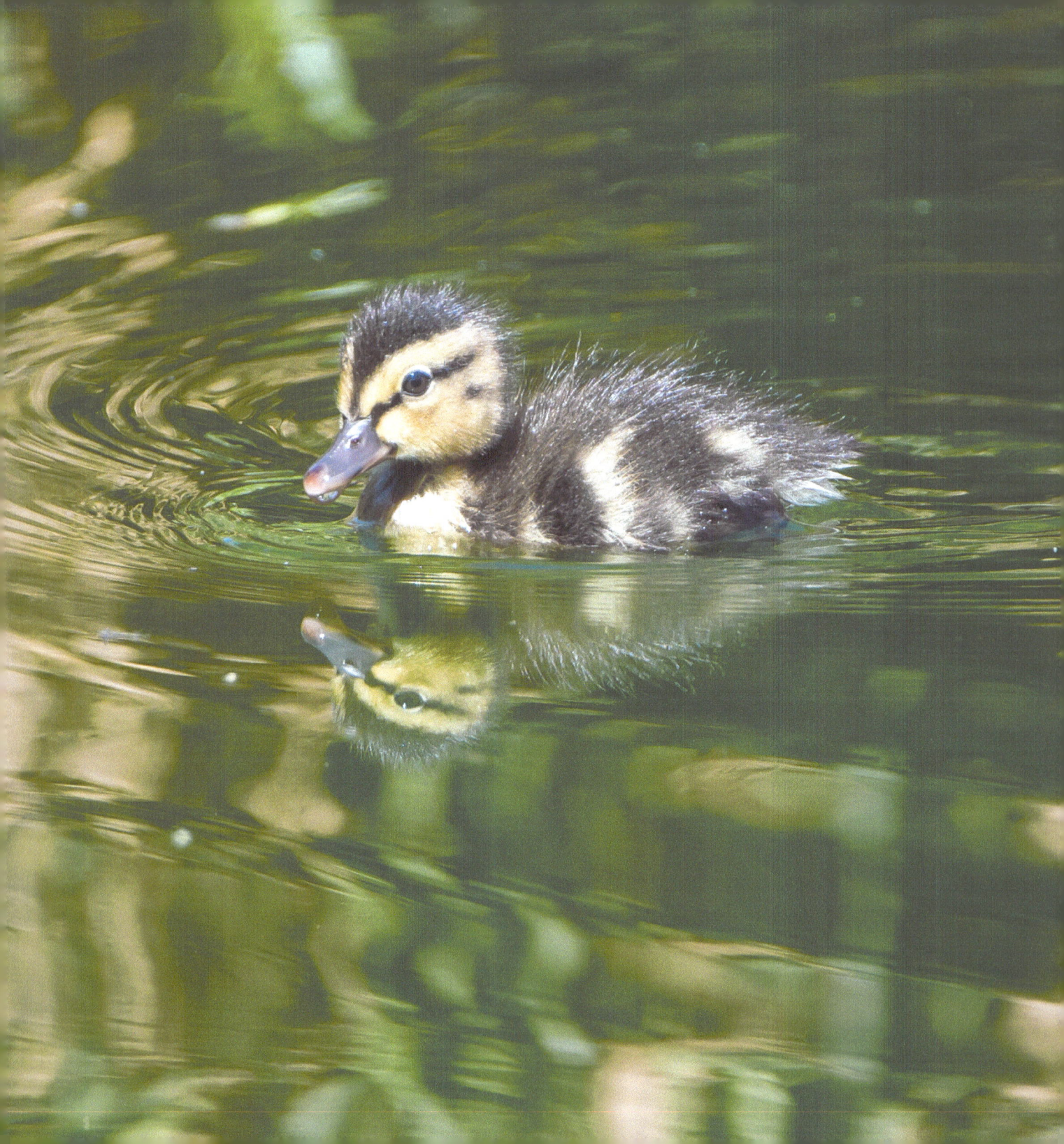

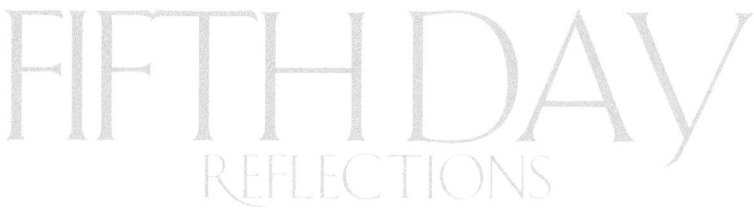

FIFTH DAY REFLECTIONS

THE GRAND AND LIFE-CHANGING CONCLUSION

Ah Lord God! Behold, You have made the heavens and the earth by Your great power and by Your outstretched arm! Nothing is too difficult for You.
JEREMIAH 32:17

When you see the intricacy and design of creation including the diversity in species of life in the ocean and the sky—multitudes of fish and birds—you cannot help but think about the fact that man could never come close to making such wonder and glory. Such creation is outside the realm of human capacity or ability. Observing God's creation brings us to the grand conclusion of the existence of God who is all-powerful. And then, we arrive at Jeremiah's conclusion, "Nothing is too difficult for You" (Jeremiah 32:17). If God can make the heavens and the earth, then He is enough for anything I face today. If you have come to this grand conclusion, then you are on your way to a deeper knowledge of God and a great trust in Him.

Lord, I look at all You have made and I am in awe of Your great power.
Nothing is too difficult for You.
I trust You today for all the impossible situations in my life. In Jesus' name, Amen.

SIXTH DAY

Now we are walking on holy and sacred ground as we watch God create His crowning achievement. The Triune God — Father, Son, and Holy Spirit — has made a decision to populate the earth He created. On the fifth day He created marine life and birds. And now, on the sixth day, God said, "Let the earth produce every sort of animal" (Genesis 1:24). Then God said, "Let us make human beings in our image, to be like us" (Genesis 1:26). This creation of human beings is so important that there is a second, more personal and detailed account in Genesis 2:7-25. And God did all of this in a day.

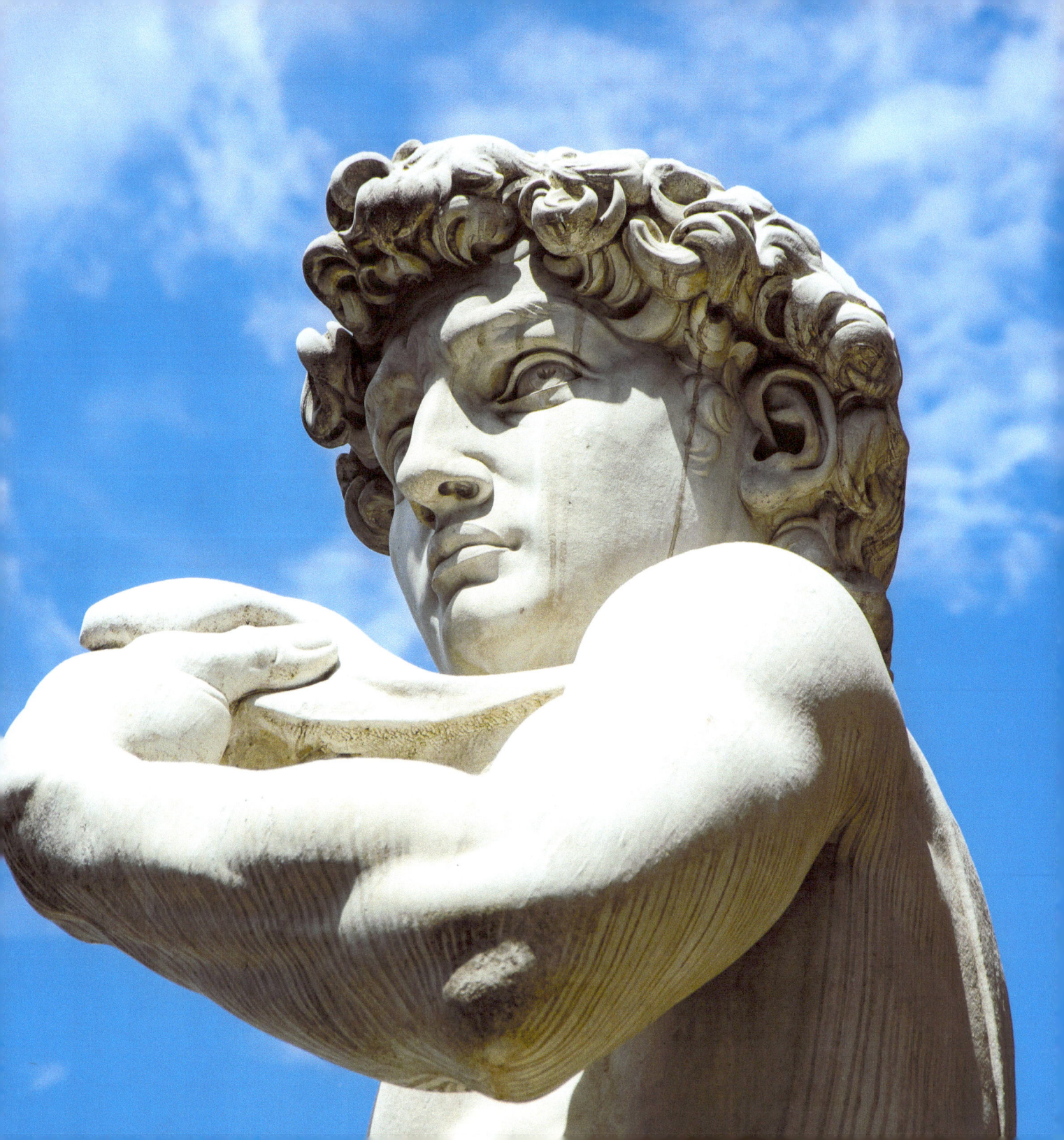

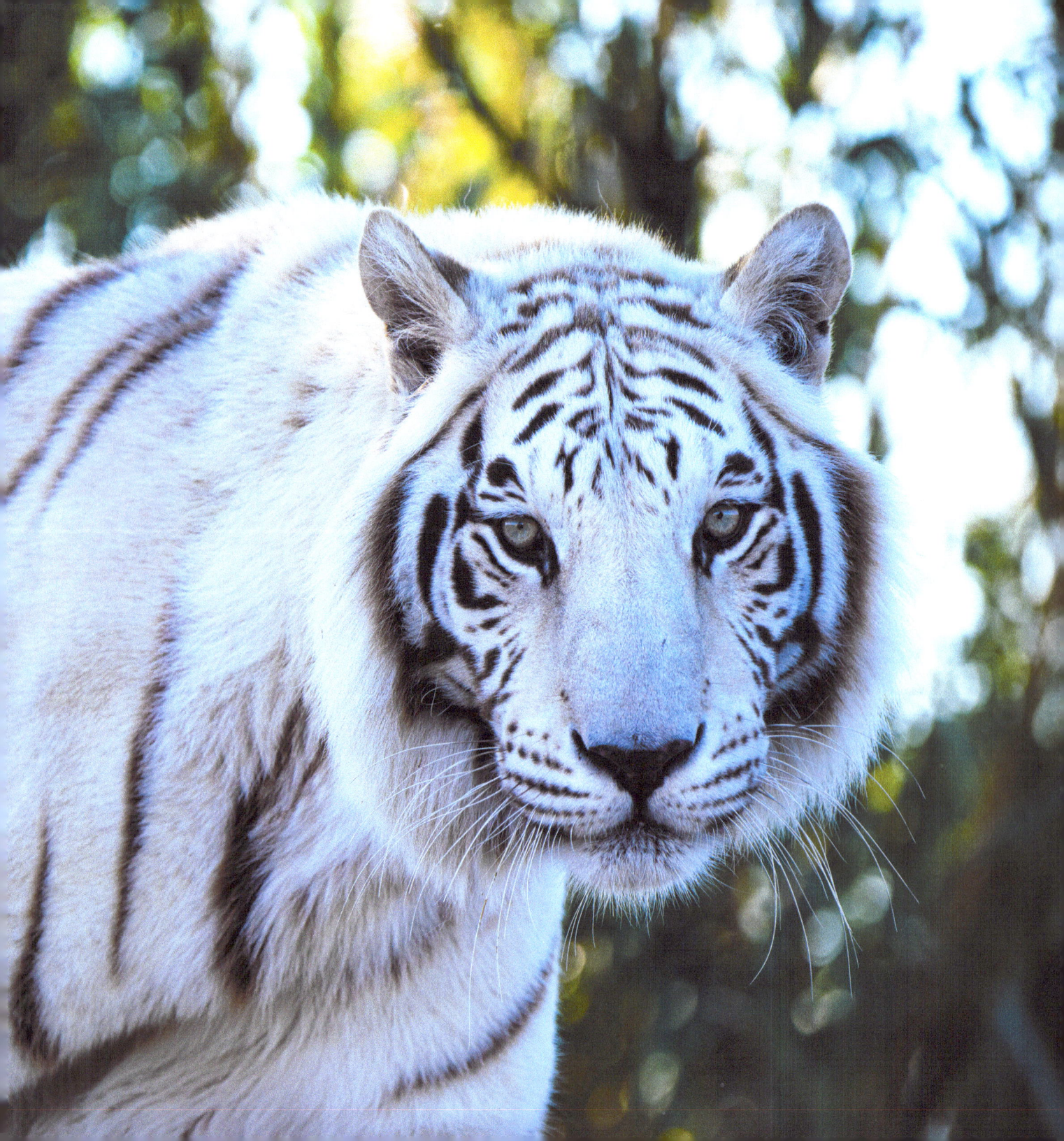

19 GOD'S CREATURES

Then God said, "Let the earth produce living creatures according to their kinds"…And it was so.

GENESIS 1:24 CSB

On the sixth day, God began His creative work commanding animals into existence. He assigned an important word to these creatures — "living." It's evident there is life in animals. Just look into the eyes of any animal. There is an exchange, depth, and personality in animals. In a difficult season of my life, when I had suffered a series of devastating losses, I spent extended time with a friend in Newport Beach. Her dog, Koko, sensed I was deeply brokenhearted. He would jump up on the couch and look into my eyes. Then, he would lay his head in my lap. We would sit there for hours together and he never left my side. The Lord used this precious dog to help comfort my wounded heart. The Lord regards these animals as His own. He says, "For all the animals of the forest are mine, and I own the cattle on a thousand hills. I know every bird on the mountains, and all the animals of the field are mine…for all the world is mine and everything in it" (Psalm 40:10-12 NLT). Just think — God created approximately 8.7 million species of animals in one day. Only God can create such wonder.

Let them praise the name of the LORD, for His name alone is exalted; His splendor is above the earth and the heavens.

PSALM 148:13 NLT

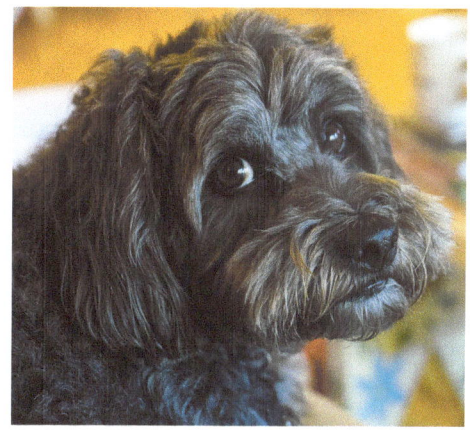

One day while visiting a friend, the gardener knocked on the door, urging us to quickly come look at something dramatic happening in the front yard. We ran outside to witness a seemingly life and death rescue mission of a mother squirrel, taking her babies (called kits or kittens), one at a time, from one tall tree that was being cut down, to another tree across the street. I grabbed my camera to capture the entire rescue, from start to finish. She put her little baby's arms around her neck, and with it hanging on for dear life, the mother squirrel raced across the street, up the new tree, depositing the young squirrel in a safe place. She did this with all three of the baby squirrels. The most dramatic part was that a neighbor's cat was chasing the mother squirrel back and forth across the street through the entire intense drama. But finally, with her babies safe and secure, that mother squirrel clung to the tree, watching constantly to guard and protect her young. We stood in awe and amazement as we witnessed the wonder of God's creation in action.

THE SQUIRREL STORY — CATHERINE MARTIN

Though not an object of God's love as man would be, animals nevertheless are objects of His care and concern.

THE GENESIS RECORD — DR. HENRY M. MORRIS

Oh LORD, what a variety of things You have made! In wisdom You have made them all. The earth is full of Your creatures…They all depend on You to give then food as they need it. When you supply it, they gather it. You open Your hand to feed them, and they are richly satisfied…May the glory of the LORD continue forever. The LORD takes pleasure in all He has made!

PSALM 104:24,27-28,31 NLT

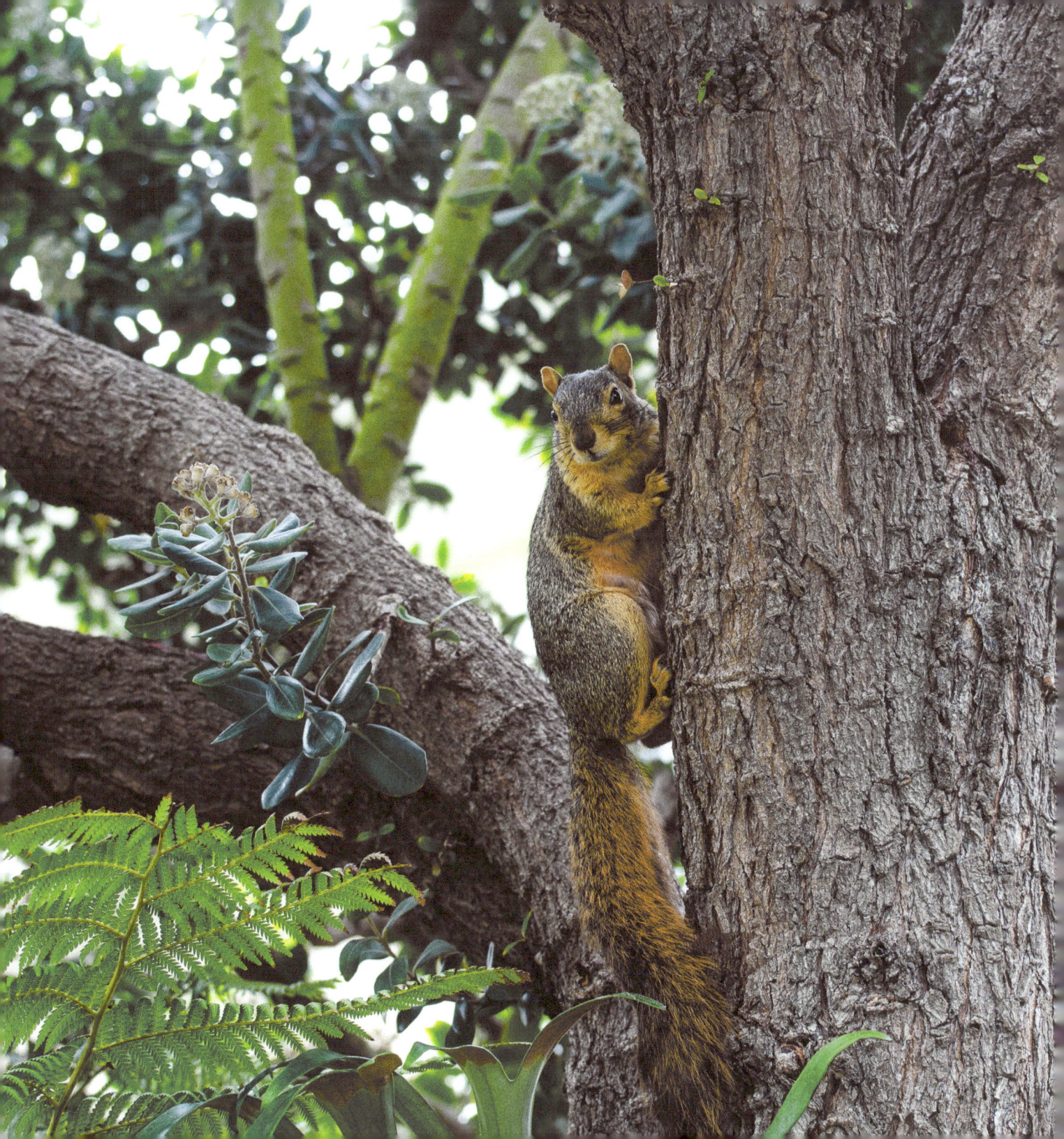

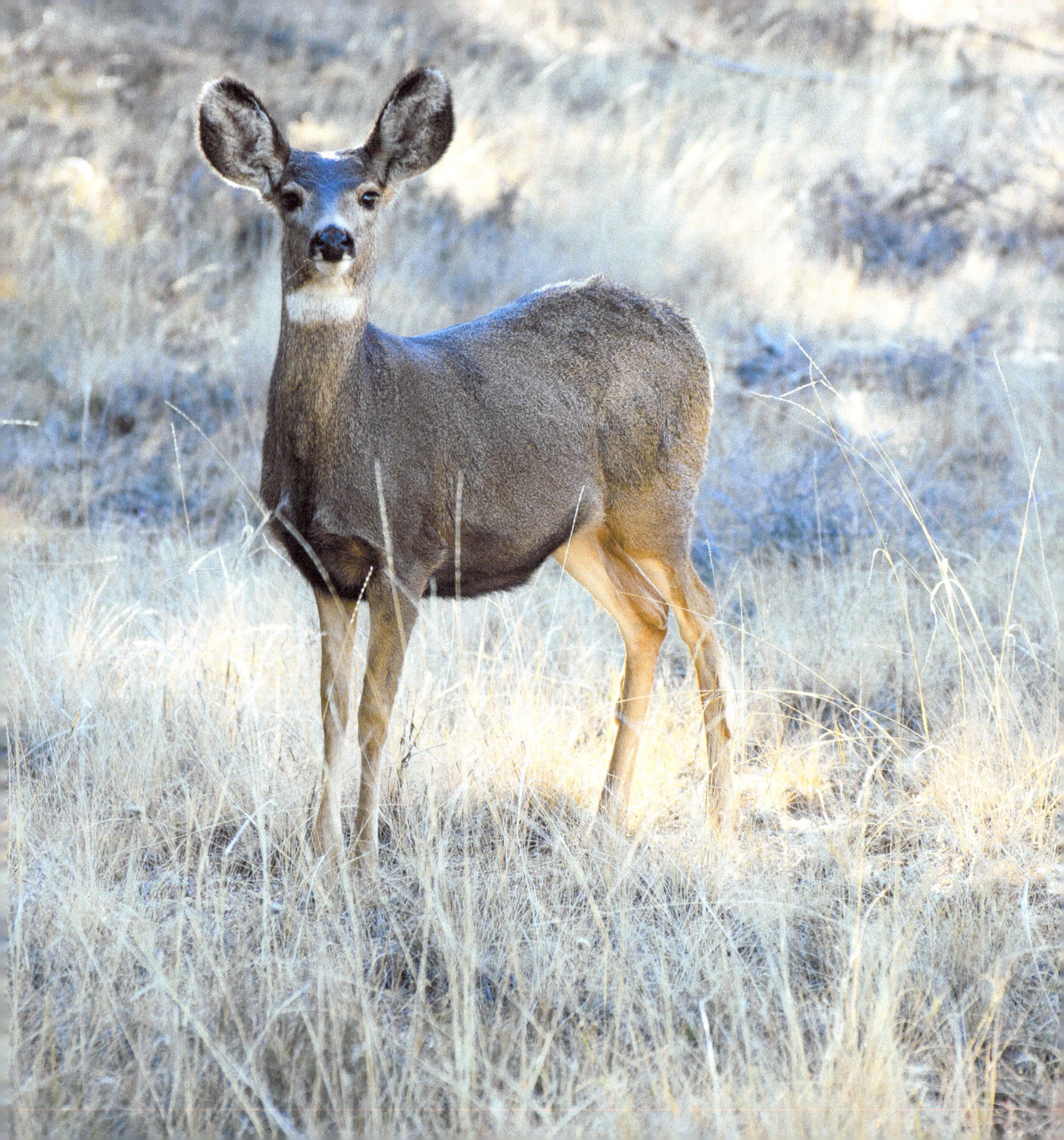

20
When God Surprises You

Just ask the animals, and they will teach you.

Job 12:7 NLT

Some of the most exciting moments in life are those times when God unexpectedly surprises you with something meaningful, custom-designed just for you. I was given the wonderful privilege to go on the photographic workshop adventure of a lifetime with the legendary photographer Bill Fortney to the Grand Circle including Monument Valley, Bryce Canyon, Zion National Park, and the Page, Arizona Slot Canyons. I was so excited to learn from one of the best photographers in the world. One morning we rose early and shot the sunrise at Inspiration Point in Bryce Canyon. As we were driving back to the hotel for breakfast, I noticed movement among the trees on the right side of the road. It was a mule deer grazing in grasses near the tall Ponderosa Pines. I had learned from another photographer, Moose Peterson, that the best way to capture images of deer is to set up your camera and tripod near a tree, stay still, and let the deer come to you. He was right! I set up my camera gear near a tree, and sure enough, to my delight, the Lord surprised me with not just one, but three deer!

But blessed are those who trust in the LORD and have made the LORD their hope and confidence.

Jeremiah 17:7 NLT

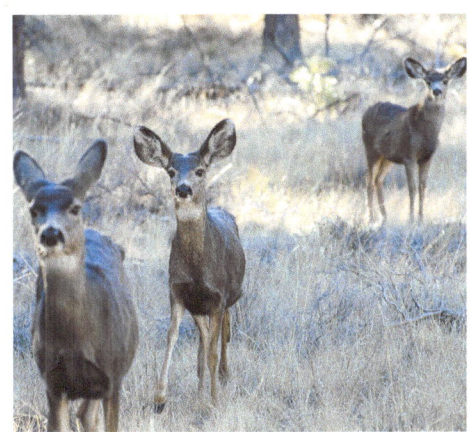

Even though the fig trees have no blossoms, and there are no grapes on the vines;
even though the olive crop fails, and the fields lie empty and barren;
even though the flocks die in the fields, and the cattle barns are empty,
yet I will rejoice in the LORD! I will be joyful in the God of my salvation!
The Sovereign LORD is my strength!
He makes me as surefooted as a deer, able to tread upon the heights.

HABAKKUK 3:17-19 NLT

Faith "grows amid storms"—just four words, but oh, how full of import to the soul who has been in the storms! Faith is that God-given faculty which, when exercised, brings the unseen into plain view, and by which the impossible things are made possible…In such an atmosphere faith finds its most productive soil; in such an element it comes more quickly to full fruition. The staunchest tree is not found in the shelter of the forest, but out in the open where the winds from every quarter beat upon it, and bend and twist it until it becomes a giant in stature…So in the spiritual world, when you see a giant, remember the road you must travel to come up to his side is not along the sunny lane where wild flowers ever bloom; but a steep, rocky, narrow pathway where the blasts of hell will almost blow you off your feet; where the sharp rocks cut the flesh, where the projecting thorns scratch the brow, and the venomous beasts hiss on every side. It is a pathway of sorrow and joy, of suffering and healing balm, of tears and smiles, of trials and victories, of conflicts and triumphs, of hardships and perils and buffetings, of persecutions and misunderstandings, of troubles and distress; through all of which we are made more than conquerors through Him who loves us. "Amid storms." Right in the midst where it is fiercest. You may shrink back from the ordeal of a fierce storm of trial…but go in! God is there to meet you in the center of all your trials, and to whisper His secrets which will make you come forth with a shining face and an indomitable faith that all the demons of hell shall never afterwards cause to waver.

E.A. KILBOURNE — STREAMS IN THE DESERT

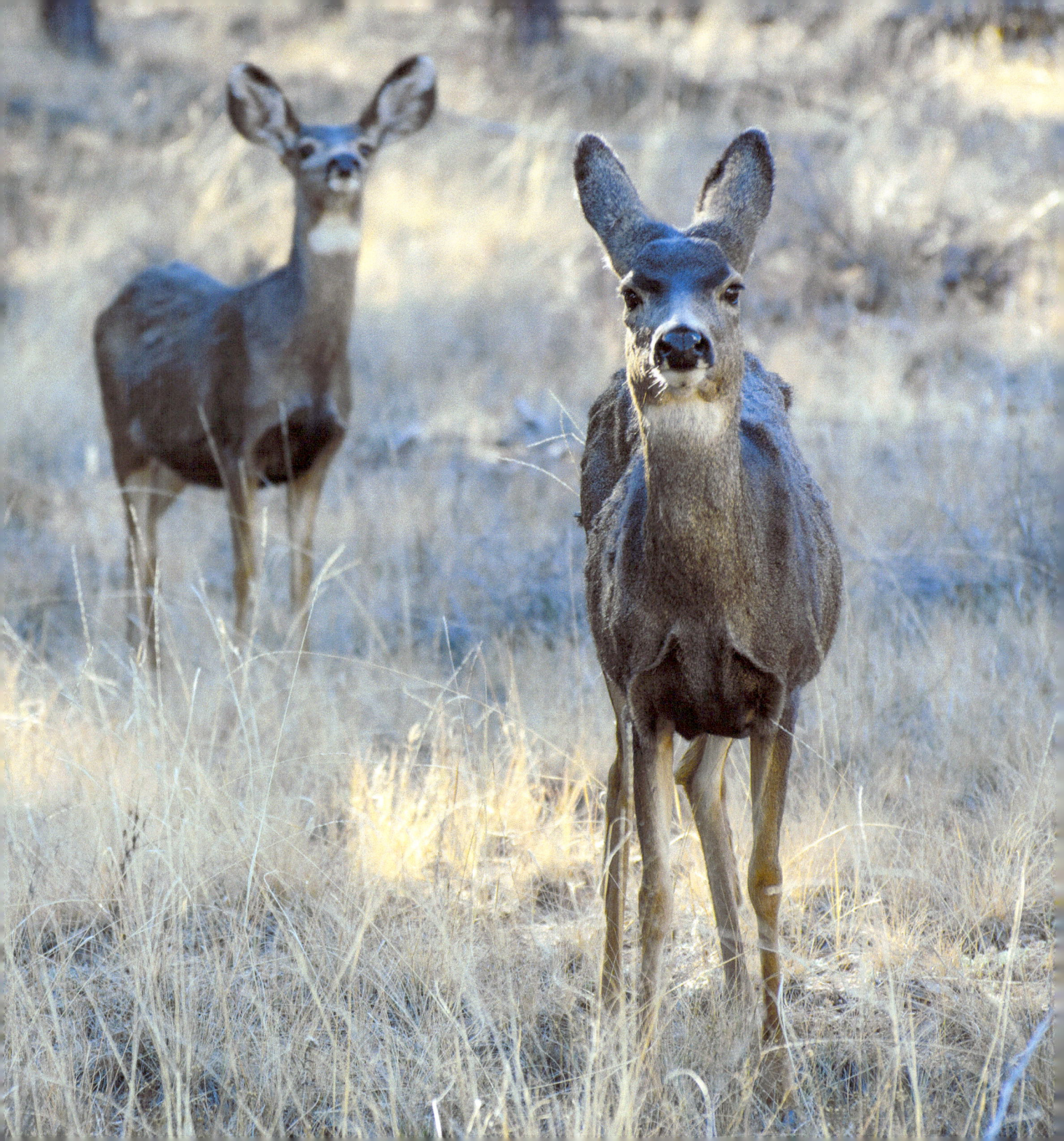

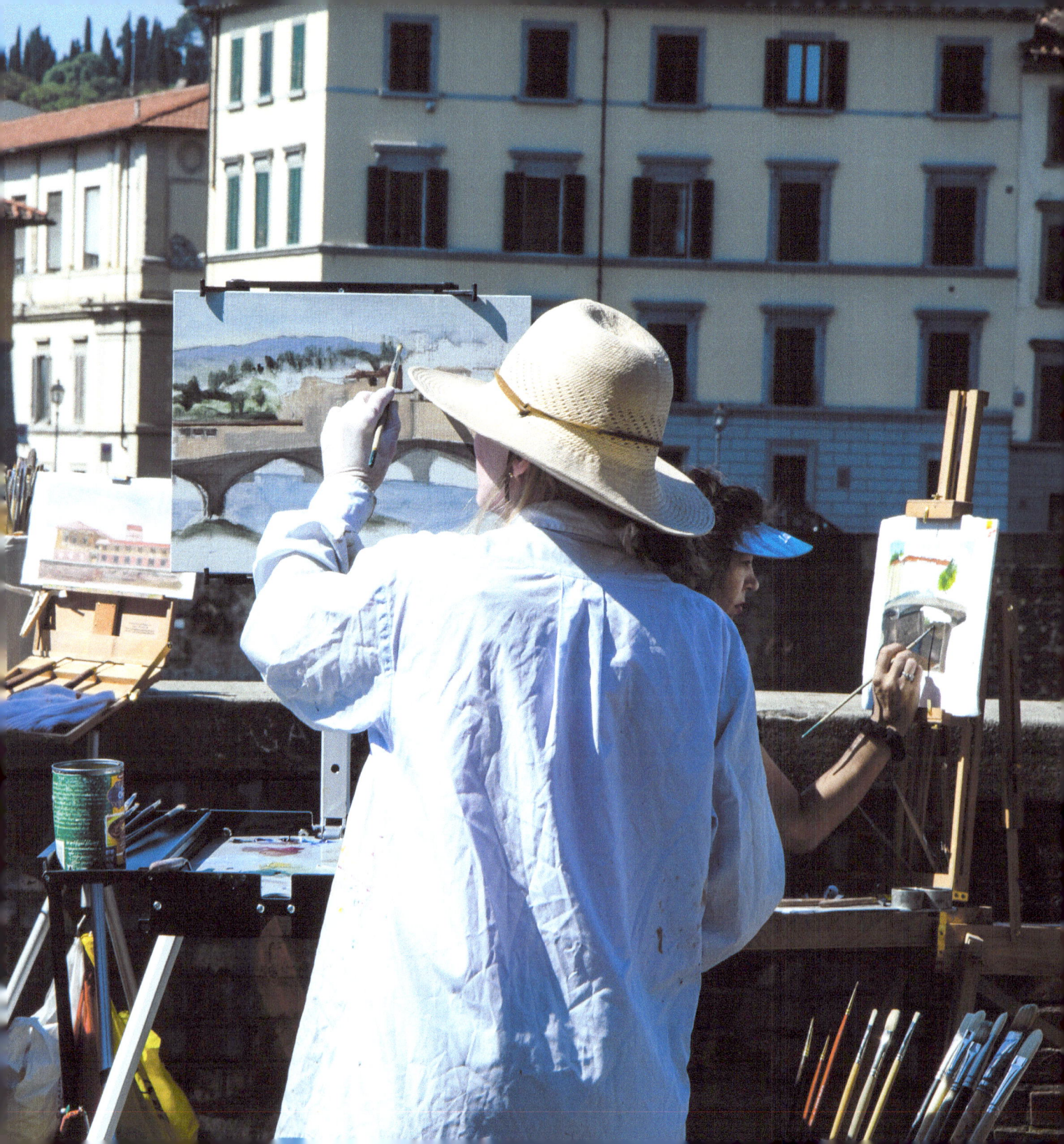

21
God's Masterpiece

Then God said, "Let Us make human beings in our image, to be like Us"…male and female He created them…And evening passed and morning came, marking the sixth day.

Genesis 1:26,27,31 NLT

God now embarks on His finest work in creation. He truly saved the best for last. In Genesis 1-2, you learn that God commanded His creation into existence. Now, we see something new, for the Triune God discusses His thought behind His next design. He has purpose, intention, detail, and artistry. Elohim said, "Let Us make human beings in our own image, to be like Us" (Genesis 1:26 NLT). Dr. Ronald Youngblood, in *How It All Began*, writes that the word "image" is understood "primarily in a spiritual sense here, including such qualities as 'knowledge' (Colossians 3:10), 'righteousness and holiness' (Ephesians 4:24)." One commentator believes image includes the ability to reason. The intricacy of the human body includes 10 major organ systems including skeletal, muscular, nervous, endocrine, cardiovascular, lymphatic, respiratory, digestive, urinary, and reproductive. What convincing proof of the presence of an all-powerful Creator! David wrote, "Thank You for making me so wonderfully complex! Your workmanship is marvelous" (Psalm 139:14 NLT).

For we are God's masterpiece. He has created us anew in Christ Jesus, so we can do the good things He planned for us long ago.

Ephesians 2:10 NLT

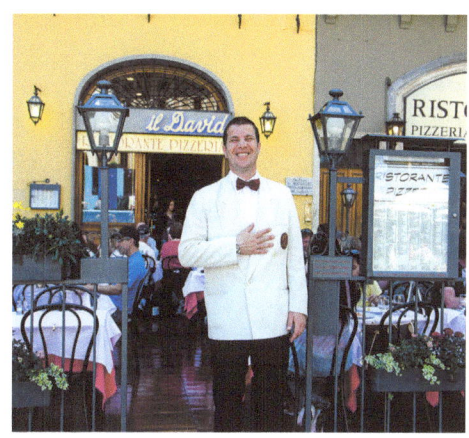

Just as a coin is stamped with a ruler's image and represents his presence and authority in his realm, so we are all stamped with God's image and should therefore not only represent him faithfully, but also acknowledge his dominion over our lives…Genesis 1 represents man as the climax of God's creative activity. God has "crowned him with glory and honor" and "made him ruler" (Psalm 8:5-8) over the rest of His creation (see Genesis 1:26)…The final verse in Genesis 1 declares all of the divine acts of creation to be "very good" indeed.

How It All Began — Dr. Ronald Youngblood

You made all the delicate, inner parts of my body and knit me together in my mother's womb. Thank you for making me so wonderfully complex! Your workmanship is marvelous—how well I know it. You watched me as I was being formed in utter seclusion, as I was woven together in the dark of the womb. You saw me before I was born. Every day of my life was recorded in your book. Every moment was laid out before a single day had passed. How precious are your thoughts about me, O God. They cannot be numbered! I can't even count them; they outnumber the grains of sand! And when I wake up, you are still with me.

Psalm 139:13-18 nlt — David, the Man After God's Own Heart

"Could there be design in the universe without a designer?" Dr. Viggo Olsen concluded there was unquestionable evidence of pattern and design in the universe and planet earth. "The millions of stars and planets track their courses precisely…The human body, whose design and function I had come to know so well, possesses a million different patterns in its many organs, groups of cells, and chemical systems." These patterns and designs led he and his wife to the conclusion that there was an intelligent power behind the universe. They realized that human beings possess something "higher and finer, called personality or soul which makes him capable of loving others." Ultimately, Dr. Olsen and his wife believed and gave their lives to Christ.

Daktar: Diplomat In Bangladesh — Viggo Olsen, M.D.

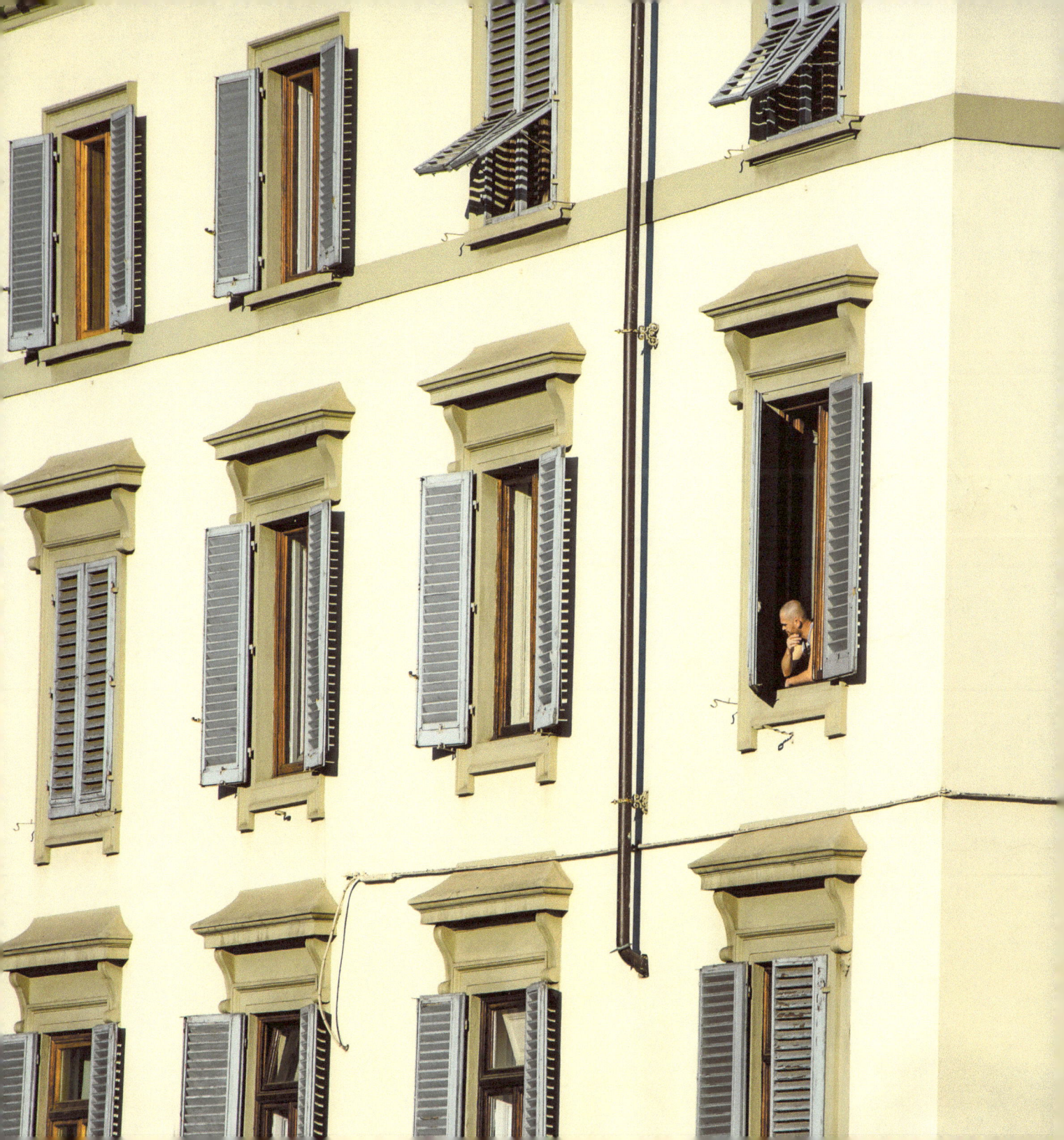

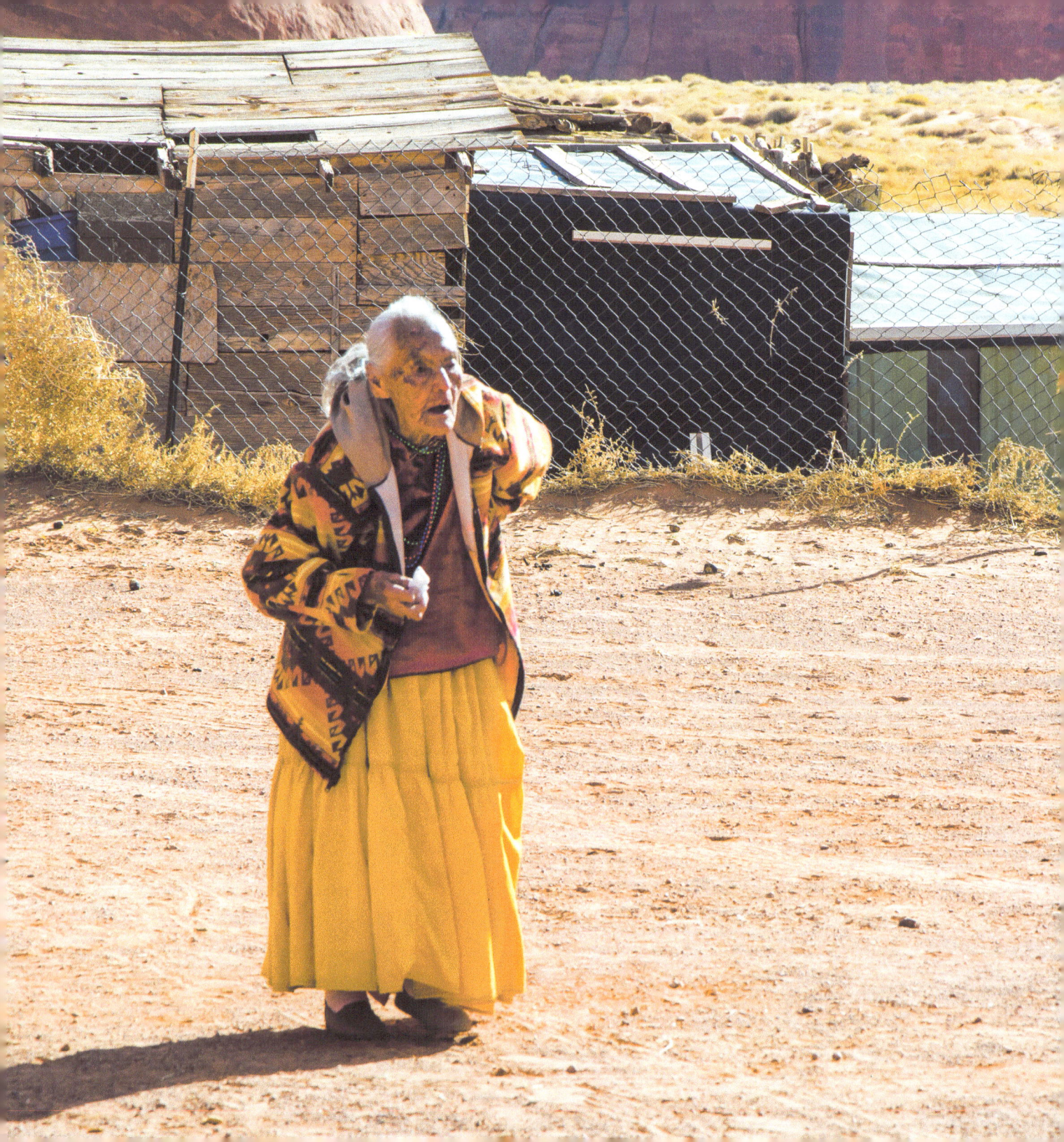

22
Every Life Tells A Story

O LORD, You have searched me and known me. You know when I sit down and when I rise up... and are intimately acquainted with all my ways.

Psalm 139:1-3

When I travel, I always stop long enough to look at the uniqueness of people. Because I am captivated by people, I love capturing images of them with my cameras. And I always conclude: *every life tells a story*. I was photographing a traditional hogan in Monument Valley — a dome-like one room hut made of Ponderosa pine and plastered with mud for insulation. And just as I had my camera poised for another photograph, an incredibly interesting woman walked into my field of vision, and I was able to capture one image of her with her yellow skirt and woven jacket. Later I was reading an article about Susie Yazzie, matriarch of Monument Valley, renowned weaver and storyteller. I looked again at the image I had captured, and sure enough, it was this renowned resident of Monument Valley. I remember special moments: like a man praying in a Santa Fe church and a guy on a bicycle with his dog in Italy. God has designed people with the purpose of knowing, loving, and glorifying Him. All are significant. He knows each person by name. What does He want more than anything? You.

Seek the LORD while you can find Him. Call on Him now while He is near.

Isaiah 55:6 NLT

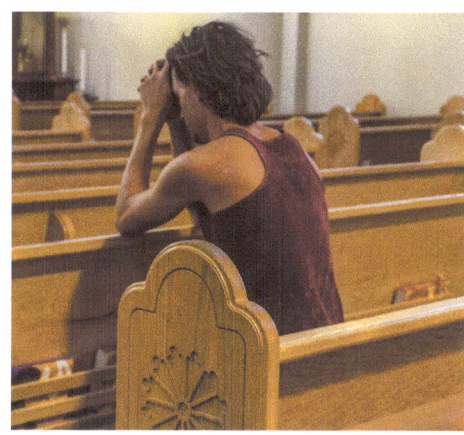

> Yet God has made everything beautiful for its own time.
> He has planted eternity in the human heart, but even so, people cannot see
> the whole scope of God's work from beginning to end.

ECCLESIASTES 3:11 NLT

In the first story [Genesis 1:1-2:3], God is the transcendant and all-powerful Creator, while in the second [Genesis 2:4-25] "the LORD God" is closely and intimately involved in the life and experiences of the people He has created. It will be observed that these differences do not amount to contradictions in any sense of the word. They are simply differences of emphasis or perspective. The two accounts look at the same or similar series of events from two distinctive points of view. The one is concerned with the big picture, the other with a few tantalizing details; the one sees the entire forest, the other a few trees…the compound name "LORD God" in 2:4-25 is intended to demonstrate that the formal God who creates man in the first creation account is identical to the personal LORD who communes with man in the second account.

HOW IT ALL BEGAN — DR. RONALD YOUNGBLOOD

The LORD God formed the man from the dust of the ground and breathed into his nostrils the breath of life, and the man became a living being…for Adam no suitable helper was found. So the LORD God caused the man to fall into a deep sleep; and while he was sleeping, he took one of the man's ribs and closed up the place with flesh. Then the LORD God made a woman from the rib he had taken out of the man, and he brought her to the man.

GENESIS 2:7,20-22 NIV

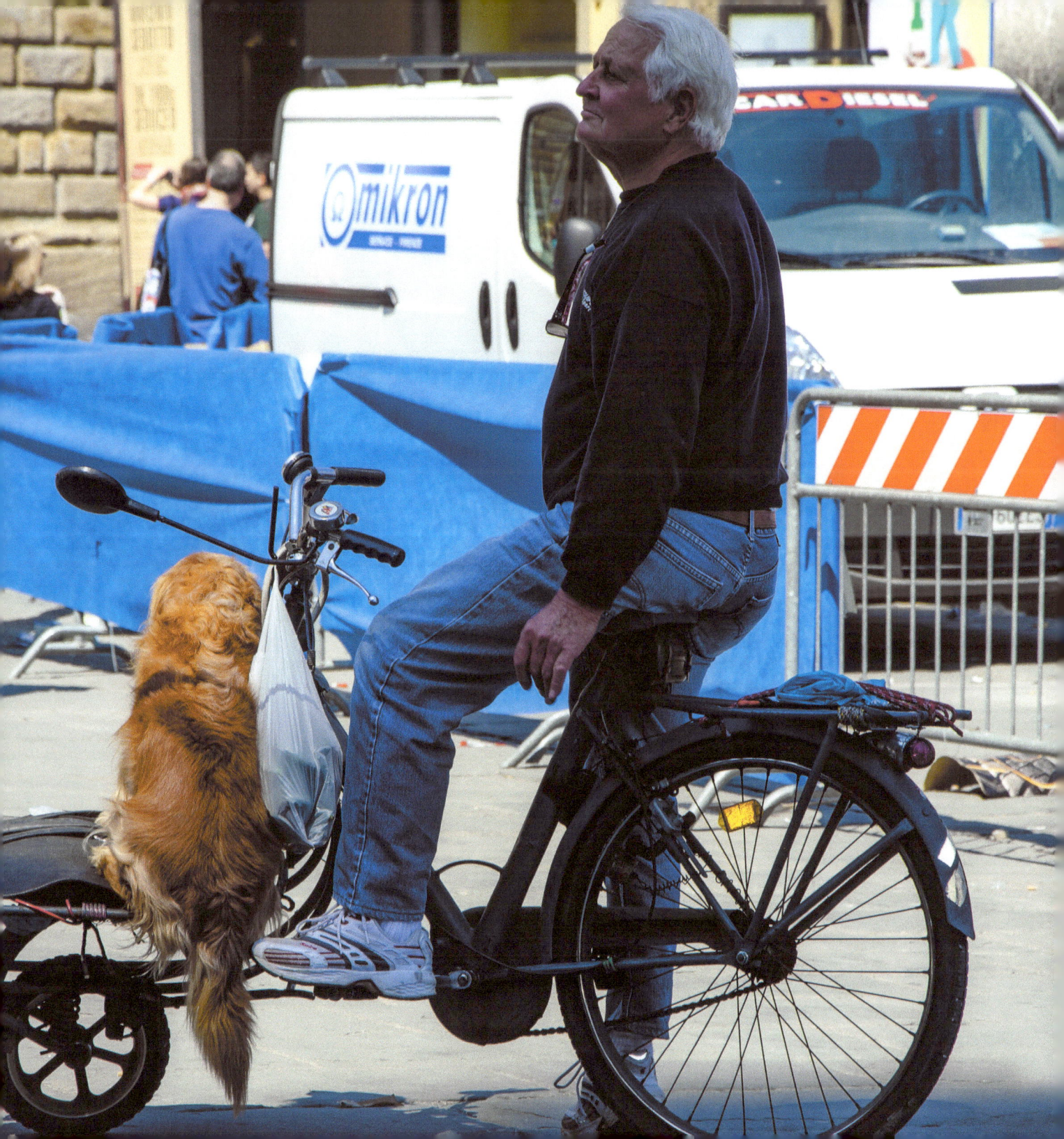

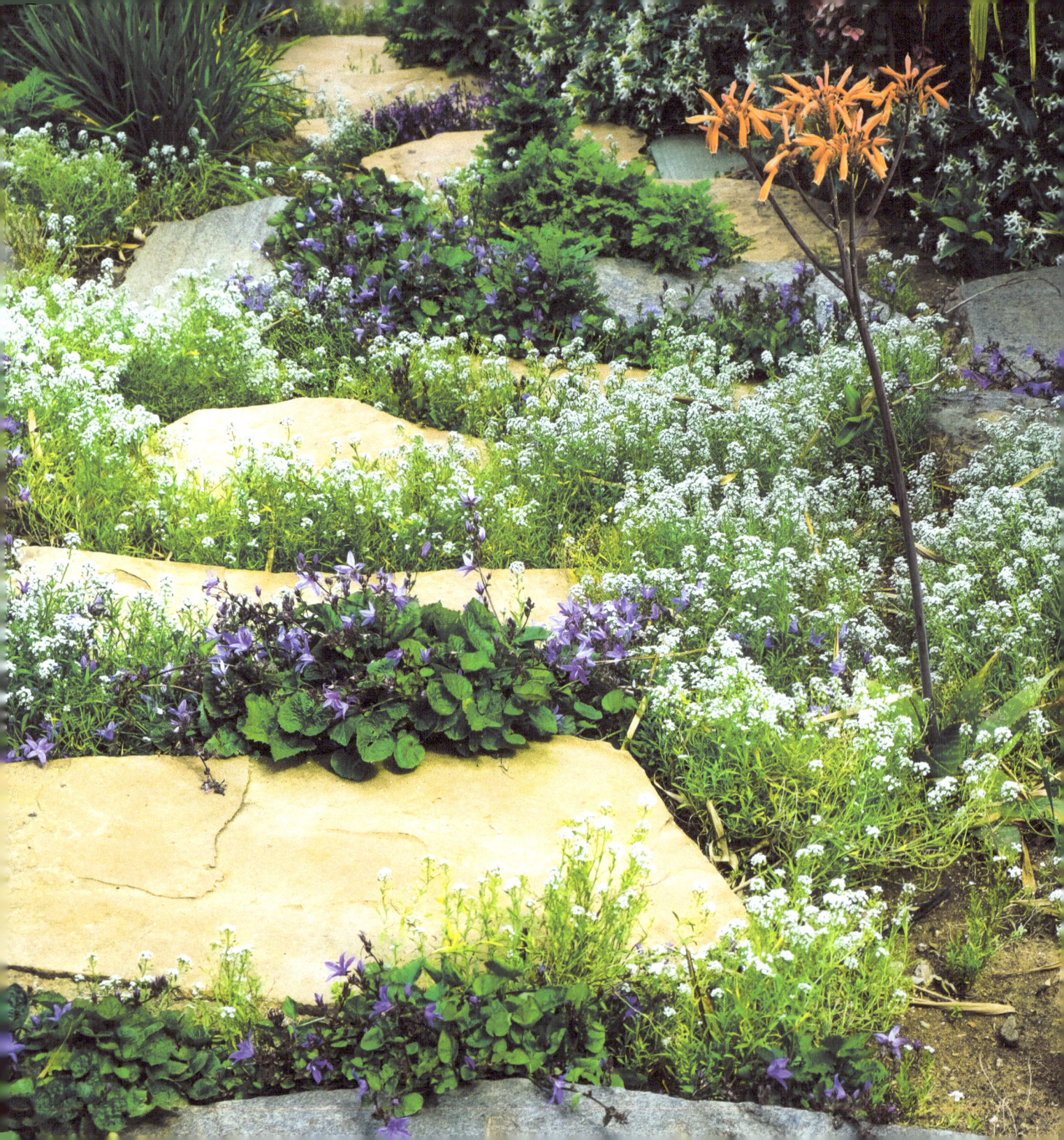

SIXTH DAY REFLECTIONS

IN THE GARDEN

*The Lord God planted a garden toward the east, in Eden;
and there He placed the man whom He had formed.*
GENESIS 2:8

God placed the man and woman He created in the Garden of Eden. God planted trees in the garden including the tree of life and the tree of the knowledge of good and evil (Genesis 2:9). They could eat from any tree except for the tree of the knowledge of good and evil. They enjoyed intimate communion with their God, and bliss, and blessing in that garden, exactly all they were designed to experience. "God saw all that He made, and behold, it was very good" (Genesis 1:31). Will you draw near and walk with your Lord today? He invites you to "come away with Me by yourselves to a quiet place and rest awhile" (Mark 6:31).

Lord, thank You for loving me so much that You long for and invite me to an intimate relationship with You. I desire to enjoy the bliss and blessing of walking in the garden with You. In Jesus' name, Amen.

SEVENTH DAY

And now, in just six days, God's work is complete in creation. "God looked over all He had made, and He saw that it was very good" (Genesis 1:31). The beginning of Genesis 2 says that everything in creation of heaven and earth was completed (Genesis 2:1). There is still one more day God describes. "On the seventh day God had finished His work of creation, so He rested from all His work" (Genesis 2:2). Following a time of work comes a time of rest and refreshment. God teaches us the necessity of stepping away from the busyness of life and enjoying a time of renewal with Him.

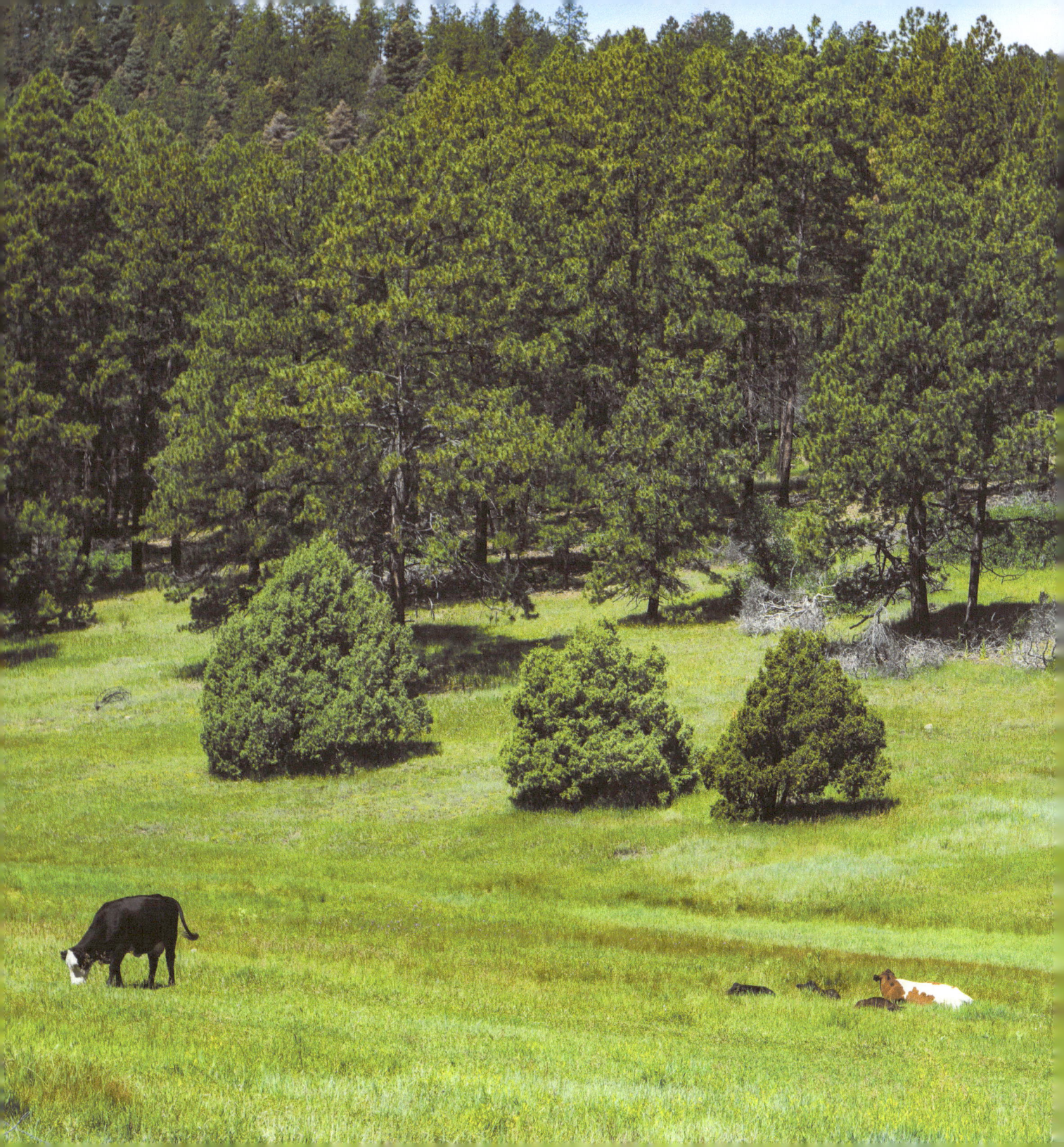

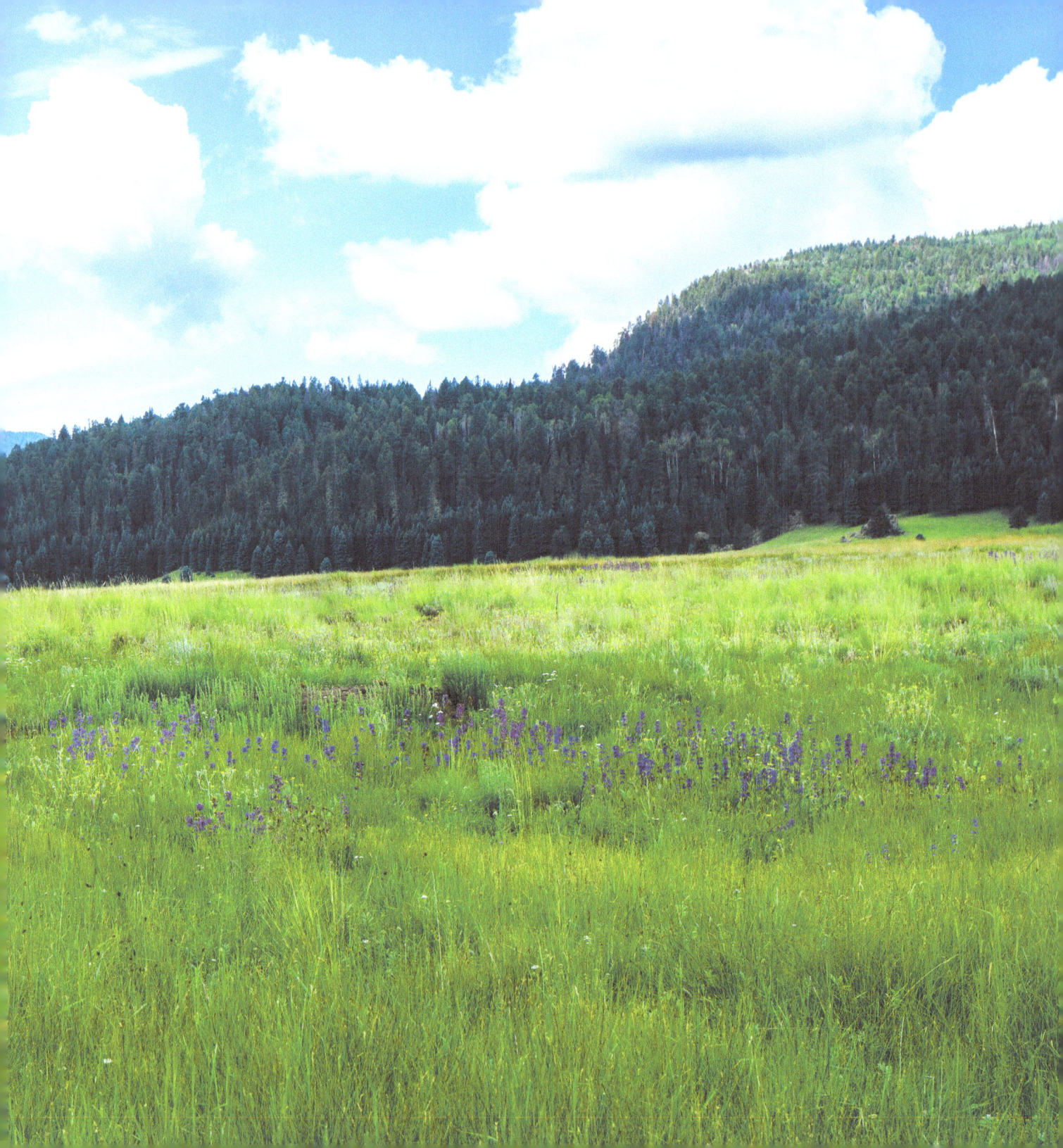

23 The Day God Rested

On the seventh day God had finished His work of creation, so He rested from all His work. And God blessed the seventh day and declared it holy…

Genesis 2:2-3 NLT

Something significant now enters the days of creation. The work is complete but there is still one more day—a seventh day. The seventh day becomes holy ground and what happens on this day can become part of our own experience with God. "On the seventh day God had finished His work of creation, so He rested from all His work. And God blessed the seventh day and declared it holy, because it was the day when He rested from all His work of creation" (Genesis 2:2-3 NLT). God never gets tired or sleeps (Psalm 121:4) so why a day of rest? Exodus 31:17 explains that on this seventh day "God stopped working and was refreshed." The seventh day became a Sabbath day for God's people (Ezekiel 20:12), a sign between God and His people, that they might know they were set apart for the Lord. Jesus, God Incarnate, interpreted the Sabbath when He said that the Sabbath was made for man and He is Lord of the Sabbath (Mark 2:27-28). We are to rest in God's work through Christ and cease from all our own efforts (Hebrews 4:9-10). Let us enter His rest—He gives us His very best.

Those who live in the shelter of the Most High will find rest in the shadow of the Almighty.

Psalm 91:1 NLT

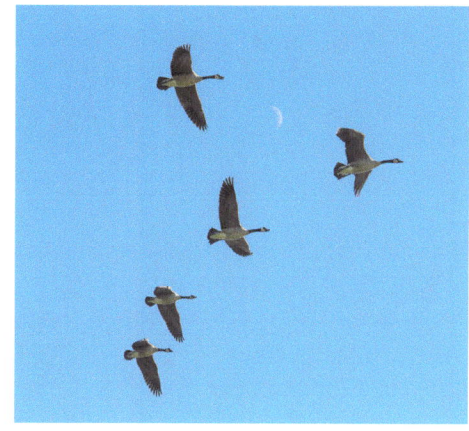

I laid it down in silence, this work of mine, and took what had been sent me—a resting time.
The Master's voice had called me to rest apart; "Apart with Jesus only," echoed my heart.
I took the rest and stillness from His own Hand, and felt this present illness was what He planned.
How often we choose labor, when He says "Rest"—our ways are blind and crooked; His way is best.
The work Himself has given, He will complete. There may be other errands for tired feet;
There may be other duties for tired hands, the present, is obedience to His commands.
There is a blessed resting in lying still, in letting His hand mould us, just as He will.
His work must be completed. His lesson set; He is the higher Workman: Do not forget!
It is not only "working." We must be trained; and Jesus "learnt" obedience, through suffering gained.
For us, His yoke is easy, His burden light. His discipline most needful, and all is right.
We are but under-workmen; They never choose if this tool or if that one their hands shall use.
In working or in waiting may we fulfill not ours at all, but only the Master's will!

MRS. CHARLES COWMAN — STREAMS IN THE DESERT

One thing I have asked from the LORD, that I shall seek; that I may dwell in the house of the LORD all the days of my life, to behold the beauty of the LORD and to meditate in His temple.

PSALM 27:4

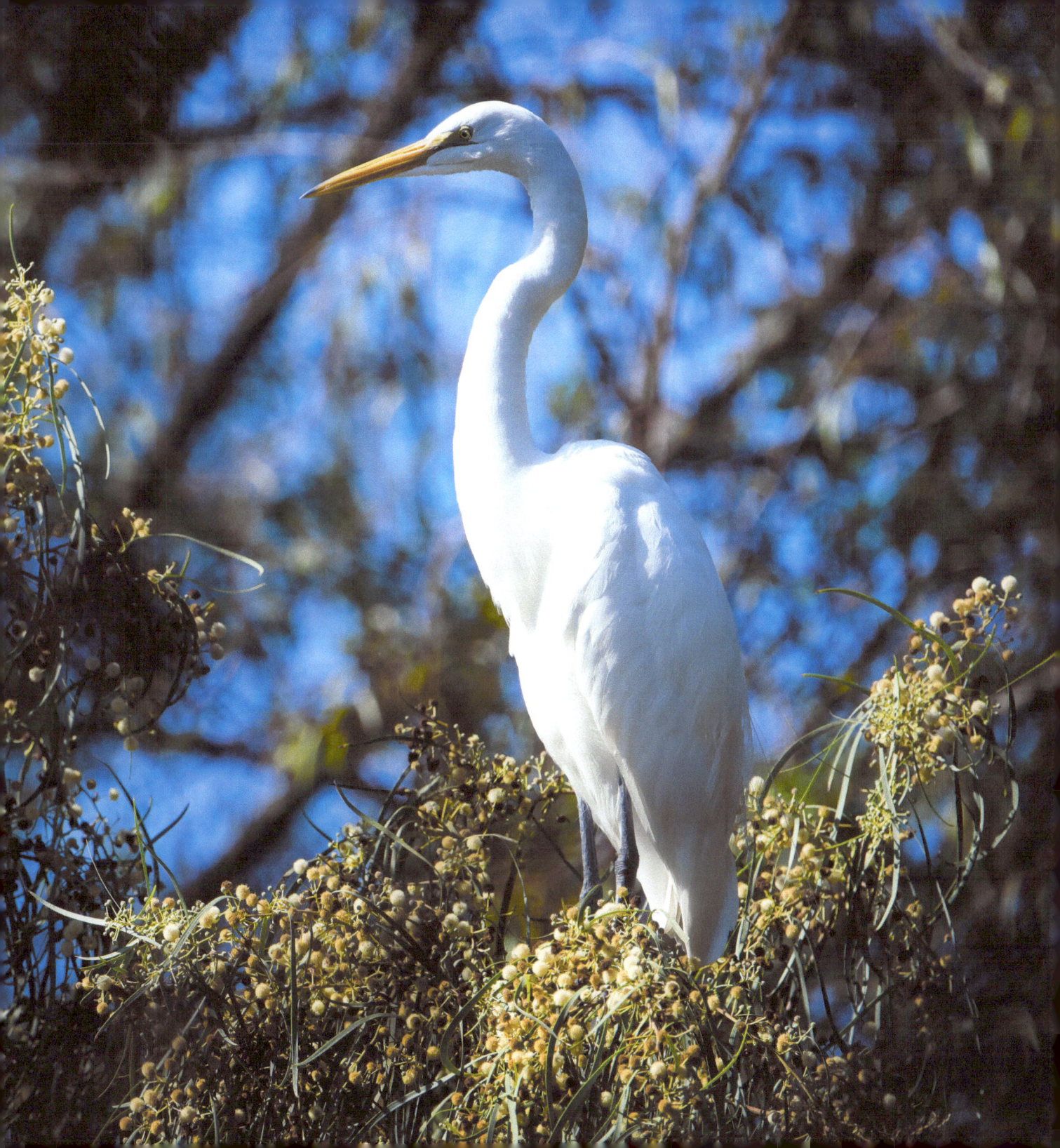

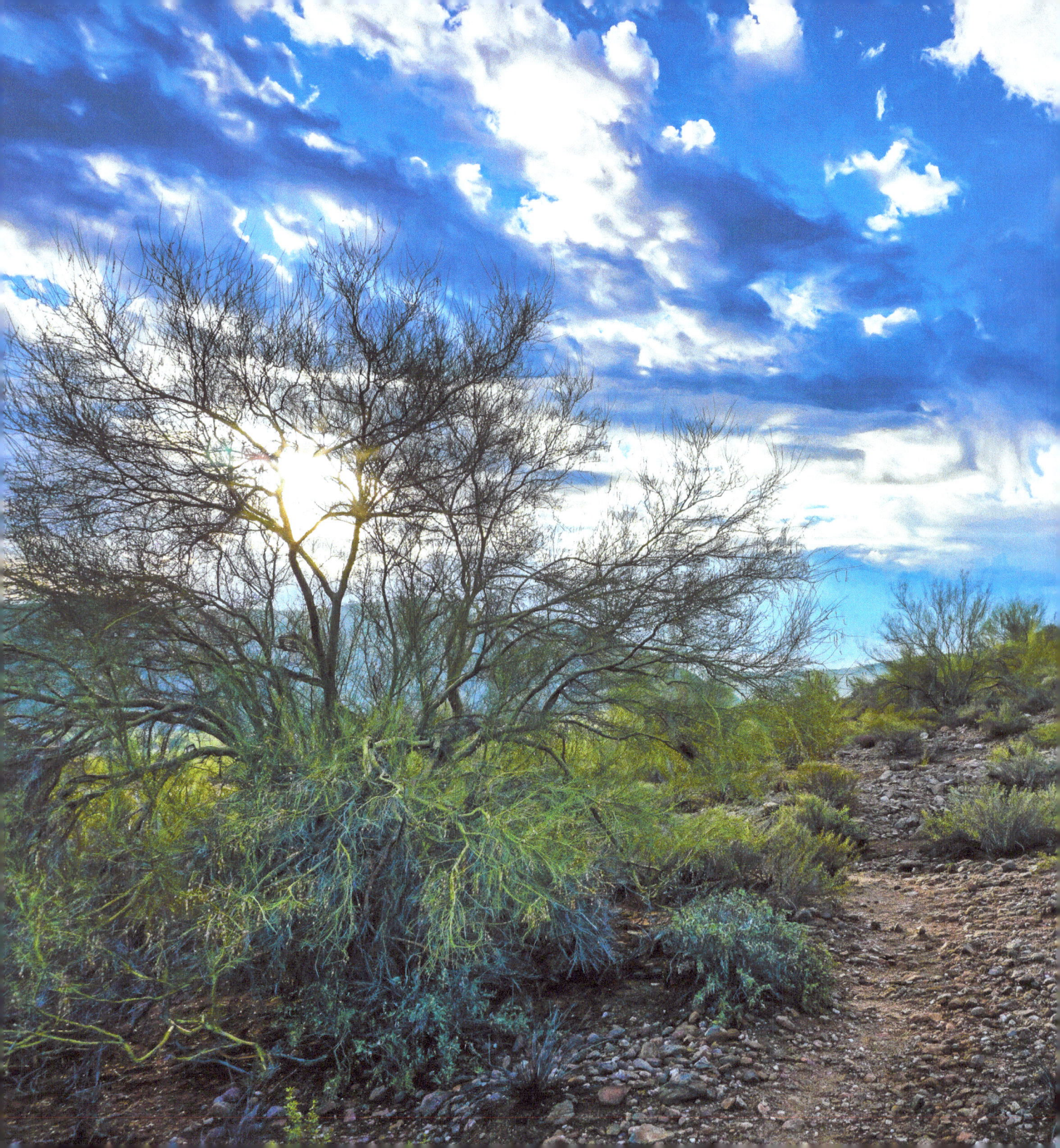

24 A Time Of Refreshing

Times of refreshing may come from the presence of the Lord.

Acts 3:19

The Lord has designed you for seasons of hard work as you run with endurance the race that is set before you (Hebrews 12:1). He has also made you for rest and refreshment. Even He rested from all His work of creation and was refreshed (Exodus 31:17). The Lord is issuing an invitation to you to step away from all that consumes your time and stresses your very soul and come to Him. He says, "Come to Me, all of you who are weary and carry heavy burdens, and I will give you rest" (Matthew 11:28). When you spend quiet time with God, draw near to Him, talk with Him, and open the pages of His Word, you are making room for a new and deeper trust in God. You are opening up to God in such a way that He can do a mighty work in you. What will it take? Purpose and intention. Set aside a time, a place, and a plan to be alone with the Lord. In this quiet time, you will "learn the unforced rhythms of grace" (Matthew 11:29 msg). And you will know by firsthand experience the time of refreshing that comes from the presence of the Lord (Acts 3:19).

Come to Me, all of you who are weary and carry heavy burdens, and I will give you rest…you will find rest for your souls.

Matthew 11:28-30 nlt

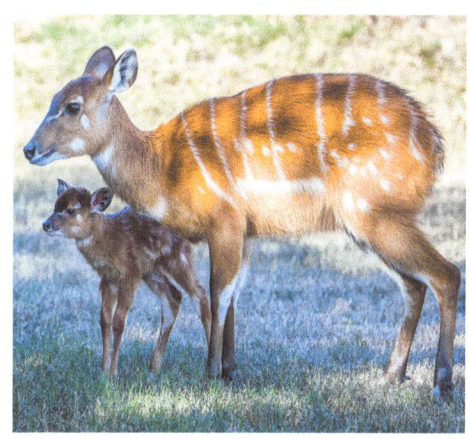

Draw near to God and He will draw near to you.

JAMES 4:8

In the spiritual life, the word *discipline* means *the effort to create some space in which God can act*. Discipline means to prevent everything in your life from being filled up. Discipline means that somewhere you're not occupied, and certainly not preoccupied… to create that space in which something can happen that you hadn't planned or counted on.

HENRI NOUWEN

In silence, our soul is quieted. Our burdens—the things we carry, can rise to the surface. Our pain and our suffering can be named. Our chaos can be calmed. Our lives can settle in the presence of God's Spirit.

ALL THAT IS MADE

God can be known in personal experience. A loving Personality dominates the Bible, walking among the trees of the garden and breathing fragrance over every scene. Always a living Person is present, speaking, pleading, loving, working and manifesting Himself whenever and wherever His people have the receptivity necessary to receive the manifestation. The Bible assumes as a self-evident fact that men can know God with at least the same degree of immediacy as they know any other person or thing that comes within the field of their experience…"O taste and see that the LORD is good" (Psalm 34:8).

THE PURSUIT OF GOD — A.W. TOZER

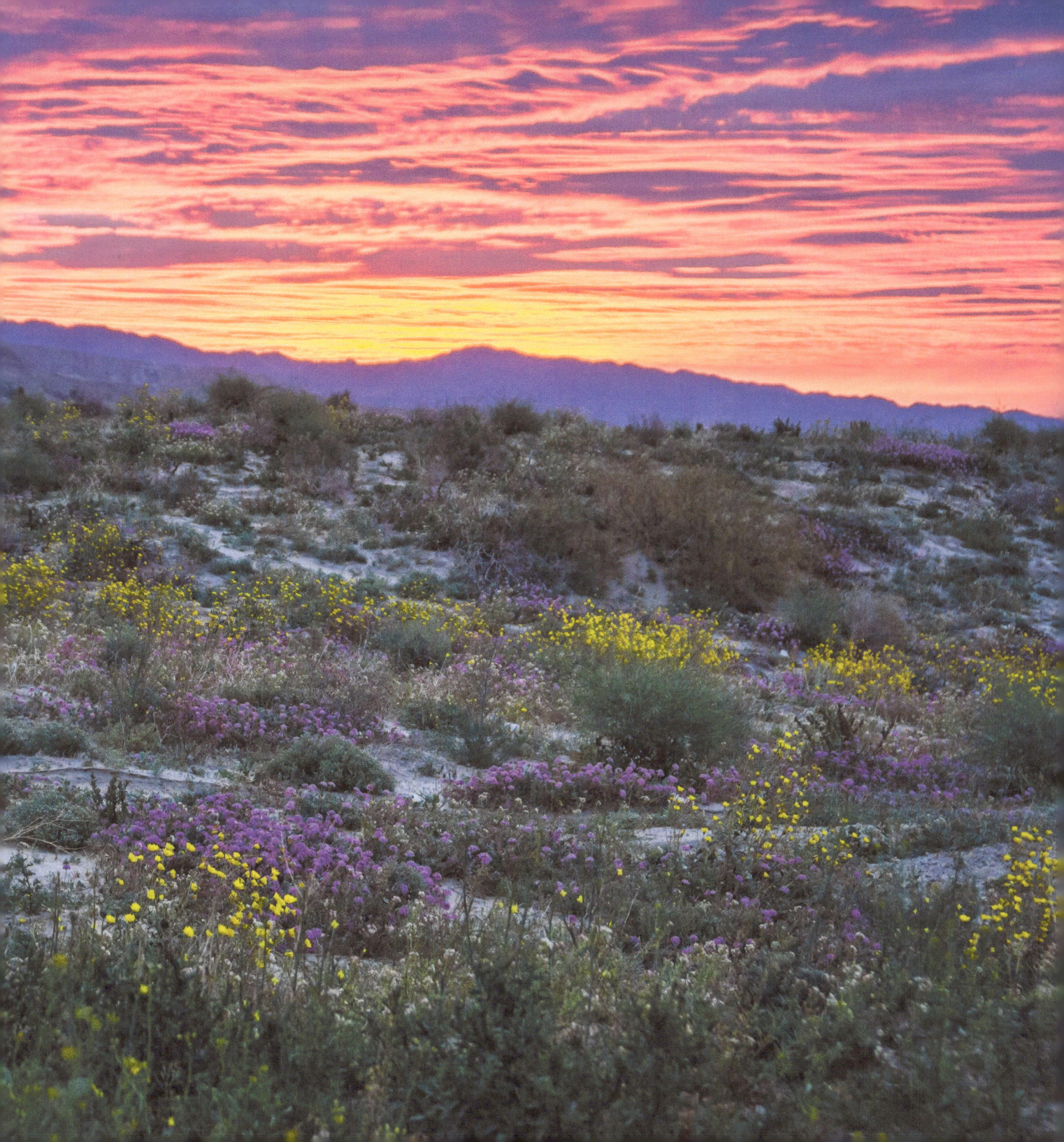

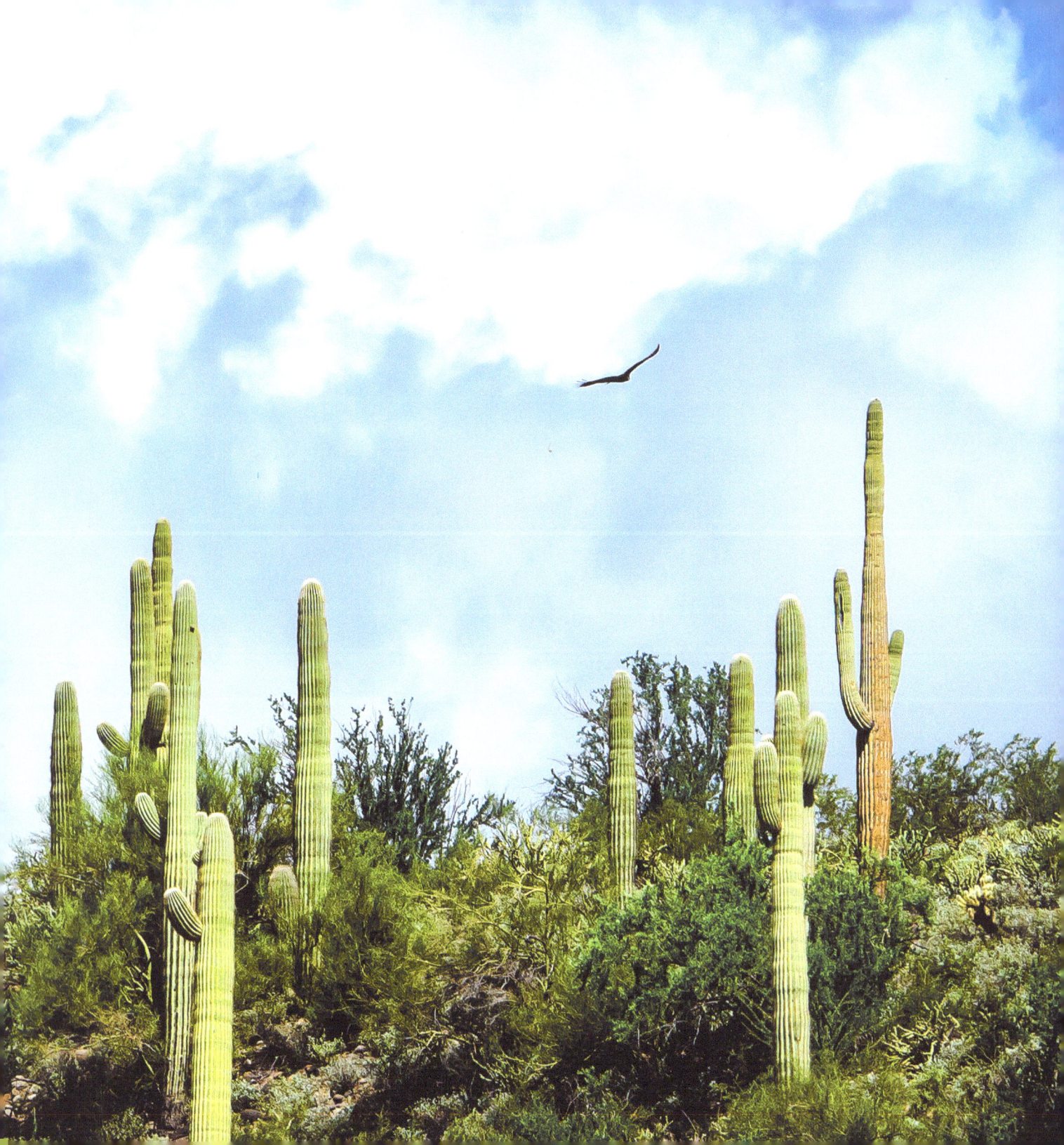

25
TRUSTING GOD

Trust in the LORD with all your heart; do not depend on your own understanding. Seek His will in all you do, and He will show you which path to take.

PROVERBS 3:5-6 NLT

God desires your wholehearted trust in Him for every detail of your life. In Proverbs 3:5, He says, "Trust in the LORD with all your heart, do not depend on your own understanding." When you stop and take time to consider all He has done in creation, you trust in a new way, realizing He is more than enough for the difficulties in your life, however tangled up or turbulent they may be. Richard A. Swenson, M.D. writes in his book, *More Than Meets The Eye*: "In the last hour, one trillion trillion of your atoms [in the cells of the human body] have been replaced…only God can monitor something of this magnitude… The point is: such a God can be trusted with the details of my life. After rearranging subatomic particles all morning, the specifics of my life probably seem a bit unchallenging to Him." When you look at God's creation and discover God in His Word, you will grow in your knowledge of God and you will trust Him more—total reliance under stress and trial. And then you will experience His plan for your life and enter in to the great adventure of knowing God.

The LORD directs the steps of the godly. He delights in every detail of their lives.

PSALM 37:23 NLT

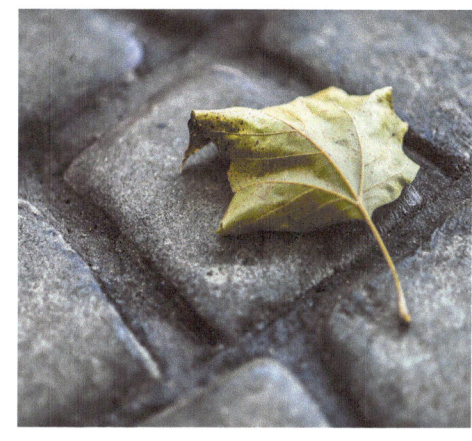

If we witness a magnetic cloud thirty million miles in diameter moving a million miles per hour—is God bigger than that? Can He move faster than that? If the center of the sun has temperatures of fifteen million degrees centigrade and pressures of seven trillion pounds per square inch—could God walk into the core of the sun, take a nap, and walk back out? Every impressive structure or event in the universe should remind us of a God who is greater than all His works. With a God this powerful, why do we doubt that He has the power to help us order our lives…What we need is a new vision of God. The real God. Not some vague image we fold up and stuff in the back drawer of life, but the kind of God who parts the Red Sea and shakes Mount Sinai. The kind of God who stuns the physicists with symmetry, the mathematicians with precision, the engineers with design, the politicians with power, and the poets with beauty…When we understand the sovereignty, power, design, majesty, precision, genius, intimacy, and caring of an Almighty God, it takes away our fear. It removes our frustration. It allows us to sleep at night and trust Him with the running of His own universe. It allows us to have margin. It allows us to resume our proper role in the order of things rather than taking over His role. It allows us to seek His will rather than follow our own mind. The more we understand about God's power, the less we worry about our weakness. The more we trust in God's sovereignty, the less we fret about our future.

More Than Meets The Eye — Richard A. Swenson, M.D.

We can trust God's ability to make sense of our lives when our world is upside down. Moreover we can trust His goodness. He will weave our failures and the evil designs of others into a covering that blesses us and accomplishes His every purpose (Genesis 50:20, Romans 8:28).

The Jeremiah Study Bible — Dr. David Jeremiah

Trust in the LORD always, for the LORD God is the eternal Rock.

Isaiah 26:4 NLT

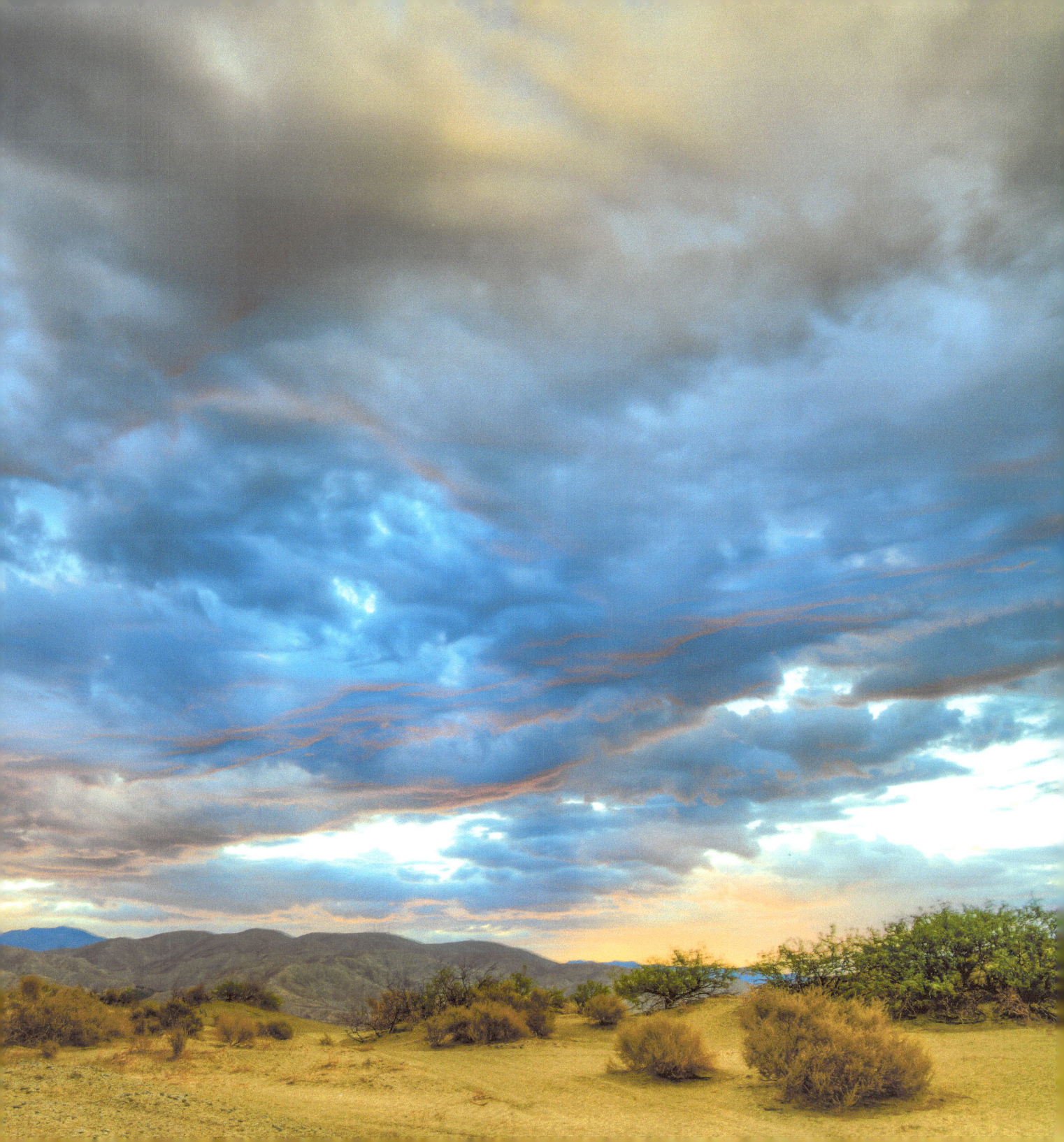

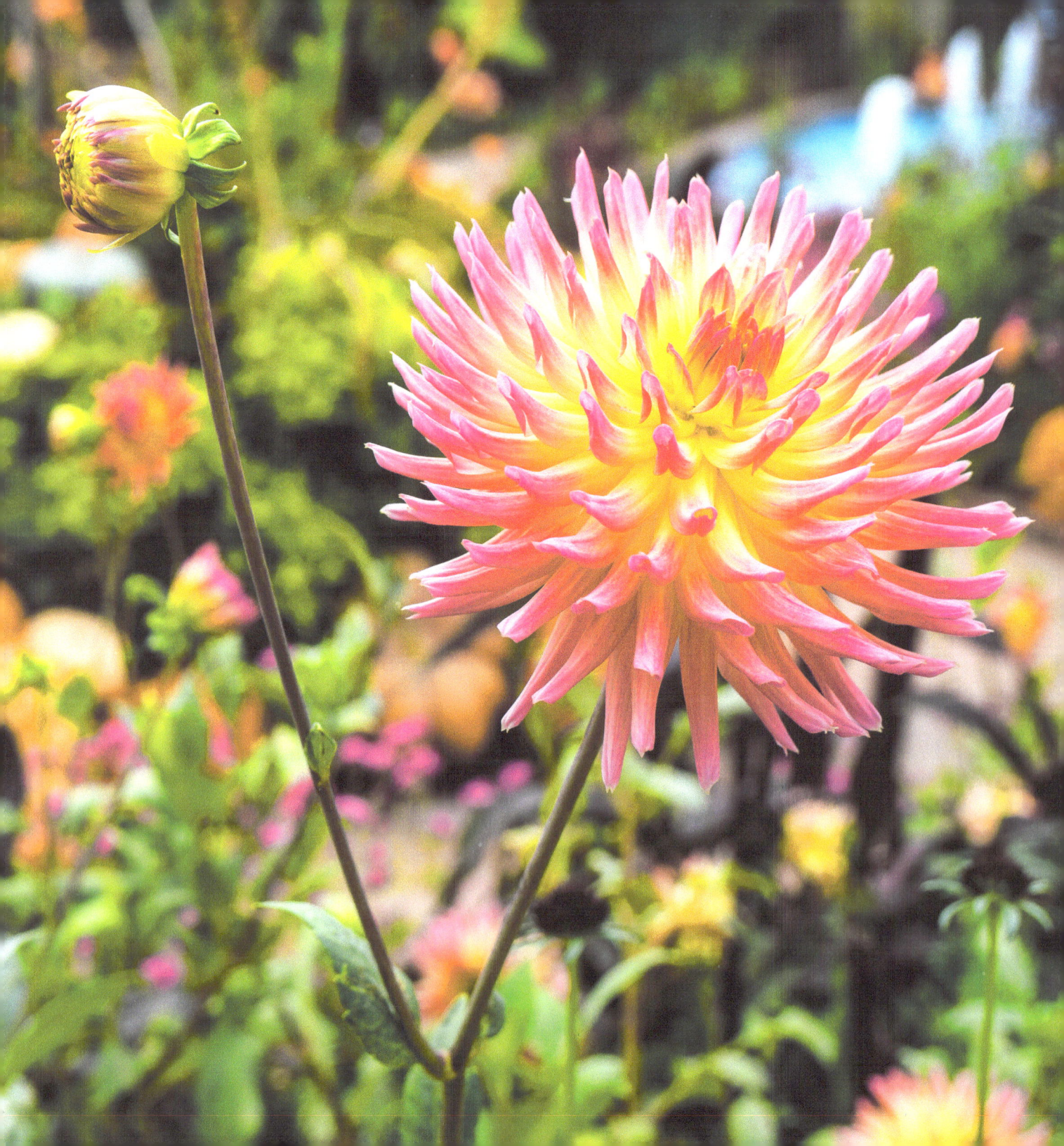

SEVENTH DAY REFLECTIONS

LIKE A WATERED GARDEN

And the Lord will continually guide you, and satisfy your desire in scorched places, and give strength to your bones; and you will be like a watered garden, and like a spring of water whose waters do not fail.

Isaiah 58:11

What is offered to the thirsty soul who is now convinced of a God who loves His creation and desires an intimate relationship? Everything you could possibly hope for and more. Jesus, God incarnate, extends this invitation to you: "'If anyone is thirsty, let him come to Me and drink. He who believes in Me,' as the Scripture said, 'From his innermost being will flow rivers of living water'" (John 7:37-38). When you come to Jesus, you experience the joys of intimacy with your great God, described so well in Isaiah 58:11. "You will be like a watered garden, and like a spring of water whose waters do not fail."

Lord, today I come to You as a thirsty soul longing to love and trust You more. Thank You for promising to make me like a watered garden with rivers of living water flowing from within. In Jesus' name, Amen.

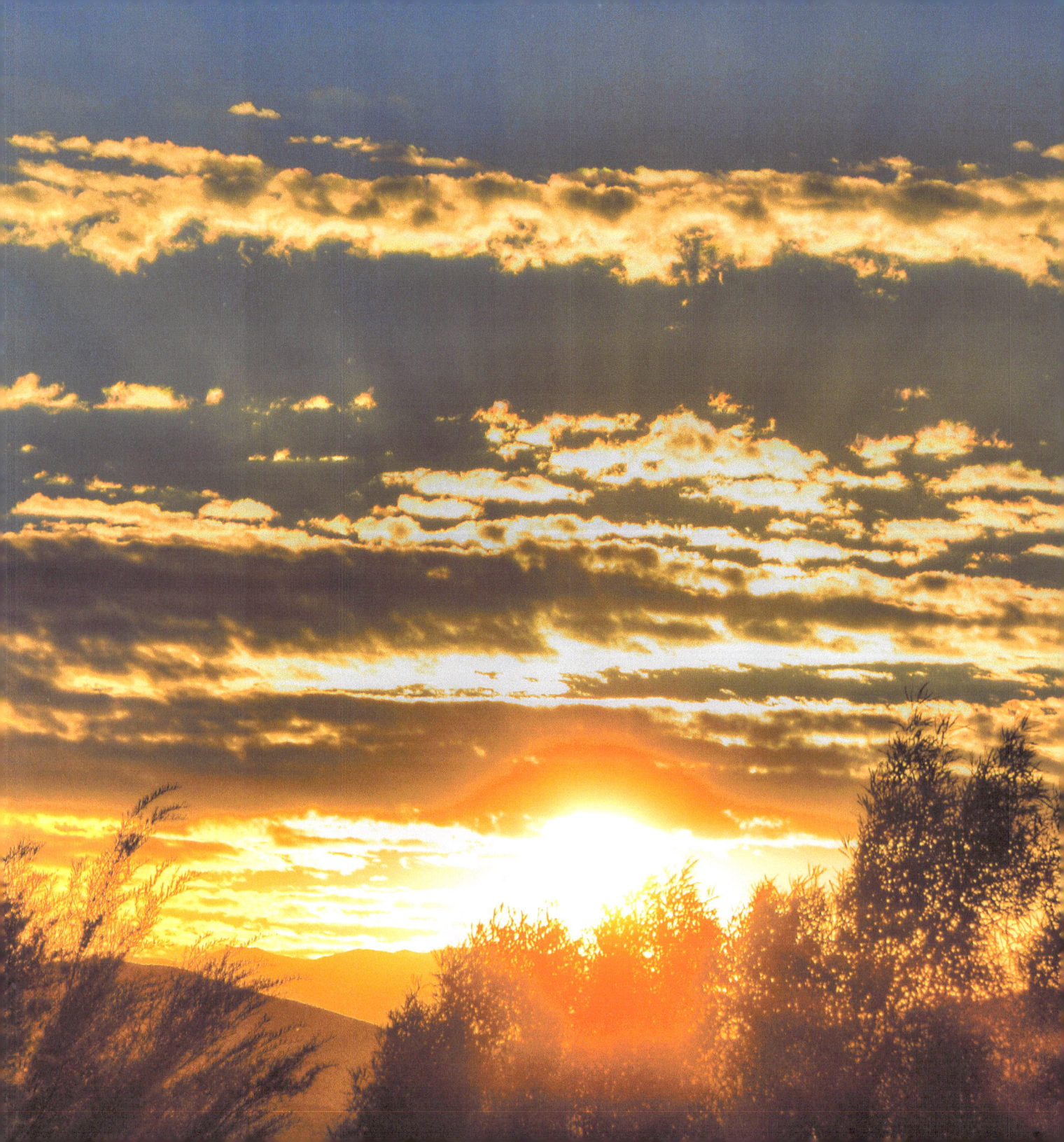

THE END OF THE BEGINNING

Have you ever been to a potluck dinner with lots of people and as the dishes are cleared away, someone leans over and says, "Keep your fork?" If you've had that experience, you know what it means. Something delicious is on its way to the table for dessert—like deep dish apple pie or chocolate cake. You know that the best is yet to come.

In this glimpse of the days of creation, you have taken time to contemplate all that God can do in a day. His power and glory have taken center stage in your thoughts. We have looked at how it all began. And all we have seen has inspired a deep and abiding trust in God.

As exciting as creation is in Genesis, we have only come to *the end of the beginning*. Wait until you read the rest of the story in the Bible—from Genesis 3 all the way through Revelation. There are lots of spectacular twists and devastating turns, but the best is truly yet to come.

When life doesn't make sense, dear friend, you can know that God never changes. He always has a plan. When you run to Him in trust, cry out to Him in your pain and brokenness, you will experience His wisdom, strength, comfort, and encouragement. Take the most difficult challenge you are facing right now and think about all you have seen God do in each day of creation. You have seen that He is indeed "able to do immeasurably more than all we ask or imagine according to the power that is at work in us" (Ephesians 3:20). He specializes in taking impossible situations and painting a new landscape of beauty into our lives that we could have never dreamed of in the middle of the trouble. You see it again and again as you continue on with God in the Bible.

When God placed man and woman in the garden of Eden, they enjoyed perfect fellowship and intimacy with God who created them. The garden of Eden was paradise filled with beauty. There were all kinds of trees planted by God including the tree of life and the tree of the knowledge of good and evil. The man and woman could eat fruit from any of the trees but not from the tree of the knowledge of good and evil. God had said they could not even touch that tree. The serpent, who is named Satan or the devil (Revelation 12:9, 20:10), deceived the woman and ultimately the man, and both disobeyed God and ate fruit from the tree.

With that one act of rebellion, sin and death entered the world. The serpent was cursed, the man and woman were sent out of the garden, intimate communion with God was broken, and physical and spiritual death entered the world.

But all was not lost. For God had a plan that He set in motion, and He shares the good news of the gospel first in Genesis 3:15. Speaking to the serpent which is Satan, God said: "Because you have done this, cursed are you…and I will put enmity between you and the woman, and between your seed and her seed; He shall bruise you on the head, and you shall bruise him on the heel" (Genesis 3:14-15).

Donald Grey Barnhouse, in his book, *The Invisible War*, describes this event in unique fashion. He writes: "War has been declared. The great, governing cherub had become the malignant enemy [Satan]. Our God was neither surprised nor astonished, for, of course, He knew before it happened that it would happen, and He had His perfect plan ready

Epilogue

to be put into effect. Although the Lord had the power to destroy Satan with a breath, He did not do so. It was as though an edict had been declared in heaven: 'We shall give this rebellion a thorough trial. We shall permit it to run its full course…we shall permit the universe of creatures to watch it, during this brief interlude between eternity past and eternity future called time. In it the spirit of independence shall be allowed to expand to the utmost. And the wreck and ruin which shall result will demonstrate to the universe, and forever, that there is no life, no joy, no peace apart from a complete dependence upon the Most High God, Possessor of heaven and earth.'"

So what was God's plan? He intended to do for man what man could not do for himself. We learn that the God of creation we see in Genesis is also the God of our redemption. God determined to pay the penalty for man's sin Himself. Romans 3:23 says that "all have sinned and fall short of the glory of God." In Romans 6:23, we see that "the wages of sin is death, but the free gift of God is eternal life in Christ Jesus our Lord." It is as though the judge has declared the person, "Guilty" with the penalty of death. But then He takes off His robes and pays the penalty Himself. Now we learn something about God we may not have known or understood. He is the "God of all grace" and grace is God's love in action. You and I are designed to be recipients of His grace and His love.

The "seed of the woman" mentioned in Genesis 3:15 is Jesus, who is called Immanual, meaning "God with us" (Matthew 1:22-23). God came to earth—Jesus is God incarnate—for one main purpose—to give His life in exchange for ours—to die on a cross and pay the price for your sin and mine. The good news is this— "For this is how God loved the world: He gave his one and only Son, so that everyone who believes in him will not perish but have eternal life. God sent his Son into the world not to judge the world, but to save the world through him" (John 3:16-17 NLT). When God said in Genesis 3:15 that the seed of the woman would be bruised on the heel, his words pointed to the crucifixion of Christ. But He also said that Christ would bruise the enemy on the head, signifying a mortal blow, and ultimately fulfilled in the destruction of Satan in the lake of fire (Romans 16:20, Revelation 20:10).

And now, here you are living in this time and place—a design of God, created by Him and for Him. He desires a vibrant, intimate, ongoing relationship with you that continues on into eternity in your heavenly home, where you will live with Him forever. Do you know Him? If you have never established a personal relationship with Him, you can by praying a simple prayer something like this: *Lord Jesus, I need You. Thank You for dying on the cross for Me. I ask You now to forgive my sins, come into my life, and make me the person You want me to be. Thank you for loving me and giving me eternal life. In Jesus' name, Amen.*

You can experience the great adventure of knowing God where you spend quiet time with Him every day, live in His Word, experience His plan and purpose for your life, and walk and talk with Him throughout the day. You will grow in the grace and knowledge of your Lord and Savior Jesus Christ (2 Peter 3:18). God is at work creating in you even now: "If anyone is in Christ, he is a new creation; the old has gone, the new has come!" (2 Corinthians 5:17 NIV).

Epilogue

What is the greatest news and the rest of the story? I encourage you to read it for yourself in the Bible. Jesus is coming again! And His return is seen in two phases—first, in the Rapture of the Church (1 Thessalonians 4:13-17), and then publicly where He is going to usher in the new heaven and new earth and all that is promised in eternity throughout the Bible. "At the name of Jesus every knee will bow, of those who are in heaven and on earth and under the earth, and that every tongue will confess that Jesus Christ is Lord, to the glory of God the Father" (Philippians 2:10-11). In Revelation 19, He is seen as the coming King who rules and reigns over all. "Now I saw heaven opened, and behold, a white horse. And He who sat on him was called Faithful and True…His name is called The Word of God… He has on His robe and on His thigh a name written: KING OF KINGS AND LORD OF LORDS" (Revelation 19:11,13,16). At His command, Satan is thrown into the lake of fire (Revelation 20:10).

And now, what shall our experience be with God in heaven? Oh friends, it is truly a beautiful story and the great hope you can have for all your days during your brief stay here on earth. Here is the pronouncement of the joy awaiting you: "Behold, the tabernacle of God is with men, and He will dwell with them, and they shall be His people. God Himself will be with them and be their God. And God will wipe every tear from their eyes; there shall be no more death, nor sorrow, nor crying. There shall be no more pain, for the former things have passed away" (Revelation 21:3-4).

There will be a new heaven and a new earth. Our experience in heaven will be something that can barely be put into words. We know that we will see the face of God and will reign forever and ever (Revelation 22:4-5). "No eye has seen, no ear has heard, and no mind has imagined what God has prepared for those who love him" (1 Corinthians 2:9 NLT).

C.S. Lewis, in his book, *The Last Battle*, describes life on earth and heaven like this: "All their life in this world and all their adventures had only been the cover and the title page: now at last they were beginning Chapter One of the Great Story which no one on earth has read: which goes on forever: in which every chapter is better than the one before."

What can you look forward to right now? Jesus is coming again. He says, "Surely I am coming quickly" (Revelation 22:20). "Amen. Even so, come, Lord Jesus!" (Revelation 22:21).

Oh yes, beloved, the best is yet to come. Until that day, may you run with endurance the race set before you, fixing your eyes on Jesus, the author and perfector of your faith (Hebrews 12:1-2). And may you live out the days the Lord is making for you with great joy in Him for "this is the day the LORD has made. We will rejoice and be glad in it" (Psalm 118:24 NLT). God bless you.

In His Love and Service,
Catherine

APPENDIX

myPhotoWalk SmugMug
Photography
About The Author
About myPhotoWalk
Ackowledgments
You Might Also Like

MYPHOTOWALK — SMUGMUG
DEVOTIONAL PHOTOGRAPHY BY CATHERINE MARTIN

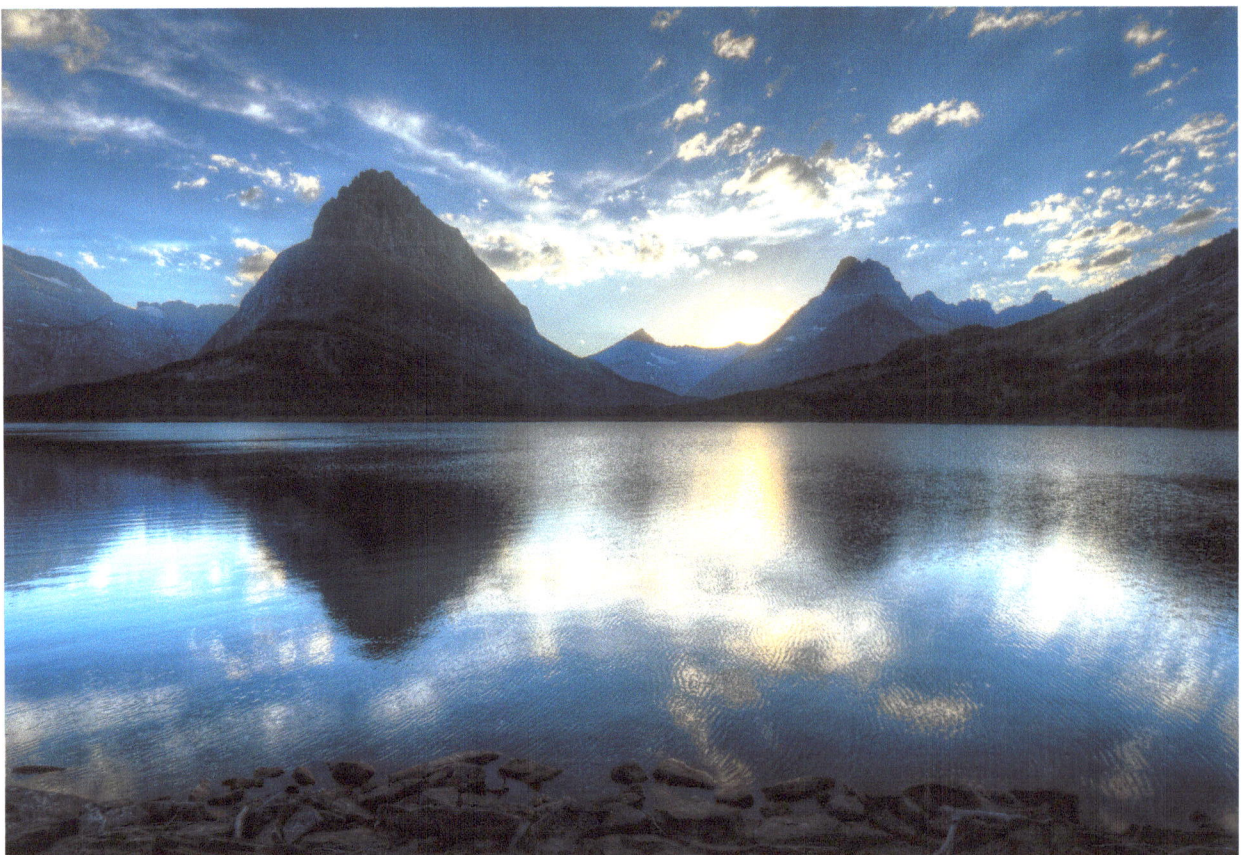

Catherine Martin | myPhotoWalk | Quiet Time Ministries — Many Glacier, Glacier National Park, Montana, USA

Your word is a lamp to my feet and a light for my path — Psalm 119:105 — His Light For Your Path

Custom Devotional Photography Prints — Spectacular photo finishes and Giclée canvas.
catherinemartin.smugmug.com

PHOTOGRAPHY

COVER

Cover and Interior Photography by Catherine Martin, myPhotoWalk—SmugMug, catherinemartin.smugmug.com, Custom Prints and Inspirational Gifts.

Seeing Jesus, 2013, Bell Rock-Courthouse Butte, Sedona, Arizona, USA, Nikon D7000, Nikor 18-105mm, FL 22mm, ISO 100, f/11, AEB.

TRUSTING OUR CREATOR IN TURBULENT TIMES

THE A DAY IN THE LIFE OF GOD SMUGMUG GALLERIES — Catherine Martin's very favorite images expressing themes from *myPhotoWalk—A Day in the Life of God,* chosen from photoshoots at Glacier National Park, Antelope Canyon, Hawaii, Tuscany, Sedona, Klamath Falls, Newport Beach, San Francisco, Los Angeles, Hollywood, Beverly Hills, Laguna Beach, Santa Monica, San Diego, and La Jolla, as well as the Mojave-Sonoran Desert. Enjoy.

Page 13: INTERLUDE, Journey With God, 2016, Tahquitz Rock, Idyllwild, California, USA, Nikon D810, Nikkor 24-120mm, FL 110mm, ISO100, f/11, AEB.

Page 14, Beginning, 2018, Coachella Valley Preserve, Palm Desert, California, USA, Sony A6000, Zeiss 16-70mm, FL 70mm, ISO 100, f/6.3, 1/200sec.

Page 15, Eternal God, 2018, Coachella Valley Preserve, Palm Desert, California, USA, Sony A6000, Zeiss 16-70mm, FL 16mm, ISO 200, f/8, 1/100sec.

Page 17, God Is Your Refuge, 2016, Mt. San Jacinto, Palm Desert, California, USA, Sony A6000, Zeiss 16-70mm, FL 70mm, ISO 400, f/5, 1/640sec.

Page 18, Beauty Of The Lord, 2017, Coachella Valley Preserve, Palm Desert, California, USA, Sony A6000, Zeiss 16-70mm, FL 25mm, ISO 100, f/11, 1/125sec.

Page 19, Simple Beauty, 2017, Shelter Island, San Diego, California, USA, Nikon D810, Micro-Nikkor 200mm, FL 200mm, ISO 500, f/7.1, 1/250sec.

Page 21, Trust In The Lord, 2017, Rancho Mirage, California, USA, Nikon D7000, Nikkor 70-300mm, FL 270mm, ISO 100, f/5.6, 1/200sec.

Page 22, Chariot Of Clouds, 2018, Coachella Valley Preserve, Palm Desert, California, USA, Sony A6000, Zeiss 16-70mm, FL 32mm, ISO 200, f/8, 1/250sec.

Page 23, Pacific Ocean Waves, 2018, Corona Del Mar State Beach, Corona Del Mar, California, USA, Fujifilm X-T2, Fujinon XF18-55mm F2.8-4 R LM OIS, FL 55mm, ISO 200, f/4.5, 1/7300sec.

Page 25, Ripples In The Sand, 2017, Coachella Valley Preserve, Palm Desert, California, USA, Sony A6000, Zeiss 16-70mm, FL 40mm, ISO 400, f/8, 1/250sec.

Page 26: INTERLUDE: REFLECTIONS, Knowing And Trusting God, 2013, Coachella Valley Preserve, Palm Deesert, California, USA, Nikon D7000, Nikkor 18-105mm, FL 40mm, ISO 100, f/11, AEB.

Page 29: FIRST DAY, Light, 2013, Coachella Valley Preserve, Palm Desert, California, USA, Nikon D7000, Nikkor 18-105, FL 34mm, ISO 100, f/11, 1/60sec.

Page 30, God's Glorious Light, 2013, Bill Williams River National Wildlife Refuge, Lake Havasu City, Arizona, USA, Nikon D7000, Nikkor 18-105mm, FL 98mm, ISO 100, f/11, AEB.

Page 31, Strong And Steadfast, 2013, Coachella Valley Preserve, Palm Desert, California, USA, Nikon D7000, Nikkor 12-24mm, FL 24mm, ISO 100, f/4, 1/40sec.

Page 33, Water In The Desert, 2013, Lake Havasu State Park, Lake Havasu City, Arizona, USA, Nikon D7000, Nikkor 12-24, FL 12mm, ISO 100, f/11, 1/5sec.

Page 34, Painting In The Sky, 2014, Upper Newport Bay State Marine Conservation Area, Newport Beach, California, USA, Nikon D7000, Nikkor 18-105mm, FL 62mm, ISO 100, f/11, AEB.

Page 35, Beauty In The Night, 2014, Upper Newport Bay State Marine Conservation Area, Newport Beach, California, USA, Nikon D7000, Nikkor 18-105mm, FL 105mm, ISO 100, f/11, 1/400sec.

Page 37, Morning Beauty, 2019, Oak Creek Canyon, Sedona, Arizona, USA, Sony A6000, Zeiss 16-70mm, FL 22mm, ISO 100, f/6.3, 1/80sec.

Page 38, Life In The Garden, 2012, Hawaii Tropical Botanical Garden, Papaikou, Island Of Hawaii, Hawaii, USA, Nikon D7000, Nikkor 12-24mm, FL 24mm, ISO 160, f/8, 1/100sec.

Page 39, Abundant Life, 2018, Newport Beach, California, USA, Fujifilm X-T2, Fujinon XF55-200mm F3.5-4.8 R LM OIS, FL 200mm, ISO 400, f/6.4, 1/420sec.

Photography

Page 41, Lighting The Way, 2018, Coachella Valley Preserve, Palm Desert, California, USA, Nikon D810, Nikkor 16-35mm, FL 16mm, ISO 100, f/8, 1/6sec.

Page 42: FIRST DAY: REFLECTIONS, The Bright Shining Light, 2014, West Fork Trail, Sedona, Arizona, USA, Apple iPhone 4S, FL 35mm, ISO 50, f/2.4, 1/1600sec.

Page 45: SECOND DAY, When God Made The Sky, 2014, Coachella Valley Preserve, Palm Desert, California, USA, Nikon D800, Nikkor 50.0mm, FL 50mm, ISO 100, f/3.5, 1/800sec.

Page 46, Looking Up To The Heavens, 2013, Lake Havasu State Park, Lake Havasu City, Arizona, USA, Nikon D7000, Nikkor 12-24mm, FL 13mm, ISO 100, f/11, AEB.

Page 47, Looking Up To God, 2019, Newport Beach, California, USA, Fujifilm X-T2, Fujinon XF18-55mm F2.8-4 R LM OIS, FL 20.5mm, ISO 100, f/11, 1/100sec.

Page 49, Believing God For The Impossible, 2014, Coachella Valley Preserve, Palm Desert, California, USA, Nikon D800E, Nikkor 24-120mm, FL 100mm, ISO 100, f/5.6, 1/1250sec.

Page 50, God's Chariot Of Clouds, 2013, Oak Creek Canyon, Sedona, Arizona, USA, Nikon D7000, Nikkor 18-105mm, FL 30mm, ISO 100, f/11, AEB.

Page 51, God's Glory In The Sky, 2015, Coachella Valley Preserve, Palm Desert, California, USA, Nikon D800E, Nikkor 50mm, FL 50mm, ISO 100, f/4, 1/400sec.

Page 53, With The Clouds Of Heaven, 2014, Coachella Valley Preserve, Palm Desert, California, Nikon D800E, Nikkor 24-120mm, FL 28mm, ISO 100, f/8, AEB.

Page 54: SECOND DAY:REFLECTIONS, God's Message In Creation, 2014, Coachella Valley Preserve, Palm Desert, California, USA, Nikon D800E, Nikkor 16-35mm, FL 35mm, ISO 100, f/16, AEB.

Page 57: THIRD DAY, The Third Day Of Creation, 2013, Lake Havasu State Park, Lake Havasu City, Arizona, USA, Nikon D7000, Nikkor 18-105mm, FL 105mm, ISO 100, f/11, AEB.

Page 58, The Glory Of God, 2017, Courthouse Butte, Sedona, Arizona, USA, Sony A6000, Zeiss 16-70mm, FL 16mm, ISO 400, f/11, 1/160sec.

Page 59, The Majesty Of God, 2014. Indian Wells, California, USA, Nikon D800E, Nikkor 80-400mm, FL 320mm, ISO 1250, f/5.6, 1/800sec.

Page 61, The Works Of God, 2013, St. Mary Village, Glacier National Park, Montana, USA, Nikon D7000, Nikkor 18-105mm, FL 28mm, ISO 100, f/11, AEB.

Page 62, When Ocean Waters Gather, 2014, Kona Coast, Kailua-Kona, Hawaii, USA, Nikon D800E, Nikkor 24-120mm, FL 38mm, ISO 100, f/22, 1/50sec.

Page 63, Faithful Creator, 2014, Kona Coast, Kailua-Kona, Hawaii, USA, Nikon D800E, Nikkor 24-120mm, FL 34mm, ISO 100, f/18, 1/80sec.

Page 65, Ocean Dance, 2018, Corona Del Mar State Beach, Corona Del Mar, California, USA, Fujifilm X-T2, Fujinon XF55-200mm F3.5-4.8 R LM OIS, FL 200mm, ISO 400, f/11, 1/1050sec.

Page 66, God's Flower Garden, 2018, Corona Del Mar State Beach, Corona Del Mar, California, USA, Fujifilm X-T2, Fujinon XF18-55mm F2.8-4 R LM OIS, FL 46.3mm, ISO 200, f/11, 1/500sec.

Page 67, The Apple Tree, 2017, Sedona, Arizona, USA, iPhone 6, FL 41.5mm, ISO 100, f/2.2, 1/30sec.

Page 69, The Sedona Sunflower, 2021, Slide Rock State Park, Sedona, Arizona, USA, Sony A6000, Zeiss 16-70mm, FL 26mm, ISO 100, f/11, 1/160sec.

Page 70, The Bee And The Butterfly, 2021, Sherman Gardens, Corona Del Mar, California, USA, Sony A6000, Zeiss 16-70mm, FL 70mm, ISO 100, f/9, 1/320sec.

Page 71, Blossom In His Presence, 2015, Phoenix, Arizona, USA, Nikon D800E, Nikkor 24-120mm, FL 120mm, ISO 250, f/5.6, 1/2000sec.

Page 73, A Heart Overflowing, 2015, Oak Creek, Sedona, Arizona, USA, Nikon D800E, Nikkor 24-120mm, FL 105mm, ISO 100, f/22, 0.4sec.

Page 74: THIRD DAY:REFLECTIONS, Reeds By The Water, 2013, Coachella Valley Preserve, Palm Desert, California, USA, Nikon D7000, Nikkor 18-105mm, FL 50mm, ISO 100, f/5, 1/160sec.

Page 77: FOURTH DAY, The Blood Red Moon, 2014, Coachella Valley Preserve, Palm Desert, California, USA, Nikon D7000, Nikkor 80-400mm, FL 400mm, ISO 200, f/5.6, 1.0sec.

Page 78, The First Gleam Of Dawn, 2014, Coachella Valley Preserve, Palm Desert, California, USA, Nikon D800E, Nikkor 24-120mm, FL 48mm, ISO 100, f/22, 1/30sec.

Page 79, Flower In The Sun, 2017, Newport Beach, California, USA, Fujifilm X-T2, Fujinon XF18-55mm F2.8-4 R LM OIS, FL 48mm, ISO 400, f/4, 1/2400sec.

Page 81, Like A Tree, 2013, Indian Wells, California, USA, Nikon D7000, Nikkor 18-105mm, FL 25mm, ISO 100, f/11, AEB.

Page 82, The Lunar Eclipse, 2014, Coachella Valley Preserve, Palm Desert, California, USA, Nikon D7000, Nikkor 80-400mm FL 380.0mm, ISO 200, f/5.6, 1.3sec.

Photography

Page 83, Light By Night, 2018, Coachella Valley Preserve, Palm Desert, California, USA, Nikon D810, Nikkor 80-400mm, FL 400mm, ISO 200, f/11, 1/200sec.

Page 85, Moon Setting In The Desert, 2012, Coachella Valley Preserve, Palm Desert, California, USA, Nikon D7000, Nikkor 18-105mm, FL 52mm, ISO 200, f/11, AEB.

Page 86, Stars In The Sky, 2014, Coachella Valley Preserve, Palm Desert, California, USA, Nikon D800E, Nikkor 24-120mm, FL 58mm, ISO 100, f/4, 1/15sec.

Page 87, Sunset In Sedona, 2019, Sedona, Arizona, USA, Fujifilm X-T2, Fujinon XF18-55mm F2.8-4 R LM OIS, FL 55mm, ISO 6400, f/8, 1/12sec.

Page 89, The Painting Of Clouds, 2014, Coachella Valley Preserve, Palm Desert, California, USA, Nikon D800E, Nikkor 24-120mm, FL 24mm, ISO 100, f/16, AEB.

Page 90: FOURTH DAY:REFLECTIONS, The Edges Of His Ways, Coachella Valley Preserve, Palm Desert, California, USA, Sony A6000, Zeiss 16-70mm, FL 67mm, ISO 400, f/4, 1/160sec.

Page 93: FIFTH DAY, Responding To The Call, 2014, Honoapiilani Kapalua, Island of Maui, Hawaii, USA, Nikon D7000, Nikkor 80.0-400.0mm, FL 320mm, ISO 400, f/5.6, 1/125sec.

Page 94, All The Beautiful Fish, 2012, Pauoa Bay, Waimea, Island of Hawaii, Hawaii, USA, . Nikon D7000, Nikkor 18-105mm, FL 42mm, ISO 500, f/4.8, 1/60sec.

Page 95, When God Blesses You, 2012, Pauoa Bay, Waimea, Island of Hawaii, Hawaii, USA, Nikon D7000, Nikkor 18-105mm, FL 92mm, ISO 200, f/6.3, 1/640sec.

Page 97, The Wonders Of Godl, 2015, San Francisco, California, USA, Nikon D810, Nikkor 70-300mm, FL 125mm, ISO 800, f/5.6, 1/50sec.

Page 98, The Dancing Hummingbirds, 2019, Sedona, Arizona, USA, Nikon D810, Nikkor 80-400mm, FL 270mm, ISO 200, f/18, 1/250sec.

Page 99, The Dancing Egrets, 2013, Coachella Valley Preserve, Palm Desert, California, USA, Nikon D7000, Nikkor 70-300mm, FL 270mm, ISO 160, f/11, 1/100sec.

Page 101, Dancing By Faith, 2013, Coachella Valley Preserve, Palm Desert, California, USA, Nikon D7000, Nikkor 70-300mm, FL 230mm, ISO 160, f/18, 1/125sec.

Page 102, Refuge In The Storm, 2013, Coachella Valley Preserve, Palm Desert, California, USA, Nikon D7000, Nikkor 18-105mm, FL 25mm, ISO 160, f/4, 1/60sec.

Page 103, Our Refuge And Strength, 2018, Coachella Valley Preserve, Palm Desert, California, USA, Nikon D810, Nikkor 80-400mm, FL 400mm, ISO 640, f/7.1, 1/160sec.

Page 105, The Little Bird, 2018, Coachella Valley Preserve, Palm Desert, California, USA, Nikon D810, Nikkor 80-400mm, FL 400mm, ISO 1600, f/5.6, 1/400sec.

Page 106: FIFTH DAY:REFLECTIONS, Trusting In Tough Times, 2015, Wildlife World Zoo, Litchfield Park, Arizona, USA, Nikon D800E, Nikkor 80-400mm, FL 400mm, ISO 400, f/5.6, 1/640sec.

Page 109: SIXTH DAY, After God's Own Heart, 2011, Piazza Della Signoria, Florence,Tuscany, Italy, Nikon D7000, Nikkor 18-105mm, FL 105mm, ISO 200, f/7.1, 1/1000sec.

Page 110, Living Creatures, 2015, Out Of Africa Wildlife Park, Camp Verde, Arizona, USA, Nikon D800E, Nikkor 80-400mm, FL 300mm, ISO 800, f/5.6, 1/1000sec.

Page 111, Koko, 2021, Newport Beach, California, USA, Sony A6000, Zeiss 16-70mm, FL 46mm, ISO 3200, f/4, 1/80sec.

Page 113, Squirrel In A Tree, 2012, Newport Beach, California, USA, Nikon D7000, Nikkor 70-300mm, FL 70mm, ISO 360, f/5.6, 1/125sec.

Page 114, Deer In Bryce, 2012, Bryce Canyon National Park, Bryce Canyon, Utah, USA, Nikon D7000, Nikkor 70-300mm, FL 145mm, ISO 450, f/4.8, 1/250sec.

Page 115, God's Surprise, 2012, Bryce Canyon National Park, Bryce Canyon, Utah, USA, Nikon D7000, Nikkor 70-300mm, FL 185mm, ISO 560, f/5.0, 1/250sec.

Page 117, Deer On The Heights, 2012, Bryce Canyon National Park, Bryce Canyon, Utah, USA, Nikon D7000, Nikkor 70-300mm, FL 155mm, ISO 500, f/4.8, 1/250sec.

Page 118, Painting On The Arno, 2011, River Arno, Florence, Tuscany, Italy, Nikon D7000, Nikkor 18-105mm, FL 90mm, ISO 125, f/18, 1/100sec.

Page 119, Waiter On The Piazza, 2011, Piazza Della Signoria, Florence, Tuscany, Italy,Nikon D7000, Nikkor 18-105mm, FL 26mm, ISO 125, f/5.6, 1/100sec.

Page 121, At The Window, 2011, Florence, Tuscany, Italy, Nikon D7000, Nikkor 18-105mm, FL 105mm, ISO 200, f/8, 1/1000sec.

Page 122, Weaver And Storyteller, 2012, Monument Valley Navajo Tribal Park, Oljato-Monument Valley, Utah, USA, Nikon D7000, Nikkor 18-105mm, FL 105mm, ISO 200, f/11, 1/200sec.

Page 123, Man In Prayer, 2015, Santa Fe, New Mexico, USA, Sony A6000, Sony 16-50mm, FL 38mm, ISO 3200, f/5.6, 1/20sec.

Page 125, A Man And His Dog, 2011, Florence, Tuscany, Italy, Nikon D7000, Nikkor 18-105mm, FL 98mm, ISO 100, f/8, 1/250sec.

Photography

Page 126: SIXTH DAY:REFLECTIONS, Walking In The Garden, 2019, Newport Beach, California, USA, Fujifilm X-T2, Fujinon XF18-55mm F2.8-4 R LM OIS, FL 42.5mm, ISO 400, f/8, 1/500sec.

Page 129: SEVENTH DAY, Resting In The Pasture, 2015, Valles Caldera National Preserve, Jemez Springs, New Mexico, USA, Sony A6000, Zeiss 16-70mm, FL 70mm, ISO 100, f/6.3, 1/250sec.

Page 130, Rest Among The Flowers, 2015, Valles Caldera National Preserve, Jemez Springs, New Mexico, USA, Sony A6000, Zeiss 16-70mm, FL 48mm, ISO 100, f/9, 1/125sec.

Page 131, Flying In Formation, 2014, Coachella Valley Preserve, Palm Desert, California, USA, Nikon D800, Nikkor 105mm, FL 105mm, ISO 320, f/8, 1/800sec.

Page 133, Resting In The Tree, 2014, Coachella Valley Preserve, Palm Desert, California, USA, Nikon D800E, Nikkor 80-400mm, FL 380mm, ISO 1000, f/5.6, 1/4000sec.

Page 134, Refreshed In The Desert, 2015, Phoenix, Arizona, USA, Sony A6000, Sony 16-50mm, FL 16mm, ISO 200, f/13, 1/200sec.

Page 135, Watching Over You, 2014, Wildlife World Zoo, Litchfield Park, Arizona, USA, Nikon D800E, Nikkor 80-400mm, FL 390mm, ISO 400, f/5.6, 1/640sec.

Page 137, Blooming Desert, 2019, Coachella Valley Preserve, Palm Desert, California, USA, Sony A6000, Zeiss 16-70mm, FL 41mm, ISO 2500, f/4, 1/160sec.

Page 138, Flying Above Saguaro, 2014, Lake Pleasant Regional Park, Morristown, Arizona, USA, Nikon D7000, Nikkor 80-400mm, FL 280, ISO 800, f/8, 1/2500sec.

Page 139, Leaf On The Path, 2014, Newport Beach, California, USA, Nikon D800E, Nikkor 105mm, FL 105mm, ISO 200, f/2, 1/250sec.

Page 141, Gazing At God's Glory, 2014, Corona Del Mar State Beach, Corona del Mar, California, USA, Nikon D7000, Nikkor 80-400mm, FL 400mm, ISO 800, f/5.6, 1/320sec.

Page 142: SEVENTH DAY:REFLECTIONS, Flower In The Garden, 2021, Newport Beach, California, USA, Sony A6000, Zeiss 16-70mm, FL 36mm, ISO 100, f/6.3, 1/200sec.

Page 144: EPILOGUE, Bright Hope Of Eternity, 2012, Coachella Valley Preserve, Palm Desert, California, USA, Nikon D7000, Nikkor 18-105mm, FL 105mm, ISO 100, f/11, 1/500sec.

About the Author

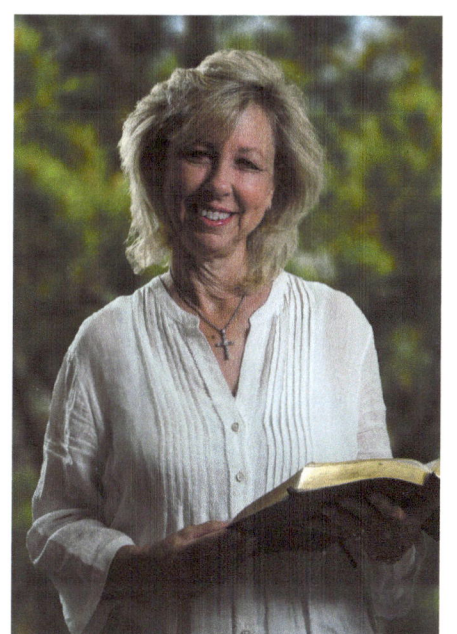

Catherine Martin is a summa cum laude graduate of Bethel Theological Seminary with a Master of Arts degree in Theological Studies. She is founder and president of Quiet Time Ministries, a director of women's ministries for many years, and an adjunct faculty member of Biola University. She is the author of *Six Secrets to a Powerful Quiet Time, Knowing and Loving the Bible, Walking with the God Who Cares, Set my Heart on Fire, Trusting in the Names of God, Passionate Prayer, Quiet Time Moments for Women,* and *Drawing Strength from the Names of God* published by Harvest House Publishers, and *Pilgrimage of the Heart, Revive My Heart* and *A Heart That Dances,* published by NavPress. She has also written *The Quiet Time Notebooks, Walk on Water Faith, One Holy Passion, A Heart on Fire, A Heart to See Forever, Run Before the Wind,* and *A Heart That Hopes in God,* published by Quiet Time Ministries Press. She is founder of myPhotoWalk.com dedicated to the art of devotional photography publishing *myPhotoWalk—Quiet Time Moments, myPhotoWalk—Savoring God's Promises of Hope,* and *myPhotoWalk—The Story of Your Life.* As a popular keynote speaker at retreats and conferences, Catherine challenges others to seek God and love Him with all of their heart, soul, mind, and strength.

About Quiet Time Ministries

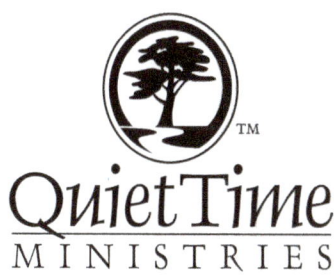

Quiet Time Ministries is a nonprofit religious organization under Section 501(c)(3) of the Internal Revenue Code. Cash donations are tax deductible as charitable contributions. We count on prayerful donors like you, partners with Quiet Time Ministries pursuing our goals of the furtherance of the Gospel of Jesus Christ and teaching devotion to God and His Word. Visit us online at www.quiettime.org to view special funding opportunities and current ministry projects. Your prayerful donations bring countless project to life!

Quiet Time Ministries | P.O. Box 14007 | Palm Desert, California 92255
1.800.925.6458 | catherine@quiettime.org | www.quiettime.org | www.myphotowalk.com

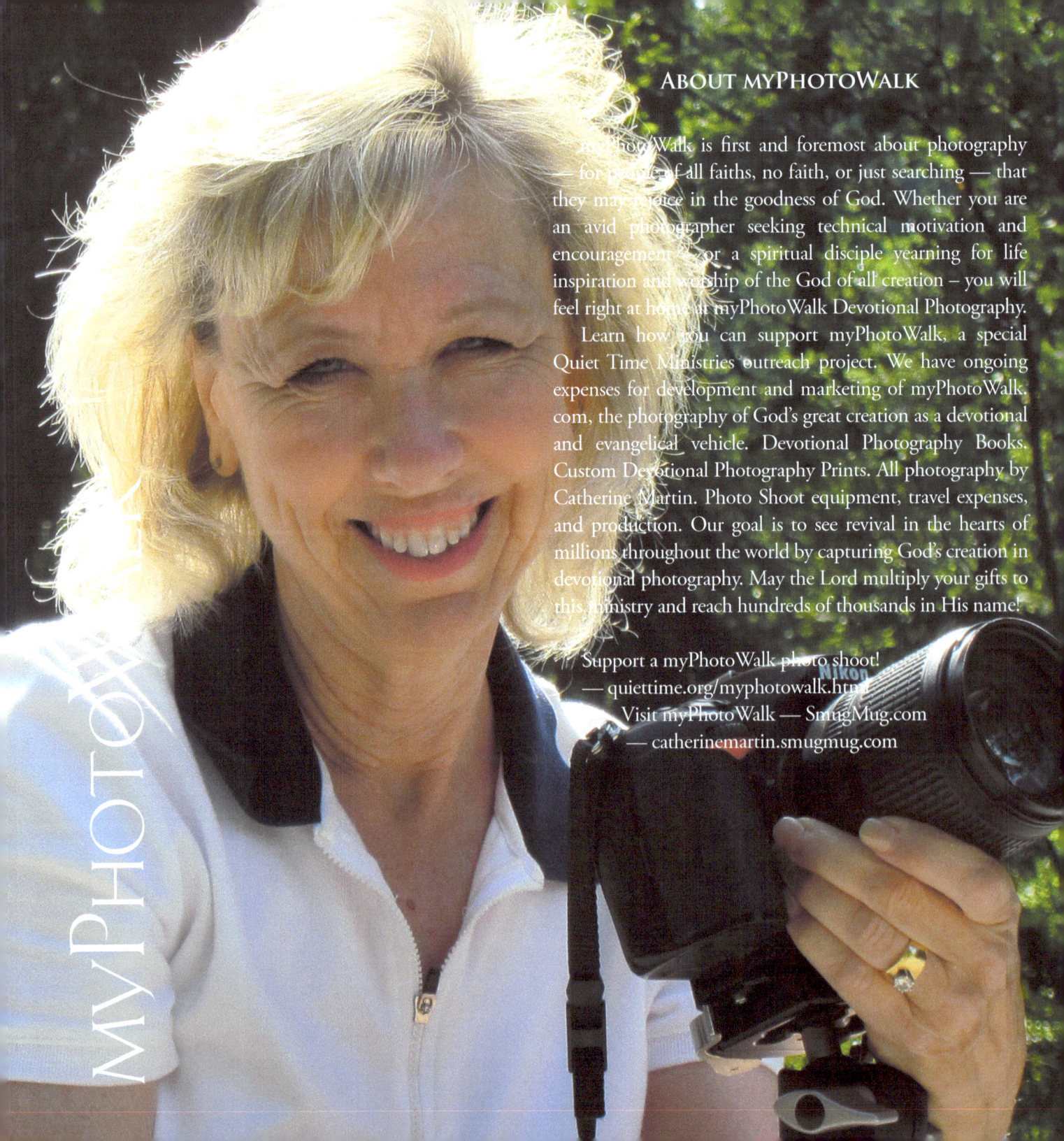

ABOUT MYPHOTOWALK

myPhotoWalk is first and foremost about photography — for people of all faiths, no faith, or just searching — that they may rejoice in the goodness of God. Whether you are an avid photographer seeking technical motivation and encouragement — or a spiritual disciple yearning for life inspiration and worship of the God of all creation – you will feel right at home at myPhotoWalk Devotional Photography.

Learn how you can support myPhotoWalk, a special Quiet Time Ministries outreach project. We have ongoing expenses for development and marketing of myPhotoWalk.com, the photography of God's great creation as a devotional and evangelical vehicle. Devotional Photography Books. Custom Devotional Photography Prints. All photography by Catherine Martin. Photo Shoot equipment, travel expenses, and production. Our goal is to see revival in the hearts of millions throughout the world by capturing God's creation in devotional photography. May the Lord multiply your gifts to this ministry and reach hundreds of thousands in His name!

Support a myPhotoWalk photo shoot!
— quiettime.org/myphotowalk.html
Visit myPhotoWalk — SmugMug.com
— catherinemartin.smugmug.com

ACKNOWLEDGMENTS

What a profound journey it has been to walk with the Lord through the days of creation in the writing of *A Day in the Life of God*. I'm so very thankful to the Lord for the idea and His guidance through the power of the Holy Spirit. Many times I experienced such intimate *aha* moments with Him as I lived in His Word. I could have never written this book without the help of my beloved husband, David. Thank you, dear husband, for serving together with me in Quiet Time Ministries and for forty years together. Thank you to my precious family for their love and encouragement—David, Mother and Dad (both now with the Lord), Robert, Kayla, Linda, Christopher, Andy, Keegan, and James.

I am so very thankful over these many years for the Quiet Time Ministries team serving the Lord together with me—Kayla Branscum, Shirley Peters, Conni Hudson, Cindy Clark, Sandy Fallon, Paula Zillmer, Karen Darras Hawley, Kelly Wysard, Maurine Cromwell, and Cay Hough. Thank you to many dear friends who have offered such words of truth, encouragement, and hope that I have needed all along the way: Beverly Trupp, Conni Hudson, Cindy Clark, Andy Kotner Graybill, Jane Lyons, Julie Airis, Stefanie Kelly, Joe and Judy Patti, Betty Mann, Kelly Wysard, Jan Lupia, Barbara Waddell, Marilyn Meberg, and Vonette Bright.

Thank you to the Board of Directors of Quiet Time Ministries: David Martin, Conni Hudson, Andy Kotner Graybill, and Jane Lyons, for your faithfulness in this ministry. And thank you to all who have partnered with us both financially and prayerfully in Quiet Time Ministries. You have helped make possible this idea the Lord gave me so many years ago called Quiet Time Ministries and have allowed us to continue to spread God's Word to men and women throughout the world. I also want to thank those who have partnered financially with Quiet Time Ministries to sponsor myPhotoWalk photo shoots and purchase photographic equipment including my Nikon cameras, my Fuji camera, lenses, tripods, and filters.

Thank you to my Bethel Seminary professors who gave me such a love for God's Word and helped me learn to study with excellence, especially Dr. Ronald Youngblood, Dr. Walt Wessel, Dr. James Smith, and Dr. Al Glenn.

Thank you to those who have encouraged me in devotional photography—especially Bill Fortney and His Light Friends, Laurie Rubin, Kevin Toohey, and Kathleen Reeder.

Thank you to Greg Johnson, my agent at WordServe Literary Agency, for all your support and encouragement.

Thank you to Friendship Church, and all the faithful women, pastors, and leaders I have had the privilege of serving with over the years in ministry. I am thankful for the beloved women I have had the opportunity to lead and pastor all these years. Thank you to all you amazing women in our online Bible study that meets on Thursday mornings—your love for God and His Word and your prayers are such a blessing in my life! A special thank you to all the groups worldwide who are drawing near to God in quiet time using the many quiet time studies and resources from Quiet Time Ministries.

Thank you to all those saints who have lived their lives with a passion for God and have encouraged me to love the Lord with all my heart and spend daily quiet time with Him.

Finally, thank You, Lord, for leading and guiding me all the days of my life. To You be the glory.

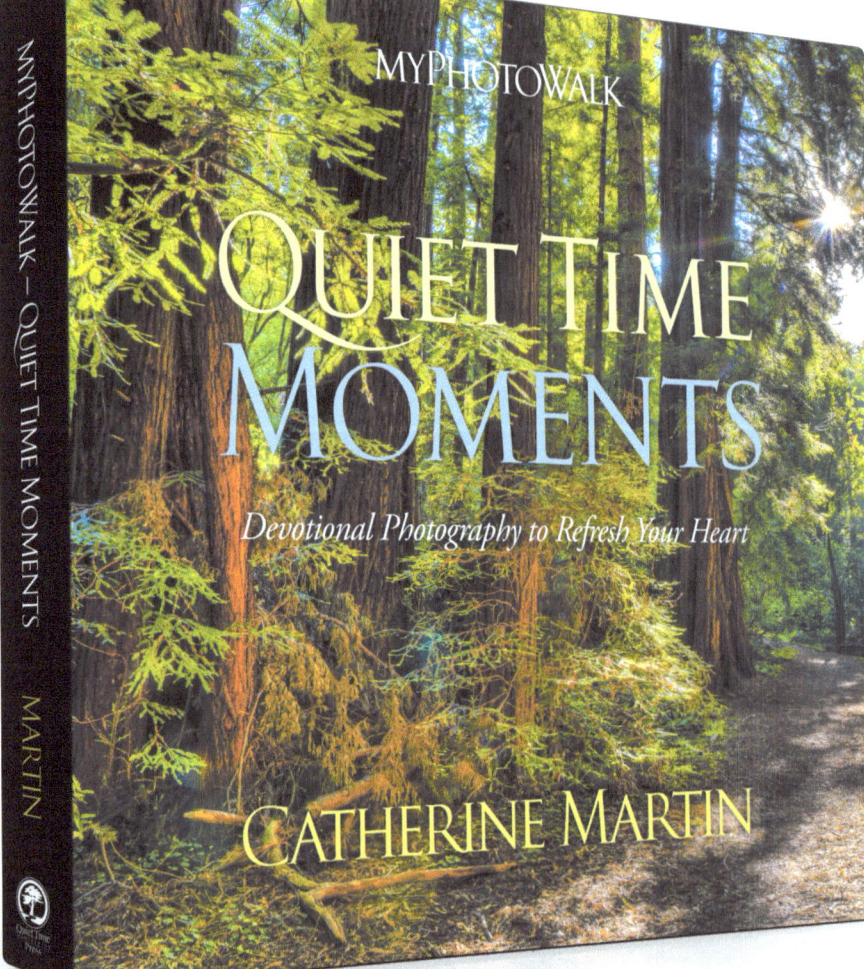

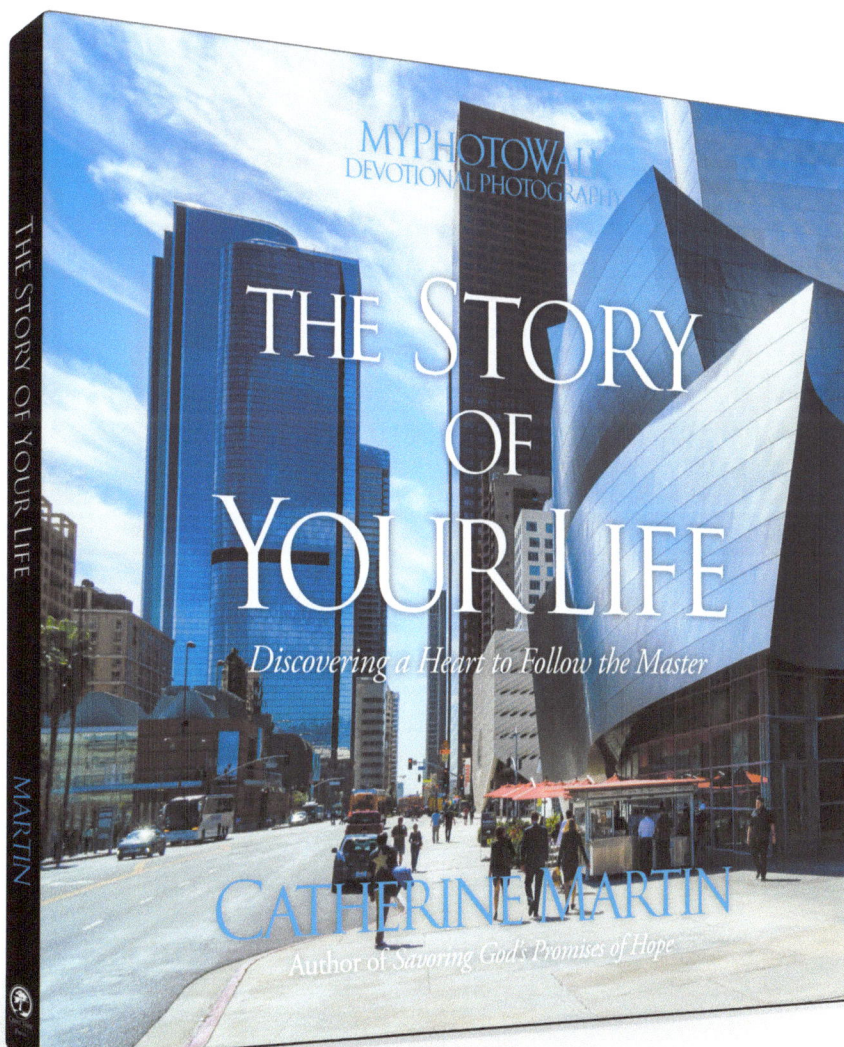

A Quiet Time Experience

TRUSTING IN THE NAMES OF GOD

EIGHT WEEKS OF GUIDED DEVOTIONS

- Inspirational Readings
- Prayer Starters and Journal Ideas
- Questions for Reflection

CATHERINE MARTIN

Author of *Knowing and Loving the Bible*

www.ingramcontent.com/pod-product-compliance
Lightning Source LLC
Chambersburg PA
CBHW051146220526
45473CB00003B/675